A Concise Glossary of
Architectural
Terms

John Henry Parker

SENATE

A Concise Glossary of Architectural Terms

First published in 1896 by
James Parker & Company, Oxford

This edition published in 1994 by Senate, an imprint of
Studio Editions Ltd, Princess House, 50 Eastcastle Street,
London W1N 7AP, England

ISBN 1 85958 069 6
Printed and bound in Guernsey by
The Guernsey Press Co Ltd

A Concise Glossary of
Architectural
Terms

PREFACE TO THE FIRST EDITION.

THE original intention of the "Glossary of Architecture" was to supply a want which had long been felt of a Manual for constant use, either for reference in the study, or to assist the student in examining buildings themselves. The great popularity of the work proves that these objects were in some degree accomplished. But in the absence of any series of engravings generally accessible to which references might be made for examples, it became necessary to supply these in the work itself. In this way its extent has been greatly increased in each successive edition, and, while these additions have added in a proportionate degree to its value, the consequent increase of bulk and of price has caused an Abridgment to be called for.

Oxford, March, 1846.

PREFACE TO THE FOURTH EDITION.

IN each succeeding Edition a few additions and corrections have been made, and a Topographical Index to the Illustrations is also given in the later Editions.

Oxford, October, 1875.

A CONCISE
Glossary of Architecture.

———•———

ABACUS (Lat. from Gr. *abax* = a board). This name
is applied in architecture to the uppermost member
or division of a capital: it is a very essential feature in
the GRECIAN and ROMAN orders.

In the Grecian Doric
the abacus has simply
the form of a square
tile without either a
chamfer or a moulding.

In the Roman Doric
it has the addition of
an *ogee* and *fillet* round
the upper edge.

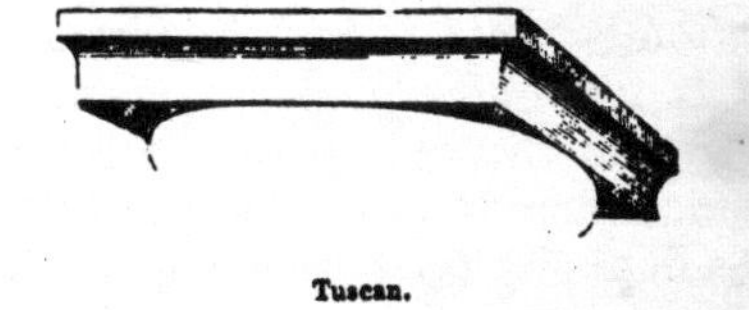

In the Tuscan a
plain fillet with a sim-
ple *cavetto* under it, is
used instead of the ogee
and fillet. In all these
orders the abacus is
of considerable thick-
ness; and the mould-
ing round the upper
edge is called the *cima-
tium* of the abacus.

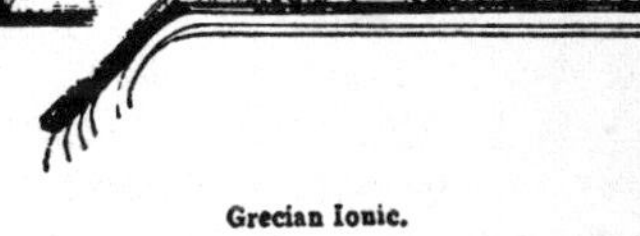

In the Grecian Ionic
it is worked very much
thinner, consisting of
an *ovolo* or *ogee*, gene-
rally *without any fillet* above it, and is sometimes sculptured.

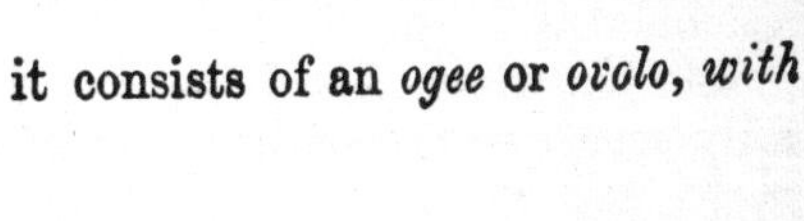

In the Roman Ionic it consists of an *ogee* or *ovolo*, *with
a fillet* above it.

Grecian Doric.

Roman Doric.

Tuscan.

Grecian Ionic.

In all the preceding orders the abacus is worked square, but in the modern Ionic, the Corinthian, and the Composite, the sides are *hollowed*, and the angles, with some few exceptions in the Corinthian order,

Corinthian.

truncated. The mouldings used on the modern Ionic vary, but an *ogee* and *fillet* like the Roman are the most common. In the Corinthian and Composite orders, the mouldings consist of an *ovolo* on the upper edge, with a *fillet* and *caretto* beneath.

Composite.

In the architecture of the MIDDLE AGES, the abacus still remains an important feature, although its form and proportions are not regulated by the same arbitrary laws as in the Classical orders: in the earlier styles there is almost invariably a clear line of separation to mark the abacus as a distinct division of the capital; but as Gothic architecture advanced, with its accompanying variety of mouldings, the abacus was subject to the same capricious changes as all the other features of the successive styles, and there is often no really distinguisnable line of separation between it and the rest of the *capital*.

It not unfrequently happens that the abacus is nearly or quite the only part of a capital on which mouldings can be found to shew its date; it is therefore deserving of close attention.

Jarrow.

In early buildings of the style spoken of as being perhaps *Saxon*, that is, previous to the twelfth century, the abacus is, in general, merely a long flat stone without chamfer or moulding; but it sometimes varies, and occasionally bears some resemblance to the Norman form.

The *Norman* abacus is flat on the top, and generally *square* in the earlier part of the style, with a plain

chamfer on the lower edge, or a hollow is used instead.
As the style advanced, other
mouldings were introduced, and
in rich buildings occasionally
several are found combined : it is
very usual to find the hollow on
the lower edge of the abacus surmounted by a small channel or
a bead. If the top of the abacus
is not flat, it is a sign that it is
verging to the succeeding style.

Whitby Church, c. 1110.

In the *Early English* style, the

Great Guild, Lincoln, c. 1160.

abacus is most commonly *cir-
cular;* it is, however, sometimes octagonal, and occasionally square, but not frequently in England, except

early in this style.
The most characteris-
tic mouldings are deep
hollows and overhang-
ing rounds ; in gene-
ral, the mouldings in
this style have con-

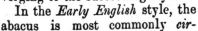

Paul's Cray, Kent, c. 1220.

siderable projections with deep and distinct hollows between them.

In the *Decorated* style, the form of the abacus is either
circular or *polygonal,* very frequently *octagonal.* The circular abacus is especially an English feature; the octagonal abacus being most common on the Continent,
especially in France. Hollows are not so frequently
to be found, nor are they in general, when used,

so deeply cut ; the
mouldings and the
modes of combining
them vary consider-
ably, but rounds are
common, particularly
a roll or *scroll-mould-*

Merton College Chapel, Oxford, A.D. 1280.

ing, the upper half of which projects and overlaps the
lower, as in Merton College Chapel; this moulding may
be considered as characteristic of the Decorated style,
although it is to be met with in late Early English work.

The round mouldings have often fillets worked on them,
and these again are also found in Early English work.

In the *Perpendicular* style, the abacus is sometimes
circular but generally octagonal, even when the shaft and
lower part of the capital are circular; when octagonal,
particularly in work of late date, the sides are often
slightly hollowed: in this style the mouldings are not
generally much undercut, nor are they so much varied as
in the Decorated. A very usual form for the abacus consists of a *waved moulding*, (of rounds and hollows united
without forming an-
gles,) with a bead un-
der it, as at Croy-
don, Surrey; the most
prominent part of this
moulding is sometimes
worked flat, as a fillet,

Croydon, Surrey, c. 1480.

which then divides it into two ogees, the upper being
reversed: the ogee may be considered as characteristic
of the Perpendicular capital: the top of the abacus is
sometimes splayed and occasionally hollowed out. [For
further illustrations see *Capital, Saxon, Norman, Early
English, Decorated and Perpendicular*.]

Abutment, the solid part of a pier or wall, etc., against
which an arch abuts, or from which it immediately springs,
acting as a support to the thrust or lateral pressure.
The abutments of a bridge are the walls adjoining to
the land which supports the ends of the road-way, or
the arches at the extremities. Also the basement projecting to resist the force
of the stream, and on which
the piers rest.

Acanthus (Lat. from
Gr.), a plant, the leaves of
which are imitated in the
capitals of the Corinthian
and Composite orders.

ABACISCI (Lat. deriv.), small
tesseræ for pavements or square
tablets.

ABAMURUS (Med. Lat.), a buttress.

ABBEY. See *Monastery*.
ABREUVOIR (Fr.), jointing in
masonry.
ABSIS, *Apsis*, or *Apse*.

Acroteria (Gr.), pedestals for statues and other ornaments placed on the apex and the lower angles of a pediment. They are also sometimes placed upon the gables in Gothic architecture, especially in canopy work.

Aisle or Aile (Fr. from Lat. *ala* = a wing), the lateral division of a church, or its wings, for such are the aisles to the body of every church. They may also be considered as an internal portico. In England there are seldom more than two, one on each side of the nave or choir, and frequently only one, but examples may be found of two aisles on one side, and one on the other, more rarely two occur on either side. In many cases the aisles have had their origin in chantry chapels. [See *Church*.]

Almery (literally a place for the alms), a cupboard; when by the side of an altar employed to contain the sacred vessels which were locked up, and hence the word *Locker*.

Almery in Lincoln Cathedral, c. 1200.

ACHELOR, ACHILER, ACHLERE = Ashlar.

ACUTE ARCH = Lancet Arch.

ADIT (Lat.), the approach to a building.

ADYTUM (Gr.), the innermost and secret part of a temple.

AEDES, generally a temple, but often used for any public building.

AILLETTES. See illustrations to *Brass*.

ALB, part of priests' robes. See illustrations to *Brass*.

ALLEY, ALLYE: used for Aisle.

It is evident, however, from many passages in ancient writers, that a more extended signification was sometimes given to the word, and that in the larger churches and cathedrals the Almeries were not only recesses in the wall, but were detached pieces of furniture, and were very numerous; they were placed in various parts of the church, or in the cloisters : they were frequently of wainscot, and sometimes of considerable size, answering to what we should now call closets. The word is also used in domestic architecture in the sense of a cupboard. It is often called the *Aumbry*. [See *Locker*.]

Almonry, (also called Aumbry). This always signified the room where alms were distributed : in monastic establishments it was generally a stone building near the church, sometimes on the north side of the quadrangle. or removed to the gate-house.

Altar (Lat.), an elevated table, slab, or board in Christian churches, consecrated for the Sacrament of the Holy Eucharist. In the third and fourth centuries, the sarcophagus or stone coffin of a martyr was frequently used as an Altar, since Pope Felix [A.D. 269—274], according to the Liber Pontificalis, " ordered masses to be celebrated over the sepulchres of the martyrs." One instance of this, as it is supposed, remains in the catacomb of S. Priscilla, with a small platform behind it for the priest to stand upon to officiate over it. [See *Cemetery*.] That they were frequently of wood during the first four or five centuries of the Christian era, is shewn by the fact that the Council of Epone in France, A.D. 517, commanded that "no altars should be consecrated with the chrism of holy oil, but such as were made of stone only." And we find this included amongst the Excerptions of Egbriht, Archbishop of York, issued about A.D. 740, in

ALORING, the parapet wall protecting the Alur.

ALTAR. The Latin *Altare* is derived either from *alta ara* = high altar, or (more probably) from *altus* only. In describing the arrangements of an altar its sides are termed the Epistle and Gospel sides or horns respectively. The Epistle side is at the left hand of a person standing with his back to the altar, and is therefore south in all churches which look eastward; the Gospel side is the north or opposite side.

this country. Later on, that is, at the Council held at Winchester, A.D. 1071, the fifth of the Canons related to altars, "that they be not of stone." And soon after, i.e. A.D. 1080, Bishop Wulstan (so William of Malmesbury records) demolished throughout his diocese the wooden altars still remaining.

Throughout the series of benefactions to the Roman churches made by successive Popes during the first seven or eight centuries, Anastasius frequently refers to their gifts of altars, and nearly always they are recorded to be covered with pure silver, and sometimes with gold. From the record of the great weight of the silver, it may be assumed that the altar was chiefly composed of the precious metal, perhaps a wooden framework only being used to keep the plates of metal in place.

It would be natural that the early Christians of Rome and elsewhere should, when they were enabled to possess or build churches, borrow much from the ancient Jewish ritual, and that the altar should thus be introduced; and it is also to be observed that some of the *Basilicæ* or justice-halls, which exercised so important an influence on the plan and design of the Christian Church, had also their altars on the chord of the bema or apse for taking oaths upon. But how far one or other of these circumstances influenced the introduction, use, or position of the altar in the very early churches, is a matter which must be left very much to conjecture, from the scanty references which we possess to ecclesiastical details of this early period. Anastasius records that Pope Sixtus, A.D. 260, ordered that altars "should be built in all the churches, and that the Sacred Mysteries should be celebrated upon them publicly before the congregation, which used not to be done before."

Although amongst the writings of the Fathers of the first four or five centuries we do not discover evidence of more than one altar in any church, it became customary

ALTAR, portable. A small slab of stone often incised or inlaid. The earliest existing is that found buried with S. Cuthbert, A.D. 687. It has the five crosses upon it. Bede mentions missionaries in 692, carrying with them a slab dedicated for an altar. See engraving of a good example, "Archæological Journal," vol. iv. p. 247.

at an early period, say the sixth and seventh centuries, to have others beside the high altar, especially at the east end of the aisles and on the east side of the transepts, each dedicated to a particular saint, as is still the custom on the Continent. For instance, Bede speaks of Acca, Bishop of Hexham (A.D. 730) collecting the relics of saints, and erecting different altars with cells (*porticos*) for them in his church. In Canterbury, Gervase reckons up twenty-five altars previous to the year 1174. From the period that stone altars were introduced, it was usual to enclose the relics of saints in them, so that they often came to be considered the actual tombs of the saints themselves. The medieval idea of the altar being connected with the departed saint may well have had its origin in Scripture. (Rev. vi. 9.)

Where the high altar is a pontifical altar, it is generally placed at the western part of the church, the priest standing behind it that he may face the east when performing the Mass. This is the case at St. Peter's at Rome, and in one or two churches specially privileged.

The slab forming the altar was sometimes supported on pillars, sometimes on brackets, but usually on solid masonry. It was frequently marked with five crosses cut on the top, in allusion, it is said, to the five wounds of Christ.

Ancient *stone altars* are very rare in this country. It is sometimes said that none exist, but this is not true. The influence of the Puritans, exercised on different occasions, has nearly swept all away; but a few of them, and some of the chantry altars in the aisles and chapels, have escaped.

The high altar of Arundel Church, Sussex, appears to be original, and was probably in imitation of the early Christian altars at Rome; it was covered with wood until a recent period, and this fact probably preserved it from destruction.

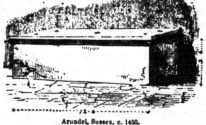

Arundel, Sussex, c. 1450.

At the Reformation the stone altars were first of all retained, and in the First Prayer-book of Edward VI. (1549), compiled under the direction of Archbishop Cranmer, the term 'altar' will be found frequently used; but in the revision of our English Liturgy in 1552, under the influence of the Continental Reformers, the word 'altar' was in all cases changed into 'table.' In the restoration of our Liturgy after Queen Mary's death, (1559,) it was a question whether to adopt Cranmer's Book of 1549, or the altered Book of 1552, there being strong parties in favour of each. The Book of 1552 was eventually adopted; but the Act of Parliament enjoining it contained the Proviso that (while the words of the 1552 Book were to be used) the ORNAMENTS of the church authorized by the Book of 1549 were to be retained.

Queen Elizabeth, in her Injunctions issued at the beginning of her reign, makes a special provision for the place of the "TABLES IN CHURCHES," to this effect :—" Whereas in many parts of the realm the Altars of the churches be removed and tables placed, and in some other places the Altars be not yet removed; in the order whereof, saving for an uniformity, there seemeth no matter of great moment, yet for observation of an uniformity through the whole realm, and for the better imitation of the law, it is ordered that no Altar be taken down, but by oversight of the Curate and Churchwarden. And that the Holy Table in every church be set in the place where the Altar stood; and there commonly covered, as thereto belongeth, and so to stand, saving when the communion of the Sacrament is to be distributed; at which time the same shall be so placed in good sort within the chancel, as whereby the minister may be more conveniently heard of the communicants, and the communicants more conveniently communicate with the said minister. And after the communion done, from time to time the same Holy Table to be placed where it stood before."

The object of this arrangement was to satisfy, as far as possible, both parties. The strong Puritan party were able to introduce the continental custom, and sit round the table; and in one or two rare instances the seats and large square tables remained, or were remaining, till a few years back (e.g. Deerhurst, Gloucestershire; Langley Chapel, near Acton Burnel, Shropshire; Shillingford, Berks, &c.); and in Jersey this Puritan position of the table is still very common: the injunctions, however, did not force the other party to move the Holy Table, provided that the communicants could hear, and be accommodated within the chancel.

The effect was, that the practices were very varied. To save the trouble, and also no doubt to prevent the irreverence ensuing from moving the Holy Table backwards and forwards, the law was seldom strictly followed. Most Curates, no doubt, left the Holy Table standing where the Altar stood, as the minister could be as well heard there as elsewhere when the communicants were gathered in the chancel. But the ultra-Puritans took advantage of the injunction to move the Holy Table, even out into the nave in some cases, and to assimilate the rite as far as possible to the Genevan model.

This practice of moving the Holy Table, may possibly be the explanation of those instances which have been observed, of the Holy Table in churches having the slab detached from the frame, or at least screwed into it, the screws appearing to be a recent addition.

Although, as has been said, a few instances of the stone altars having been suffered to remain can be found, in most cases the Commissioners ordered them to be removed, and the parish was bound to supply a Communion Table, or as it is more fully expressed in Archbishop Parker's Advertisements of March 28, 1566,—" a decent table standing on a frame for the Communion-table." But the practice of moving it backwards and forwards fell into desuetude, and though the Injunctions of Queen Elizabeth were not definitely repealed, the Holy Table now stands in all the churches in England " where the altar stood," not only before and after, but during the administration of the Holy Communion. The Communion Tables of the time of Elizabeth and James I. are frequently found remaining in churches, though from the plain character of the majority it is difficult to assign dates to these.

ALTAR-PIECE. See *Reredos.*	ALTO-RELIEVO. See *Basso-relievo.*
ALTAR-SCREEN. See *Screen.*	AMBRY, AMBRE = Almery.

Altar-tomb, a raised monument resembling a solid altar. This appears only to be a modern term, descriptive of the character and shape of the Tomb. It is equivalent to the expression High - tomb, used by Leland. Tombs on the north side of the altar, used for the ceremonies of the Easter *Sepulchre* were of this character.

Altar-tomb, Porlock, Somerset, c. 1500.

Alur (Old Eng. *alours*). This word appears generally to have signified the gutter, passage, or gallery, in which persons could walk behind a parapet on the top of a wall, or in other situations, especially in military architecture, where the Alur becomes of the highest importance. The term, however, was sometimes used for passages of various kinds. Lydgate used the word for covered walks in the streets. [See *Ambulatory*.]

A. Alur. B. Parapet. M. Machicolation.

Ambo (Gr. possibly from *anabainein* = to ascend), a kind of pulpit. Zosimus and Socrates the historians inform us, that St. Chrysostom preached from the *Ambo*, for the greater convenience of the people. St. Augustin also tells us, that for the same reason he preached from the

Epistle Ambo, St. Clement's, Rome, A.D. 1110.

Exedra or *Apse* of the church behind the altar. It appears from early writers, that the name of *Ambo* was especially applied to a reading-desk, which was raised on two steps, and was sometimes situated immediately within the entrance to the choir, at others on one side, as in the church of the Holy Cross at Jerusalem.

The *Ambo* is a prominent feature in the furniture of the churches at Rome, but the earliest now existing there are of the twelfth and thirteenth centuries, those in St. Clement's are of about A.D. 1110. The low marble screen was brought up from the lower church or crypt, which was filled with earth to support the pavement of the upper church when it was rebuilt at that period. The screen itself is of the eighth century, but the arrangement of it has evidently *been altered* when it was moved, and the *Ambones* inserted at that time; they are built partly upon the old screen, but are of a different work, and a different kind of marble.

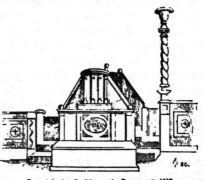

Gospel Ambo, St. Clement's, Rome, A.D. 1110.

All the *Ambones* in Rome are made of the same kind of marble, evidently the fashion of the twelfth century.

Amphitheatre, an oval theatre, with tiers of seats, used chiefly by the Romans to exhibit the combats of gladiators or wild beasts. The galleries with the seats were covered with awning. The general taste of that people for these amusements is proverbial, and they appear to have constructed amphitheatres at all their principal settlements. There are still considerable remains of them: in this country the earthworks only exist, at Cirencester, Sil-

---

Ambulatory, a place to walk in, such as *cloisters*. Lydgate, in his "Boke of Troye," writes—

"Freshe *Alures* with lustye hye pynacles..
...that called were deambulatoryes,
Men to walke togither twaine and
twaine
To keep them drye when it happed to
rayne."

Amphiprostyle, Amphyprostylos, a temple with a Portico at each end. See *Temple*.

Amphithura (Gr.), the curtain hanging like doors between nave and chancel.

Ancones = Consoles.

chester, and Dorchester: in France, much of the masonry exists at Arles, and at Nismes in Languedoc; in Istria at Pola; and in Italy, the well-known Colosseum at Rome, at Verona, Capua, Pompeii, and many other places, the buildings exist with their masonry very perfect.

Andirons, a term of frequent occurrence in old inventories, &c., and one which is still well known in some parts of the country, for the Fire-dogs: they are generally enumerated as a "pair of andirons," but occasionally only one is mentioned. In the hall at Penshurst, Kent, the hearth still remains in the middle of the room, and there stands on it *one* large fire-dog, consisting of an upright standard at each end, and a bar between. Although used chiefly for the braziers in the middle of the hall, they were also used in the fireplaces in the chambers.

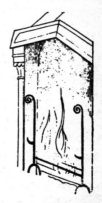

Andirons from MS. Illustration.

Annulet (lit. *a ring*), a small flat fillet, encircling a column, &c., used either by itself or in connection with other mouldings: it is used, several times repeated, under the *Ovolo* or *Echinus* of the Doric capital.

Annulets repeated.

Antæ (Lat.), a species of pilasters used in Greek and Roman architecture to terminate the *pteromata* or side walls of temples, when they are prolonged beyond the face of the end walls. The first order of temples, according to Vitruvius, is called "*in antis*," because the *pronaos* or porch in front of the cell is formed by the projection of the pteromata terminated by antæ, with columns between them. They may be said to correspond to the 'respond' in English architecture.

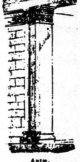

Antæ.

Ante-chapel, a term used in the Universities for the outer part at the west end of a chapel. It would form the transept of a cruciform church were a nave added, as was evidently intended at Merton College, Oxford. The plan was followed by Wykeham in New College, and Waynflete in Magdalen, and hence became a common feature in a collegiate chapel, both in Oxford and Cambridge.

Antefixæ, or Antefixes (Lat.), ornamented tiles on the top of the cornice or eaves, at the end of each ridge of tiling, as on the choragic monument of Lysicrates, at Athens; sometimes of marble, but generally of *terra cotta*, and ornamented with a mask, honeysuckle, or other decoration moulded on them. Also lions' heads carved on the upper mouldings of the cornice, either for ornament, or to serve as spouts to carry off the water, as on the Temple of the Winds at Athens.

Antepagmenta (Lat.), dressings or architrave of a doorway. This term does not include the frame of the door, which is of wood, but only the stone decorations, or stucco, when that material is used.

Apophyge (Gr.), the small curvature given to the top and bottom of the shaft of a column where it expands to meet the edge of the fillet. [See *Column.*]

Apse (Gr.), the semicircular or polygonal termination to the choir or aisles of a Basilica. This form was almost universally adopted in Germany, France, and Italy. A similar termination is sometimes given to the transepts and nave, and is also called by the same name. The use of the word *Porticus*, as a recess for a tomb or an altar, by Bede and other early historians, e.g. Gervase, is thought often to imply the apsidal termination of an aisle. There are a few churches with the semicircular apse at the east end in different parts of England, chiefly in the Norman style, and some in which this form has evidently been

---

ANTEPENDIUM, the frontal hangings of the Altar.

ANTISTITIUM = Monastery.

APODYTERIUM, a dressing-room next the bath in Roman villas.

In Oxford the atrium to the Convocation House is so called.

APOTHESIS, APOPHYSIS = Apophyge.

altered at a subsequent period. In several cases the crypts beneath have retained the old form when the superstructure has been altered.

On the Continent the apse continued in use much later than in England, where the practice of making the east end of the churches square began early in the Norman period. In the Gothic style the form of the apse was frequently changed from semicircular to polygonal.

Apse, Dalmeny, Linlithgowshire, c. 1150.

Arabesque, a species of ornament used for enriching flat surfaces, either painted, inlaid in mosaic, or carved in low relief: it was much used by the Arabs, as also by the Saracens or Moors in Spain. In the domestic architecture of this country in the sixteenth and seventeenth centuries, this mode of ornamentation is very frequent.

Arabesque.

Araeostyle, that style of the Grecian temple in which the columns are placed at the distance of four (and occasionally five) diameters apart.

APTERAL TEMPLE, Temple without columns on the sides.

ARBALISTERIA. See *Loopholes*.

ARCA or ARK, a chest; also a coffin.

Arcade, a series of arches, either open, or closed with masonry, supported by columns or piers. The term is more generally applied to the closed arches which are used for the decoration of the walls of churches, both on the exterior and interior: on buildings in the Norman style of the twelfth century, we frequently find them consisting of semicircular arches intersecting each other, supposed by some to have suggested the pointed arch. In later styles they are excessively ornamented, as for example at Lichfield, an illustration of which will be found under *Canopy;* a plainer example from Lincoln is given under *Perpent.*

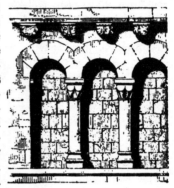

St. Peter's, Northampton, c. 1140.

Aqueduct (Lat.), an artificial channel for conveying water from one place to another, very frequently raised on arches, but sometimes carried underground or on the surface. The Roman aqueducts rank amongst their noblest designs and greatest works.

Arch. Primarily a construction of bricks, or stones, so arranged as by mutual pressure to support each other, and to become capable of sustaining a superincumbent weight.

Secondarily, any construction whether of wood, iron, or of other material, although in one piece, assuming the same form as the above. (Lat. *Arcus* = a bow.)

With whatever people the arch may have originated, it is certain that the Romans were the first to bring it into general use. The influence which the arch has had in effecting changes in architecture is much greater than is generally supposed: not only may the deterioration which took place in the Roman be ascribed to it, but even the introduction of Gothic architecture may be said to be

ARCH. The sides of an arch are termed its *haunches* or *flanks,* and the highest part the *crown.*

owing to it, for the arch gradually encroached upon the leading principle of Classical architecture, namely, that the *horizontal lines* should be dominant, until that principle was entirely abrogated, and the principle of the Gothic, namely, the *dominant vertical line*, took its place.

In the early Christian Churches in Rome the arches are usually of brick, resting upon marble columns, and are frequently concealed behind a horizontal entablature. When once the open application of the arch above the columns had been introduced, it appears never to have been abandoned, and the *entablature* was interrupted to suit the arch, the principal object aimed at being an appearance of height and spaciousness; and in some instances in late Roman work the entablature is omitted entirely, and the arch rises directly from the capital of the column, as in Gothic architecture. In the fifth and sixth centuries, a piece of entablature is preserved over the capital in Byzantine work, as at Ravenna, and in the church of S. Stefano Rotondo in Rome. When, after the dominion of the Romans was destroyed, and the rules governing the true proportions of architecture, from which they had themselves so widely departed, were entirely lost, the nations of Europe began again to erect large buildings, they would naturally endeavour to copy the structures of the Romans; but it was not to have been expected, even supposing they were capable of imitating them exactly, that they would have retained the clumsy, and to them unmeaning appendage of a broken entablature, but would have placed the arch at once on the top of the column, as

Roman Arch, Brixworth.

we know they did; hence arose the various national styles which preceded the introduction of the pointed arch, including the Norman.

The earliest Norman arches are semicircular and square-edged, as in the remains of the work of Edward the Confessor at Westminster, not recessed (or divided into orders), and not moulded. As the Norman style advanced, the arches became much enriched with mouldings and ornaments, and recessed, often doubly or trebly recessed, or what Professor Willis called divided into two or more orders. The *form* of the arch also by this time begins to vary very much; a stilted arch is often used, sometimes for greater convenience in vaulting, in other instances, like the horse-shoe arch, apparently from fashion only. The form, however, is of very little use as a guide to the date of a building, either in this or in the later styles; it is dictated always by convenience rather than by any rule, and it is probable that the pointed arch came in exceptionally much earlier than has been generally supposed. The mouldings and details, both of the arch itself and of the capitals, are a much better guide to the date than the form of the arch.

Antiquaries are not agreed upon the *origin of the pointed arch*, some contending that it is an importation from the East, and others that it is the invention of the countries in which Gothic Architecture prevailed. It is perhaps more true that the Gothic style in which the pointed arch is so chief a feature was gradually developed from the mixture of the Romanesque and Byzantine, and that the origin of the pointed arch was rather constructional than ornamental. But be its origin what it may, the pointed arch was not introduced to general use on this side of Europe till the latter half of the twelfth century. From that time it continued, under various modifications, to be the prevailing form in the countries in which Gothic architecture flourished, until the revival of the Classical orders: one of the best-authenticated instances of the earliest use of the pointed arch in England is the circular part of the Temple Church of London, which was dedicated in 1185. The choir of Canterbury Cathedral, commenced in 1175, is usually referred to as the earliest example in England, and none of earlier date has been authenticated; although it seems probable that many pointed arches of the transitional character with Norman details are at least as early as the middle of the twelfth century, if not earlier, as at Malmesbury Abbey, St. Cross, &c.

The only forms used by the ancients were the *semicircle* (fig. 1), the *segment* (fig. 2, 3), and *ellipse* (fig. 4),

all which continued prevalent till the pointed arch appeared, and even after that period they were occasionally
employed in all the styles of Gothic architecture.

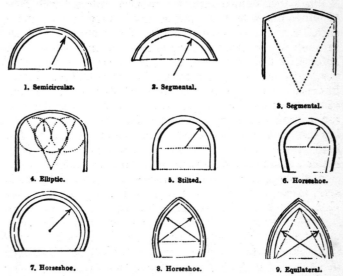

1. Semicircular.   2. Segmental.

3. Segmental.

4. Elliptic.   5. Stilted.   6. Horseshoe.

7. Horseshoe.   8. Horseshoe.   9. Equilateral.

In the Romanesque and Norman styles, the centre, or
point from which the curve of the arch is struck, is not unfrequently found to be above the line of the impost, and the
mouldings between these two levels are either continued
vertically (to which arrangement the term *stilted* has been
applied, (fig. 5), or they are slightly inclined inwards
(fig. 6), or the curve is prolonged till it meets the impost
(fig. 7): these two latter forms are called *horse-shoe*
arches: pointed arches are sometimes elevated in a similar manner, especially in the Early English style, and
are called by the same names (fig. 8), but they are principally used in Moorish architecture. The proportions
given to the simple *Pointed Arch* (Fr. *Ogive*) are threefold: viz. the equilateral (fig. 9), which is formed on an
equilateral triangle; the lancet (fig. 10), formed on an
acute-angled triangle, and the drop arch (fig. 11), formed
on an obtuse-angled triangle; these, together with the
segmental pointed arch (fig. 12), are the prevailing forms
used in Early English work, although trefoiled arches

(figs. 13, 14, 15), cinquefoiled, &c. (figs. 16, 17), of various proportions, are frequently met with, especially towards

10. Lancet.   11. Drop.   12. Segmental Pointed.

13. Trefoil.   14. Trefoil.   15. Trefoil.

16. Cinquefoil.   17. Multifoil.   18. Ogee.

the end of the style, but they are principally used in panellings, niches, and other small openings.

Simple pointed arches were used in all the styles of Gothic architecture, though not with the same frequency; the lancet-arch is common in the *Early English,* and is sometimes found in the *Decorated,* but is very rarely met with in the *Perpendicular;* the drop-arch and the equilateral abound in the two first styles, and in the early part of the Perpendicular, but they afterwards in great measure gave way to the four-centred. Plain and pointed segmental arches also are frequently used for windows in the Decorated and Perpendicular styles, but not often for other openings. With the Decorated style was introduced the *ogee* arch, Fr. *Arcade en talon* (fig. 18), which continued to be used throughout the Perpendicular style, although less frequently than in the Decorated; it is very common over niches, tombs, and small doorways, and in Northamptonshire over doors or windows, [see pp. 89, 100] but the difficulty of constructing it securely precluded its general adoption for large openings. About the commencement of the Perpendicular style the *four-centred*

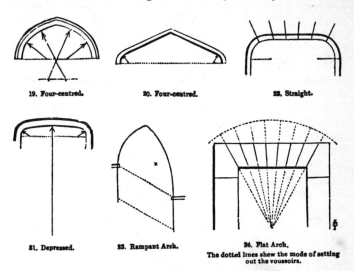

19. Four-centred.   20. Four-centred.   22. Straight.

21. Depressed.   23. Rampant Arch.   24. Flat Arch.
The dotted lines shew the mode of setting out the voussoirs.

arch (fig. 19) appeared as a general form, and continued in use until the revival of Classical architecture: when first introduced the proportions were bold and effective, but it was gradually more and more depressed until the whole principle, and almost the form, of an arch was lost, for it became so flat as to be frequently cut in a single stone, which was applied as a lintel over the head of an opening. In some instances an arch, having the effect of a four-centred arch, is found, of which the sides are perfectly straight, except at the lower angles next the impost (fig. 20); it is generally a sign of late and bad work, and prevailed most during the reigns of Henry VIII., Elizabeth, and James I. The four-centred arch appears never to have been brought into general use out of England, although the Flamboyant style of the Continent, which was contemporary with our Perpendicular. underwent the same gradual debasement; the *depressed* arches used in Flamboyant work are flattened ellipses (fig. 21), or sometimes, as in late Perpendicular, ogees, and not unfrequently the head of an opening is made *straight*, with the angles only rounded off (fig. 22); this last form and the flattened ellipse are very rarely met with in England.

There is also the *rampant* arch (fig. 23), the imposts of which are at different levels; and what is called a *flat* arch (fig. 24), which is constructed with stones cut into wedges or other shapes so as to support each other without rising into a curve, and considerable ingenuity is often displayed in the formation of these. This form is commonly used over fire-places.

Notice must also be taken of a construction which is not unfrequently used as a substitute for an arch, especially in the style which is referred to as perhaps being Saxon, and which produces a very similar effect (fig. 25); it consists of two straight stones set upon their edge and leaning against each other at the top, so as to form two sides of a triangle and support a superincumbent weight; excepting in the style just alluded to, these are seldom used except in rough work, or in situations in which they would not be seen. It does, however, sometimes occur in good Early English work, as in Hereford Cathedral, and Uffington Church, Berkshire.

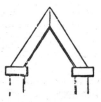

25. Triangular.

There is one form given to the heads of openings, which is frequently called an arch, although it is not one. It consists of a straight lintel, supported on a corbel in each jamb, projecting into the opening so as to contract its width; the mouldings, or splay of the jambs and head being usually continued on the corbels, producing an effect something like a flattened trefoil (fig. 26); the corbels are usually cut into a hollow curve on the under side, but they occasionally vary in form. This form has been called the *shouldered* arch, from its resembling a man's shoulders with the head cut off. These heads are most commonly used for doorways: especially in domestic work, and in the thirteenth and fourteenth centuries.

26. Shouldered.

As the arch forms so important an element in the Gothic style, as distinguished from the entablature of the Greek and Roman styles, it is introduced in every part of the building and receives a great variety of ornamentation. In the *Norman* style such ornaments as the zigzag and *beak-head* are most usual; in the *Early English* style the dog's-tooth in the hollows is very frequent; in the *Decorated* style the arches are not usually more rich than in the Early English; the mouldings are not so bold nor the hollows so deep, and the plain chamfered arch is very common in this style. When ornament is used, the ball-flower or the four-leaved flower take the place of the dog's-tooth. The arches of the *Perpendicular* style are often profusely moulded, but the mouldings less bold and less deep even than in the previous style; they are sometimes ornamented with the foliage peculiar to that style, and sometimes also quite plain.

Illustrations of the various forms of arches will be found more or less under *Doorway, Window,* &c., and the examples of their ornamentation under *Mouldings.*

Architecture, (Gr. *Archi-tekton* = chief builder or architect). The history of Architecture is the history of civilization written on stone, in a language easily learned, and which cannot deceive. Every nation has an architecture of its own, just as distinct as its language, and there is a remarkable analogy between the two, as in both cases there are provincialisms also. Each succeeding century has a very distinct character of its own, but modified by the different countries and provinces to which the buildings belong; it is therefore necessary to know something of the history of the country before we can properly understand its architecture. The Eastern nations have left us many magnificent buildings in a variety of styles, some of which belong to a very early period in the history of the world: the great empires of antiquity, the Assyrian, the Egyptian, the Persian, and the Indian, may all be traced by their buildings. The Greeks have left us their beautiful temples, which the Romans vainly strove to excel. In Western Europe Roman architecture gradually died out along with Roman civilization; from the fourth to the tenth century there is a gradual decay of art of all kinds, with a great struggle to revive it in the ninth century, when numerous buildings were erected under the influence of Charles the Great, in rude imitation of the early Roman buildings; but this effort did not last more than half a century, and we have scarcely any buildings of the tenth century in any part of Western Europe.

But during this period the Eastern Empire was far more flourishing and more civilized than the Western; that variety of the Roman style which was established in the East, distinguished especially by the use of the Dome or cupola, and called the Byzantine style [see *Byzantine Architecture*] is very superior to the Western style of the same period. When the Crusaders visited Byzantium, Palestine, and Syria, they found buildings there very superior to any they had at home, and they brought home with them drawings, and probably workmen also, to improve their own buildings.

The revival of civilization, and with it architecture, had indeed begun about the beginning of the eleventh century, and the distinct architecture of the different countries of Western Europe begins from that period. Previously to that time the Celtic nations were accustomed to build of wood only (with a few rare exceptions). The first stone buildings in England, the church towers called Anglo-Saxon, are in imitation of wooden buildings [see *Saxon* style], the cut stones are not laid in beds as a mason would place them, but upright at the angles, and horizontally, through the walls of rubble and rough stone, to tie them together, like the wooden frame of a house.

In the different provinces of Gaul which were then separate kingdoms, now included in the general name of France, the Roman buildings which there remained served as models to copy from, and each nation formed a peculiar style of its own, derived originally from the peculiar characteristics of each Roman building which had served as the model for that country. There is a very marked difference in the architecture north of the Loire and that of the south. In Normandy, with which England was more immediately connected, there were few or no Roman buildings to copy; but the Normans were a very energetic race,

ARCH-BUTTRESS. See *Buttress*.

and not to be left behind in the general march of civilization—they were driven to invent for themselves. Their
early buildings of the eleventh century were very plain
but very substantial, and in many instances the ornamentation was entirely added in the twelfth century, after
the return of the Crusaders, without rebuilding. [See
Norman style.] All our rich Norman ornament belongs
to the twelfth century, when the arts of building and
stone carving had arrived at great perfection, and each succeeding generation has left lasting marks of its progress.

During the second half of the twelfth century, in
the long peaceful reign of Henry II., this progress was
particularly rapid, and it was during this period that
the Gothic style was developed both in England and
France. The movement had been begun by Suger, at
St. Denis, about 1140, but the remains of his work there
are quite of early transitional character; the new style
was not developed until the following generation. The
Early English or the early French Gothic style cannot
be considered as more than varieties of the same style
with certain national distinctions. [See *Early English*
style.] This style continued for about a century, and
gradually changed into the Decorated style of the latter
part of the thirteenth and early part of the fourteenth
centuries. This style, sometimes called the "Perfect
Gothic style," is remarkably alike in both countries,
and in Germany also. [See *Decorated* style.] From this
perfection the art soon began to decline, and the later
Gothic styles of each country are more distinct and separate than the earlier ones. The Flamboyant style of
France is quite different from the Perpendicular style of
England. The Flamboyant styles of Germany, Belgium,
and Holland, all have national or provincial characters of
their own. The Gothic of Italy was at first a manifest copy
of the Western Gothic, but was developed into a style of
its own, which is not without merit. In the fifteenth
century the revival of classical literature was naturally
accompanied by the revival of Classical or pagan art, and
at a time when the Latin language was attempted to be
revived as the universal language, the same pedantry was
applied to architecture, and the style called *The Renais-*

sance, a bad imitation of the Roman, became almost universal, and it was not until the middle of the nineteenth century that the national styles of the different countries of modern Europe were revived.

Architrave (Gr. and Lat. = chief-beam), the lowest division of the *entablature,* in Classical architecture, resting immediately on the abacus of the capital: also the ornamental moulding running round the exterior curve of an arch; and hence applied to the mouldings round the openings of doors and windows, &c. [For illustration, see *Column* and *Order.*]

Archivolt (Fr. from Lat. *arcus, volutus*), the under curve or surface of an arch, from impost to impost. The ar hivolt is sometimes quite plain, with square edges, in which case the term *soffit* is applicable to it; this kind of archivolt is used in the Roman and Romanesque styles, including those buildings in this country which are by some considered as Saxon, and in the early Norman. In later Norman work it usually has the edges moulded or chamfered off; and towards the end of that style, and throughout all the Gothic styles, it is frequently divided into several concentric portions, each projecting beyond that which is beneath (or within) it.

Arena (Lat.), the floor of an amphitheatre, a wooden floor covered with sand for the athletes to wrestle upon: sometimes applied to the amphitheatre itself; often confounded with the *area* or open space, and in that sense applied also to the body of a church.

Ashlar, Achelor, Ashler, hewn or squared stone used in building, as distinguished from that which is unhewn, or rough as it comes from the quarry: it is called by different names at the present day, according to the way in which it is worked, and is used for the facings of walls. "Clene hewen" or finely worked ashlar is frequently specified in ancient contracts for building, in contradistinction to that which is roughly worked.

ARMARIUM (Lat.), same as Aumbry, probably = Fr. *Armoire.*

ARMATURE (Fr.), iron bars or framing employed for the consolidation of a building.

ARRIS (Fr. *Arête*), the edge of a roof, or of a stone, or of a piece of wood.

ASHLER, piece in a roof. See *Roof.*

Astragal (Gr. = a knuckle-bone), a small semicircular moulding or bead, either encircling a column, or in other situations. [See *Column.*]

Atlantes, male figures used in the place of columns to support entablatures, &c.: so called by the Greeks, but by the Romans *Telamones*.

Atrium (Lat.), the entrance court or hall of a Roman dwelling. In a large and complete house it was enclosed on all sides by a series of chambers, which opened into it, and to which it gave access and light. It was roofed so as to leave a large opening (*compluvium*) in the centre to admit light, and consequently rain: the latter was received in a cistern (*impluvium*). There was frequently a colonnade round it, as in several houses at Pompeii. Afterwards an arcade was often substituted for the colonnade. In houses where there were many courts, the word would more properly be applied to the one nearest the entrance, also called the Porticus or Peristyle.

In the large Early Christian churches an atrium was built before the principal entrance doors, and this practice, as well as the name, was retained to the eleventh century, and in some cases even later. When the practice, however, of constructing such an enclosed court was abandoned, the name was transferred to the churchyard and cemetery.

Attic, a low story above an entablature, or above a cornice, which limits the height of the main part of an elevation: it is chiefly used in the Roman and Italian styles.

Bailey (Lat. *Ballium*), a name given to the courts or wards of a castle formed by the spaces between the circuits of walls or defences which surrounded the keep: sometimes there were two or three of these courts between the outer wall and the keep, divided from each other by embattled walls. The name is frequently retained long after the castle itself has disappeared; as the Bailey in Lincoln, the Old Bailey in London, St. Peter's-in-the-Bailey in Oxford.

ASPERSORIUM (Lat.), a holy-water basin, used for the stone *stoup*.

AUMBRY. See *Almonry*.

AUTER, AWTER = Altar.

BACKS (in carpentry), the principal rafters of a *Roof*. The upper side of any piece of timber is also termed the *back*, the lower side being called the *breast*.

Ball-flower, an ornament resembling a ball placed in a globular flower, the three petals of which form a cup round it: this ornament is usually found inserted in a hollow mould- ing, and is generally characteristic of the Decorated style of the fourteenth century; but it sometimes occurs, though rarely, in buildings of the thirteenth century, or Early English style, as in the west front of Salisbury Cathedral, where it is mixed with the tooth ornament: it is, however, rarely found in that style, and is an indication that the work is late. It is the prevailing ornament at Here- ford Cathedral, in the south aisle of the nave of Glou- cester Cathedral, and the west end of Grantham Church; in all these instances in pure Decorated work. Sometimes it is mixed with foliage, more rarely alone. A flower resem- bling this, except that it has four petals, is occasionally found in very late Norman work, but it is used with other flowers and ornaments, and not repeated in long suits, as in the Deco- rated style. A similar ornament is of frequent occurrence in the twelfth century in the west of France, but not in the fourteenth century. As to its origin there are several theories. One that it represented the Pomegranate, and was introduced out of compli- ment to Queen Eleanor of Castile. The probabilities, however, are that it was brought from the East.

Spire, Salisbury Cathedral, c. 1300.

Examples of the use of the ball-flower will be found in the illustrations given under *Moulding, Niche, Rib, Win- dow,* &c.

BAGUETTE (Fr.), a small mould- ing.

BALCONY, a projecting gallery in front of a window, supported usually by consoles, brackets, cantalivers, or pillars, and fre- quently surrounded by a *Balus- trade.*

BALDACHINO, BALDEQUIN (Lat. *Baldakinus,* Anglicè Bawde- kin), 1. a rich embroidered cloth used for copes; 2. The port- able canopy borne over shrines, &c. in procession; 3. The cibo- rium.

Baluster, corruptly banister and ballaster, a small pillar usually made circular, and swelling in the middle or towards the bottom (*entasis*), commonly used in a balustrade. A rude balustre-shaft occurs in the Romanesque styles of the eleventh and twelfth centuries in England and elsewhere, where it occupies the place of a mid-wall shaft to the tower windows. Some of the examples have evidently been turned in a lathe, and it has been observed that they bear a great resemblance to the spokes of a cart-wheel at the present day, also turned in a lathe in the same manner. From the eleventh century it was disused till the revival of Classical architecture in the sixteenth.

St. Alban's, c. 1070.

Balustrade, a range of small balusters supporting a coping or cornice, and forming a parapet or enclosure.

Band, a flat face or fascia, a square moulding, or a continuous tablet or a series of ornaments, &c., encircling a building or continued along the wall. Bands of panelling on the external surface of a

Band of Panelling, Cranford St. John's, c. 1490.

wall are very usual in rich work of the Perpendicular style, especially on the lower part of a tower, and sometimes higher up between the stories also, as in the rich Somersetshire towers, and in Northamptonshire and Oxfordshire, and indeed wherever rich churches of this style are found. This kind of ornament is however used in the earlier styles also, though less frequently. See also a good illustration from Yelvertoft Church under *Perpendicular.*

BALUSTRARIA. See *Loop-holes.*
BANKER, a cushion or covering for a seat.

Also the moulding, or suite of mouldings which encircles the pillars and small shafts in Gothic architecture, the use of which was most prevalent in the Early English style. Bands of this description are not unfrequently met with in very late Norman work, while they are occasionally to be found in early Decorated work. When the shafts are long they are often encircled by several bands at equal distances apart between the cap and base. [See *Tablet*.]

Band of a Shaft. Whitby Abbey
c. 1250.

Baptistery, sometimes a separate building; sometimes the part of a church in which baptism was performed by immersion. Baptisteries are frequently found in Italy, and rare cases occur in France and Germany. The name is also applied occasionally to the enclosure containing the font, as at Luton, Bedfordshire, which is an ornamented erection of Decorated work, forming a canopy over the font.

A separate building was usual with the Early Christians, and there are many fine baptisteries in Italy, some of them as early as the fourth century. In Germany also, especially near Vienna, there are very fine medieval baptisteries. In England the climate was not favourable for baptism by immersion, and instances of it are rare. At Cranbrook, in Kent, the entrance, or approach, to the room over the porch is used as a baptistery for adult persons.

Barbican, an advanced work before the gate of a castle or fortified town; or any outwork at a short distance from the main works, generally serving the purpose of a watch-tower. There are barbicans remaining at York, Scarborough, Alnwick, and Carlisle Castles. This term is especially applied to the outwork intended to defend the drawbridge, called in modern fortifications the *Tête du Pont*. It was frequently constructed of timber. It often consists of two walls parallel to each other with an arch or a gate at each end to defend the principal gate, which is midway between them.

Barge-board, Verge-board, a board generally used on the verge of gables where the covering of the roof extends over the wall; it usually projects from the wall, and either covers the rafter, that would otherwise be exposed, or occupies the place of a rafter. On the gables of houses and church porches, and particularly on those of wood, barge-boards are very extensively used, but on the gables of the main roofs of churches they occur very rarely. The earliest barge-boards known to exist are of the fourteenth century.

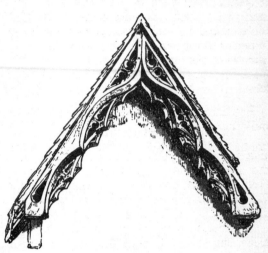

George Inn, Salisbury, c. 1350.

After that time they were used most abundantly, and were of very various designs, and in later examples they not unfrequently supported a *hipknob* on the point of the gable; they are usually either feathered, or panelled, or pierced with a series of trefoils, quatrefoils, &c., and the spandrels carved with foliage; when feathered, the cusps or points of the principal featherings have flowers sometimes carved on them. As Gothic architecture advanced, the barge-boards continued gradually to lose much of their rich and bold effect. There are few of the old towns where examples do not still occur, but they become fewer and fewer every year.

BARREL-VAULT. See *Vault.*
BAR-TRACERY, a term to dis-
tinguish the later from the earlier tracery. See *Tracery.*

Bartizan, the small overhanging turret which projects from the angles on the top of a tower, or from the parapet or other parts of a building. They are not so common in England as on the Continent.

Base, the lower part of a pillar, wall, &c.; the division of a column on which the shaft is placed: the Grecian Doric order has no base, but the other Classical orders have each their appropriate bases, which are divided into *plinth* and *mouldings*, though in some examples the former of these divisions is omitted.

In middle-age architecture, the forms and proportions of the various members not being regulated by arbitrary rules, as in the Classical orders, the same capricious varieties are found in the bases, as in all the other features of each of the successive styles. In the Norman style the mouldings of the base often bear a resemblance to those of the Tuscan order, with a massive plinth which is most commonly square, even though the shaft of the pillar and the moulded part of the base may be circular or octagonal. There is often a second

Door, Haddiscoe, Norfolk.

or sub-plinth, under the Norman base, the projecting angle of which is chamfered off. In the earlier period of this style the bases generally have but few mouldings, but as a rule they increase in numbers, and vary in their arrangement as the style advances. There is a very great variety of bases in the Norman style; often in the same building scarcely any two are alike: this seems to be especially the case in the earlier division of the style both in Normandy and in England, and the bases in the two countries are often exactly alike. In Gundulph's crypt, in Rochester Cathedral, this variety of bases is found, and it continues until quite late in the style.

At the commencement of the *Early English* style the bases differ but little from the Norman, having very frequently a single or double plinth, retaining the square form, with leaves springing out of the mouldings lying on the angles; at a later period the plinth commonly takes the same form as the mouldings, and is often made so high as to resemble a pedestal, and there is frequently a second moulding below the principal suite of the base, as at the Temple Church, London:

Window Shaft, Stanton Harcourt, Oxon.

in this style the mouldings of the base sometimes overhang the face of the plinth. The mouldings of the Early English bases do not vary so much as those of the other styles, and those which are most usual approach very nearly to the Attic base. One of the characteristics of early examples of the transitional Norman and the Early English base is that the moulding will hold water, which is not the case in any other style.

In the *Decorated* style there is considerable variety in the bases, although they have not generally many mouldings: the plinths, like the mouldings, conform to the shape of the shaft, or they are sometimes made octagonal, while the mouldings are circular, and in this case the mouldings overhang the face of the plinth; in some examples, where the shaft of the pillar is circular, the upper member only of the base conforms to it, the other

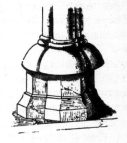

Dorchester, Oxon.

mouldings, as well as the plinth, becoming octagonal: the plinths are often double and of considerable height, the projecting angle of the lower one being worked either with a splay, a hollow, or small moulding. A common suite of mouldings for bases in this style consists of a torus and one or two beads above.

In the *Perpendicular* style the plinths of the bases are almost invariably octagonal, and of considerable height,

and very frequently double, the projection of the lower
one being moulded with a reversed ogee or a hollow:
when the shaft is circular, the whole of the mouldings of
the base sometimes follow the same
form, but sometimes the upper member
only conforms to it, the others being
made octagonal like the plinth: in
clustered pillars in which there are
small shafts of different sizes, their
bases are often on different levels, and
consist of different mouldings, with
one or two members only carried round
the pillar, which are commonly those
on the upper part of the lower plinth.
The characteristic moulding of the Perpendicular base is the reversed ogee,
used either singly or double; when
double there is frequently a bead between them; this moulding when used
for the lower and most prominent
member of the base, has the upper
angle rounded off, which gives it a
peculiar wavy appearance: the mouldings in this style most commonly overhang the face of the plinth.

Pier, Ewelme, Oxon.

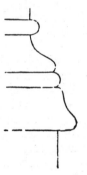

The above descriptions apply only
where a single shaft occurs. In compound piers, which are made up of
groups of single pillars, the bases become more complex.

Basement, the lower story or floor of a building, beneath
the principal one. In ordinary houses the lower story is
not called a basement unless partly below the surface of
the ground. In larger buildings, in which an architectural arrangement is introduced, the lower story, even
if above the ground, is called a basement, if in the composition it serves as a pedestal or substructure for the
main order of the architecture.

Base Court, the first or outer court of a large mansion.

Base-moulding, or base-table, a projecting moulding or band of mouldings near the bottom of a wall, &c.; it is sometimes placed immediately upon the top of the plinth, and sometimes a short distance above it, in which case the intervening space is frequently panelled in circles, quatrefoils, &c.

Basilica, the name applied by the Romans to their public halls, either of justice, of exchange, or other business. The plan was usually a rectangle divided into aisles by rows of columns, that in the middle being the widest, with a semicircular apse at one end in which the tribunal was placed. Many of these buildings were afterwards converted into Christian churches; and their ground-plan was generally followed in the early churches, which also long retained the name, and it is still applied to some of the churches in Rome by way of honorary distinction.

This name became synonymous with Church, and was applied by some writers even to the small burial-chapels in the Catacombs at Rome; the original meaning is, however, that above mentioned, and the name is applied in Rome in an especial manner to the seven principal churches founded by Constantine. The usual arrangements of a church on this plan are borrowed from the halls of justice, in which there was an altar on the chord of the apse for administering oaths, separated from the nave by a low screen or cancellus; the seat for the judges was against the wall in the centre of the apse, raised on steps, and these steps were continued round the wall of the apse, with seats upon them. The basilica in the palace of the Cæsars at Rome, which was never converted into a church, has remains of the altar and the *cancelli*. [See *Chancel*.]

In the time of Constantine the *apse* appears to have been considered a necessary part of a church, as in the church of Santa Croce: when one of the halls of the palace, which had no apse, was converted into a church, an apse was added to it. The Basilica Constantia at Rome on the Velia was originally built by Maxentius as the Temple of Peace, and an apse was added to it by Constantine

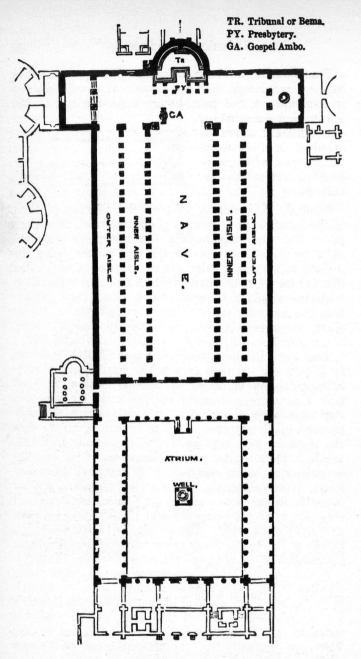

TR. Tribunal or Bema.
PY. Presbytery.
GA. Gospel Ambo.

TR.
PY
GA
OUTER AISLE
INNER AISLE.
N A V E.
INNER AISLE.
OUTER AISLE.
ATRIUM.
WELL.

Original Plan of the Basilica of St. Peter at Rome.

when it was made into a Basilica. The apse, therefore, belongs to the earliest idea of a public church; those previously existing had been either rooms or chapels. The basilican plan almost requires that the altar should stand detached on the chord of the apse, and this was probably the case in the early churches in England, as is shewn in the case of Canterbury, but after the revival of the building art in the eleventh century the apse was soon abandoned, and the custom of placing the altar against the east wall became universal in this country.

Bas-relief, or Basso-relievo, sculptured work, the figures of which project less than half their true proportions from the wall or surface on which they are carved: when the projection is equal to half the true proportions it is called *Mezzo-relievo;* when more than half it is *Alto-relievo.*

Batter, a term applied to walls built out of the upright, or gently sloping inwards: for example, the towers of the Castle, and of St. Peter's Church, Oxford, of Isham Church, Northants, and some others, *batter;* that is, they are smaller at the top than at the bottom, the walls all inclining inwards. Wharf walls, and walls built to support embankments and fortifications, generally batter.

Battlement, an indented parapet originally used only on fortifications and intended for service, but afterwards employed on ecclesiastical and other edifices and intended for ornament only. The solid parts of a battlement are called *merlons,*

Tower of Oxford Castle, A.D. 1070.

BASINET. See illustrations to *Brass.*

BASTILE, a castle or tower used as a prison.

BASTION, a bulwark or tower projecting from the face of a fortification.

and the intervals between them *embrasures,* but these are rather military terms than ecclesiastical. In the earlier battlements the *embrasures* appear to have been narrow in proportion to the size of the *merlons.* On ecclesiastical buildings the battlements are often richly panelled, or pierced with circles trefoils, quatrefoils, &c., and the coping is frequently continued up the sides of the merlons so as to form a continuous line round them, as at St. George's, Windsor. On fortifi-

St. George's Chapel, Windsor.

cations the battlements are generally quite plain, or pierced only with a very narrow, cruciform, or upright opening, the ends of which often terminate in circles, called *loopholes* or *oillets,* through which archers could shoot : sometimes the coping on the top of the merlons is carried over the embrasures, producing nearly the appearance of a pierced parapet, as at the leaning tower at Caerphilly. Occasionally on military structures figures of warriors or animals are

Walls of York.

carved on the tops of the merlons, as at Alnwick and Chepstow Castles.

In the fourteenth century, and afterwards, battlements are very frequently used in ecclesiastical work as ornaments on cornices, tabernacle work, and other minor features, and in the Perpendicular style are sometimes found on the transoms and bases of windows. It is remarkable that the use of this ornament is almost entirely confined to the English styles of Gothic architecture. In Wales a peculiar battlement is used, as at Swansea and St. David's, which has a hollow space under it to allow of the free passage of the water from the roof, an ingenious contrivance suitable to the climate : it is used chiefly in the fourteenth century.

The Irish battlements are also very peculiar, consisting

of a sort of double battlement, one rising out of the other; they are very picturesque, but very liable to decay. The idea of them was probably taken from the Venetian battlements, which bear some resemblance to them. In Ireland there is frequently a row of holes on a level with the gutter to let off the water, instead of the English gurgoyles or the Welsh openings.

Bay, a principal compartment or division in the architectural arrangement of a building, marked either by the buttresses or pilasters on the walls, by the disposition of the main ribs of the vaulting of the interior, by the main arches and pillars, the principals of the roof, or by any other leading features that separate it into corresponding portions. The word is also sometimes used for the space between the mullions of a window, properly called a *light;* it is occasionally found corrupted into *Day.*

Bay-window, a window forming a bay or recess in a room, and projecting outwards from the wall either in a rectangular, polygonal, or semicircular form, often called a *bow*-window. Bay-windows do not appear to have been used earlier than the Perpendicular style, but at that period they were very frequently employed, particularly in halls, where they are invariably found at one end, and sometimes at both ends, of the dais, and the lights are generally considerably longer than those of the other windows, so as to reach much nearer to the floor. Semicircular bay-windows were not used till Gothic architecture had begun to lose its purity, and were at no period so common as the other forms. Windows of this kind are

Compton Winyate, Warwickshire.

sometimes used in upper stories, and in such cases are supported on corbels or on projecting suites of mouldings. [See *Oriel.*]

Beak-head, a term applied to an ornament which is
very frequently
used in rich
Norman door-
ways, resem-
bling a head
with a beak:
there are many
varieties of this
ornament. An-
other similar
form having a
tongue hanging
out, instead of
a beak, is call-
ed the *Catshead.*

Beak-heads, Iffley Church.

Beam, this term appears formerly, as at present, to have
been applied generally to the principal horizontal timbers
of a building, an additional epithet being used to point
out the particular application of such of them as have no
other specific names. [See *Roof.*]

Belfry, a bell-tower, or campanile, usually forming part
of a church, but sometimes detached from it, as at Evesham,
Berkeley, Chichester Cathedral, Walton, Norfolk, and Led-
bury, Herefordshire, &c. At Lapworth, Warwickshire, the
belfry is connected with the church by a covered passage.
This term is also applied to the room in the tower in
which the bells are hung. At
Pembridge in Herefordshire, there
is a detached belfry built entirely
of wood, the frame in which the
bells are hung rising at once from
the ground, with merely a casing
of boards. [See *Tower.*]

Bell. The body of a Corinthian
or Composite capital, supposing

Bell of a Capital.

the foliage stripped off, is called the bell; the same name
is applied also to the Early English and other capitals in
Gothic architecture which in any degree partake of this
form.

Bells. The use of bells in churches for the purpose of assembling the congregation appears to have been introduced into England at a very early period, and are supposed to have had their origin at Nola (whence *nola*, "a bell") in Campania (whence *campana* and *campanile*). The illumination of St. Æthelwold's Benedictional shews that they were in use in the tenth century; this seems intended to represent five bells hanging in a tower and not in an open turret. And as early as A.D. 674 Bede mentions the "hearing the well-known sound of a bell."

The inscriptions on bells are mostly pious aspirations, frequently addressed to the patron saint in whose name the bell, or the church containing it, had been consecrated.

Bell-gable, Bell-turret, or Bell-cot: in small churches and chapels that have no towers, there is very frequently a bell-gable or turret at the west end in which the bells are hung; sometimes these contain but one bell, sometimes two, and occasionally three, as at Radipole, near Weymouth: a few of these erections may be of Norman date, but the greater number are later;

Bell-gable, Little Casterton, Gloucestershire.

BEAD, 1. Small round moulding, same as *Astragal*; 2. A moulding in Norman work, like a row of beads.

BEAM. Chief names of beam are—Binding-, Collar-, Dragon-, Girding-, Hammer-, Straining-, Tie-, Somer-.

BED, the stratum or direction in which the stone naturally lay in the quarry.

BED - MOULD, in Classical architecture, mouldings of cornice immediately below corona.

many of them are Early English, in which style they appear to have been very frequent. Besides the bell-gables above referred to, there is often found a smaller erection, of very similar kind, on the apex of the eastern end of the roof of the nave. This is for the *Sancte-bell*, which see.

Bench-table, or Bench, a low stone seat on the inside of the walls, and sometimes round the bases of the pillars in churches, porches, cloisters, &c.

Bevel, a sloped or canted surface resembling a chamfer or splay, excepting that in strictness this latter term should be applied only to openings which have their sides sloped for the purpose of enlarging them, while a sloped surface in another situation would be a bevel; this distinction, however, is seldom regarded, and the two terms are commonly used synonymously. [See *Splay* and *Cant*.]

Blind-story, a term sometimes applied to the triforium as opposed to the clear-story.

Blocking-course, the plain course of stone which surmounts the cornice at the top of a Greek or Roman building : also a course of stone or brick forming a projecting line without mouldings at the base of a building.

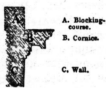

A. Blocking-course.

B. Cornice.

C. Wall.

Boast. To boast or block out a piece of stone or wood is to shape it into the simple form which approaches nearest to its ultimate figure, leaving the smaller details to be worked out afterwards. Sometimes capitals, corbels, &c., especially of the thirteenth century, are found in this state, never having been finished. A good example occurs in the crypt at Canterbury.

Crypt, Canterbury.

BELVEDERE, a room built above the roof for the purpose of obtaining a "fine view."

BEMA (Gr.), the raised portion at the end of the early Christian Churches with the apse, used afterwards to signify the presbytery or *chancel*, q. v.

BENCH-END. See *Pew*.

BENITIER (Fr.), Holy-water basin or *stoup*.

Bonders, Bond-stones, Binding-stones, stones which reach a considerable distance into, or entirely through a wall for the purpose of binding it together : they are principally used when the work is faced with ashlar, and are inserted at intervals to tie it more securely to the rough walling or backing. [See *Perpent-stone* and *Through.*]

Boss, a projecting ornament placed at the intersections of the ribs of ceilings, whether vaulted or flat ; also used as a termination to weather-mouldings of doors, windows, &c., called then a *Corbel* or *Dripstone Termination ;* and in various other situations, either as an ornamental stop, or finishing, to mouldings, or to cover them where they intersect each other ; but their principal application is to vaulted ceilings. In *Norman* work the vaults are most commonly without bosses until the latter part of the style, and when used they are generally not very prominent nor very richly carved. In the succeeding styles they are used in profusion, though less abundantly in the Early English than in the Decorated and Perpendicular, and are generally elaborately carved. The *Early English* bosses are usually sculptured with foliage characteristic of the style, among which small figures and animals are at times introduced, but occasionally a small circle of mouldings, in continuation of those of the ribs, is used in the place of a carved boss.

Chapter-house, Oxford Cathedral, c. 1220.

BICOCA (Low Lat.), a turret or watch-tower.

BILECTION MOULDINGS, those surrounding the panels and projecting before the face of a door, &c.

BILLET Ornament. See *Moulding.*

BLADES, the principal rafters or backs of a roof, q. v.

BOTERAS = Buttress.

BOWER, the ladies' chamber or boudoir in ancient castles and mansions.

Bow, an arch or gateway.

In the *Decorated* style the bosses consist of foliage, heads, animals, &c., or of foliage combined with heads and animals, and sometimes shields charged with armorial bearings are used. Many of the *Perpendicular* bosses bear a strong resemblance to the Decorated, but there is generally the same difference in the execution of the foliage that is found in all the other features of the style: shields with armorial bearings are used abun-

St. Alban's Abbey, Herts., c. 1320.

dantly in Perpendicular work, and there is considerably greater variation in the bosses of this style than any other; sometimes they are made to represent a flat sculptured ornament attached to the underside of the ribs; sometimes they resemble small pendants, which are occasionally pierced, as in the south porch of Dursley Church, Gloucestershire, but it is impossible to enumerate all the varieties.

Bracket, an ornamental projection from the face of a wall, to support a statue, &c.; they are sometimes nearly plain, or ornamented only with mouldings, but are generally carved either into heads, foliage, angels, or animals. Brackets are very frequently found on the walls in the inside of churches, especially at the east end of the chancel and aisles, where they supported statues which were placed near the altars.

York Cathedral, c. 1350.

Bowtell, or Boltell (Old Eng.), term for a round moulding, or bead; also for the small shafts of

BRACES, certain timbers of the *Roof.*

clustered pillars, in window and door jambs, mullions, &c.,
probably from its resemblance to the shaft of an arrow or
bolt. It is the English term for the *torus*.

Brasses, Sepulchral, monumental plates of brass or the

SIR ROGER DE TRUMPINGTON, 1289,
Trumpington Church, Cambridgeshire.

SIR JOHN DE CREKE,
Westley Waterless 1337.

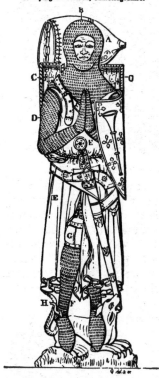

A. Heaume, or Basinet. On its apex is a staple for
   appending the Kerchief of Plesaunce, and it is
   furnished with a chain attached to the girdle, to
   enable the Knight t· recover his head-piece, if
   knocked off in the fray.
B. Coif de Mailles.   F. Chausees de Mailles.
C. Ailettes.   G. Genouilleres of Plate.
D. Hauberk.   H. Spur with a single point,
E. Surcoat.   or Prick spur.

A. Roundels, in the form of lions'
   heads, serving as Epaulieres.
B. Demi - Brassarts over the
   sleeves of the Hauberk, with
   vambraces of plate under them
   to protect the fore-arms.
C. Cyclas, over the pour-point.
D. Coutes, or elbow-pieces, orna-
   mented with lions' heads.
E. Gamboison.
F. Genouilleres.
G. Greaves, or shin-pieces.

mixed metal anciently called latten, inlaid on large slabs
of stone, which usually form part of the pavement of the
church, and representing in their outline, or by the lines

engraved upon them, the figure of the deceased. In many instances in place of a figure there is found an ornamented or foliated cross, with sacred emblems, or other devices. The fashion of representing on tombs the effigy of the deceased, graven on a plate of brass, appears to have been adopted about the middle of the thirteenth century; this was imbedded in melted pitch, and firmly fastened down by rivets leaded into a slab, of some hard material, such as the Sussex or the Purbeck marble.

HENRY DENTON,
Chaplain of Chilston, Higham Ferrars Church.

These memorials, where circumstances permitted, were often elevated upon altar - tombs, but more commonly they are found on slabs, which form part of the pavement of churches; so that the area of the church, and especially the choir, was not thereby encumbered, as was the case when effigies in relief were introduced.

The Sepulchral Brass in its original and perfect state was a work rich and beautiful in decoration. It is by careful examination sufficiently evident that the incised

A. Apparel or Parura of the Amice.
B. Stole.   D. Chasuble or Chesible.
C. Maniple, or fanon.   E. Alb, with apparel at the feet.

lines were filled up with some black resinous substance; the armorial decorations, and, in elaborate specimens, the whole field or background, which was cut out by the chisel or scorper, were filled up with mastic or coarse enamel of various colours, so as to set off the elegant tracery of tabernacle-work, which forms the principal feature of ornament

The earliest specimen of a brass that has been noticed
in this country is that at Stoke Dabernon, Surrey, apparently the memorial of Sir John d'Aubernoun, who died
1277. And next in date that of Sir Roger de Trumpington, at Trumpington, Cambridgeshire, who died 1289.

In speaking of these as the two earliest known examples, it should be added that Jocelyn, Bishop of Wells,
who died 1247, is recorded to have had a brass on his
tomb; and on that of Bishop Bingham, who died the same
year, the matrix or incision of the stone in which the
brass was laid still exists.

The Brasses afford good illustrations of the armour and
costume of the period. The two first given represent
knights. That of Sir Henry Denton affords illustrations
of the several portions of the priests' robes.

Breast-summer (old form *Bressumer*), a beam, after the
manner of a lintel, but extending beneath the whole superstructure of wall, &c., instead of only a small portion over
an opening. A good example will be found in the illustration accompanying *Timber-built Houses.*

Brick. The Romans used brick extensively in this
country. Roman bricks were flat, like tiles, often a foot
square, and were chiefly employed in this country in
courses between stone or rubble masonry. Though it
might seem singular that such an art when once learnt
should have been lost, nevertheless, in our numerous
twelfth-century buildings no traces of brick occur except
in a few instances; the using them up as old material
from buildings left by the Romans, as at Colchester and
St. Alban's Abbey suggested making others in imitation.
Perhaps the earliest true brick-building existing is that of
Little Wenham Hall (c. 1260). A few instances of early
fourteenth-century brickwork occur, and towards the close
of the style, and in the fifteenth century, it becomes common. The most elaborate mouldings and ornamentation
are exhibited in some of the remains of brickwork; and
the numerous and fine sixteenth-century chimneys are
for the most part built of brick.

BRATTISHING, BRANDISHING,
BRETIZMENT, BRETASYNG, BRETIN,
BRETISEMENT, all various terms
for a crest-battlement or parapet.

BURSARY (Lat), the exchequer
in collegiate and conventual
houses.

It may be said, however, that the use
of brick seems to have been confined to
civic buildings, and very seldom used in
ecclesiastical work.

Broach, or Broche, an old English
term for a spit, and applied to a spire;
still in use in some parts of the country,
as in Northamptonshire, Leicestershire,
&c., where it is used to denote a spire
springing from the tower without any
intermediate parapet. [See *Spire*.] The
term " to broche" seems to be also used in
old building accounts, perhaps for cutting
the stones in the form of voussoirs.

Horsley Church, Derby.

Buttress, a projection from a wall to
create additional strength and support.
Buttresses, properly so called, are not
used in Classical architecture, as the projections are formed into pilasters, antæ,
or some other feature in the general
arrangement, so as to disguise or destroy
the appearance of strength and support.
Norman buttresses, especially in the
earlier part of the style, are generally
of considerable breadth and very small
projection, and add so little to the substance of the wall that it may be supposed they were used at least as much
for ornament as for support: they are
commonly not divided into stages, but
continue of the same breadth and thickness from the ground to the top, and
either die into the wall with a slope
immediately below the parapet, or are
continued up to the parapet, which frequently overhangs the perpendicular face
of the wall as much as the buttresses
project in order to receive them, as at

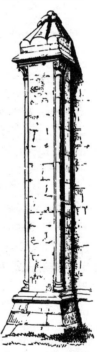

Glastonbury Abbey, (Norman),
c. 1180.

BUTTERY, the place for bottles,
the butler's pantry, usually be- | tween the hall and the kitchen.
See *Pantry*.

the nave of Southwell Minster. Occasionally small shafts
are worked on the angles of Norman buttresses, but
these generally indicate that the work is late.

Early English buttresses have usually considerably less
breadth and much greater projection than the Norman,
and often stand out very boldly; they are sometimes continued throughout their whole height without any diminution; but are oftener broken into stages with a successive

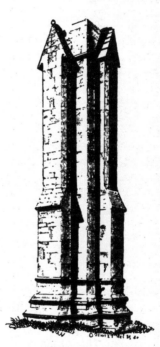

Irthlingborough (Early English),
c. 1220.

Higham Ferrers (Early English),
c. 1250.

reduction in their projection, and not unfrequently in their
width also, in each; the sets-off dividing the stages are
generally sloped at a very acute angle; the buttresses
terminate at the top either with a plain slope dying into
the wall, or with a triangular head (or pediment) which

sometimes stands against the parapet, sometimes below it, and sometimes rises above it, producing something of the effect of a pinnacle, as at Salisbury. Actual pinnacles on buttresses in this style are very rare, and are indications that the work is late: the angles of Early English

buttresses are very commonly chamfered off, and are occasionally moulded. With this style *flying or arch buttresses* seem first to have been used, but they did not become common till a subsequent period.

In the *Decorated* style the buttresses are almost invariably worked in stages, and are often ornamented with niches, with crocketed canopies, and other carved decorations; in large buildings they often terminate in pinnacles, which are sometimes of open work, forming niches or canopies for statues; with the introduction of this style the angle buttresses began to be set diagonally.

In the *Perpendicular* style, the buttresses differ but little in general

St. Mary Magdalene, Oxford, (Decorated), c. 1330.

form and arrangement from the Decorated; but the ornaments of the buttresses in each of the styles partook of the prevailing character of the architecture, and varied with it; thus in the latter specimens of the fifteenth century they are more frequently panelled than at any previous period.

St. Lawrence, Evesham, (Perpendicular), c. 1460.

Byzantine Architecture. The style of architecture in-troduced at Byzantium in the fifth century, derived from the Roman, but dis-tinguished from it by the plans of the buildings, and by the general use of the dome or cupola. The plan of the Grecian or Byzan-tine churches was usually that of the Greek cross, with a large cupola rising from the centre, and smaller cupolas crowning the four arms. The arches were

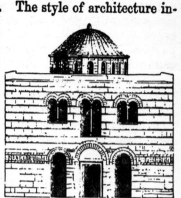

St. Nicodemus, Athens.

generally semicircular, sometimes segmental, or of the horse-shoe form. The capitals of columns were little more than square blocks, tapered downwards, and adorned with foliage or basket-work. The doorways were com-monly square-headed, with a semi-circular, and occasionally, in later specimens, a pointed arch over the flat lintel. The Byzantine style had great influence on subsequent styles, both in this country and on the Continent. The Gothic styles are derived quite as much from this as from the Roman.

Cabling, a round moulding frequently worked in the flutes of columns, pilasters, &c., in Classical architecture, and nearly filling-up the hollow part: they seldom extend higher than the third part of the shaft.

Canopy, in Gothic architecture an ornamented projec-tion over doors, windows, &c.; a covering over niches, tombs, &c. Canopies are chiefly used in the Decorated

CAISSONS, a French term for sunk panels of ceilings, soffits, &c.
CALYON, flint or pebble stone, used in chalk districts.
CAMPANILE, Italian for *Belfry,* q. v. See also *Tower.*

and Perpendicular styles, although they are not uncommon in the Early English, and are occasionally found over the heads of figures, &c., in late Norman work.

Early English canopies over niches and figures are generally simple in their forms, often only trefoil or cinquefoil arches, bowing forwards, and surmounted by a plain pediment, as on the west front of the cathedral at Wells: the canopies over tombs are sometimes of great beauty and delicacy, and highly enriched, as that over the tomb of Archbishop Gray in York Minster.

In the *Decorated* style, the canopies are often extremely elaborate, and are so various in their forms that it is impossible to particularize them; some of the more simple of those over figures, niches, &c., consist of cinquefoiled or trefoiled arches, frequently ogees, bowing forwards, and surmounted with crockets and finials; some are like very steep pediments with crockets and finials on them; others are formed of a series of small feathered arches, projecting from the wall on a polygonal plan, with pinnacles between and subordinate canopies over them, supporting a superstructure somewhat re-

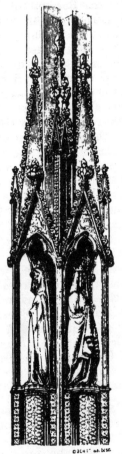

Queen Eleanor's Cross, Geddington,
Northamptonshire, A.D. 1294.

sembling a small turret, or a small crocketed spire; of this description of canopy good specimens are to be seen at the sides and over the head of the effigy of Queen Philippa in Westminster Abbey. The canopies over tombs in this style are often of great beauty; some consist of bold and well-proportioned arches with fine pediments over them, which are frequently crocketed, with buttresses and pinnacles at the angles; many tombs of this style, when made in a wall, have an ogee arch over them, forming a kind of canopy.

In the *Perpendicular* style, the canopies are

Lichfield Cathedral, c. 1320.

more varied than in the Decorated, but many of them are in general character nearly alike in both styles; the high pointed form is not to be met with in Perpendicular work; a very usual kind of canopy over niches, &c., is a projection on a polygonal plan, often three sides of an octagon, with a series of feathered arches at the bottom, and terminating at the top either with a battlement, a row of Tudor flowers, or a series of open carved work.

The canopies of tombs are frequently of the most gorgeous description, enriched with a profusion of the most minute ornament, which is sometimes so crowded together as to create an appearance of great confusion. Most of our cathedrals and large churches will furnish examples of canopies of this style, not only in stone, but frequently in wood also.

Gloucester Cathedral, c. 1430.

CANTHARUS, a vase or cistern in the atrium of the early churches.

Cant, and Canted, a term in common use among carpenters to express the cutting off the angle of a square. Any part of a building on a polygonal plan is also said to be *canted*, as a *canted* window, or oriel, &c.

Cantaliver, a kind of bracket, whether of stone, wood, or iron, used to support eaves, cornices, balconies, &c., usually of considerable projection.

Capital, or Cap, the head of a column, pilaster, &c. In Classical architecture, the orders have each their respective capitals, which differ considerably from each other, but their characteristics are easily distinguished: there are, however, considerable differences to be found in a few of the ancient examples, as in the Corinthian orders of the Temple of Vesta at Tivoli, and of the Choragic monument of Lysicrates at Athens; there are also a few capitals totally unlike those of any of the five orders, as in the Temple of the Winds, at Athens. In English architecture they are endlessly diversified.

A very common form for plain *Norman* capitals, especially on small shafts, is one called the cushion capital, resembling a bowl with the sides truncated, so as to reduce the upper part to a square; there is also another form which is extremely prevalent, very much like this, but with the under part of the bowl cut into round mouldings which

Cassington, Oxon, c. 1120.

Steetley, Derbyshire, c. 1160.

stop upon the top of the necking; these round mouldings are sometimes ornamented, but more often plain; this kind of capital continued in use till quite the end of the style.

At a later period the capitals are ornamented with con-

ventional fo-
liage, which
gradually ap-
proaches to
the prevalent
ornamenta-
tion of the
next style.
In the early
work of the
style they are

Easton, Hants, c. 1180.

Byland Abbey, Yorkshire, c. 1180.

generally rather short in proportion to the height, but
they afterwards become more
elongated, and the foliage
and other decorations became
lighter in character, approxi-
mating to the Early English.

Early English capitals are not so much diversified as
Norman, although there are many varieties; they are very
frequently entirely devoid of carving, and consist of suites
of plain mouldings, not, however, very numerous, which
are deeply undercut so as to produce fine bold shadows,
and there is usually a considerable plain space, of a *bell*
shape, between the upper mouldings and the necking.

Occasionally a series
of the toothed orna-
ment, or some other
similar enrichment,
is used between the
mouldings. When
foliage is introduced
it is placed upon
the bell of the
capital, and for the
most part, but few

Hereford Cathedral, c. 1220.

Rushden, Northants, c. 1250.

if any mouldings beyond the abacus and necking, are
used with it; the leaves have generally stiff stems; but
almost always stand out very boldly, so as to produce
a very striking and beautiful effect, and they are generally

very well carved, and often so much undercut, that the stalks and more prominent parts are entirely detached. The character of the foliage varies, but by far the most common, and that which belongs peculiarly to this style, consists of a trefoil, the two lower lobes of which (and sometimes all three) are worked with a high prominence or swelling in the centre, which casts a considerable shadow; the middle lobe is frequently much larger than the others, with the main fibre deeply channelled

Presbytery, Lincoln Cathedral, A.D. 1260.

in it. Occasionally animals are mixed with the foliage, but they are usually a sign that the work is late. Some of the richest specimens of thirteenth-century foliage are to be found in the presbytery of Lincoln Cathedral.

In the *Decorated* style, the capitals very often consist of plain mouldings either with or without ball-flowers or other flowers worked upon the bell, though they are frequently carved with very rich and beautiful foliage; the mouldings usually consist of rounds, ogees, and hollows, and are not so deeply undercut as in the Early English style; the foliage is very different from Early English work, and of a much broader character, many of the leaves being representations of those of particular

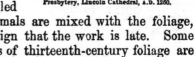

Beverley Minster

plants and trees, as the oak, ivy, maple, white-thorn, vine,

Hampton Poyle, c. 1320.

&c.; which are often worked so truly to na-ture as to lead to the sup-position that the carver used real leaves for his pattern: they are also generally ex-tremely well arranged, and without the stiffness to be found in Early English foliage.

Sandhurst, c. 1350.

Perpendicular capitals are most usually plain, though

Ewelme, c. 1460.

in very large and ornamented build-ings they are some-times enriched with shallow foliage, espe-cially early in the style, when the shafts are circular; it is very common for the necking only, or for

Christ Church, Oxford, c. 1500.

the necking, the bell, and the first moulding above it, to follow the same form, the upper mouldings being changed into an octagon; ogees, beads, and hollows are the prevailing mould-ings; much of the foliage bears considerable resemblance to the Decorated, but it is stiffer and not so well combined, and the leaves in general are of less natural forms and frequently square; towards the latter part of the style there is often a main stalk continued un-interruptedly in a waved line, with the leaves arranged alternately on opposite sides. [See *Abacus.*]

Howden, c. 1480.

Caryatides (Gr.), a name given to statues representing draped female figures, applied instead of columns in Grecian architecture, as at the Erectheum at Athens.

Casement, (1) a frame enclosing part of the glazing of a window, with hinges to open and shut. (2) An old English name for the deep hollow moulding, similar to the *Scotia* of Italian architecture, which is extremely prevalent in Gothic architecture, in cornices, door and window jambs, &c., especially in the Perpendicular style, and which is frequently enriched with running patterns of foliage.

Cathedral (Lat. from Gr.), a church which contains the *cathedra* or seat of the bishop. In the earliest cathedrals, the basilicas or large churches in Rome, the bishop's seat was a marble chair attached to the end wall behind the altar, which was at the west end of the church, and he officiated over the altar, looking towards the east. This marble chair is often called the Cardinal's chair, because when the church was served by a cardinal it was his seat. Some few examples of the Bishop's chair remain on the Continent. The best in this country is that behind the altar in Norwich Cathedral.

Of the foundation of the first cathedral in this country, *circa* A.D. 600, the Venerable Bede tells us in these words: "Augustine having his episcopal see granted to him in the royal city [Canterbury], recovered therein a church, which he was informed had been built by the ancient Roman Christians, and consecrated it in the name of our Lord Jesus Christ, and there established a residence for himself and all his successors."

We learn, incidentally, that the cathedral church was re-constructed by Archbishop Odo, *c.* 950, and finally

CAPPING, same as *Coping.*

CAROL, a small closet or enclosure to sit and read in, as in the cloisters at Gloucester. A bay-window may thus be called a Carol.

CARTOUCH. 1. French name for a tablet or stone to receive an inscription, formed like a sheet of paper with the edges folded round. 2. Applied to modillons under a cornice.

CATACOMBS. See *Cemetery.*

CATAFALQUE, a hearse; or the frame of wood used in funeral processions.

CATAPULT, a military engine for throwing stones, arrows, and other missiles.

CAT'S-HEAD. See *Beak-head.*

rebuilt by Lanfranc. Although no traces of Odo's church
remain, we learn from one of the chroniclers that, as regards the apse, it was like that of St. Peter's at Rome,
and it is therefore exceedingly probable that the original
church of all was of the same character, and that Odo in
rebuilding, and possibly enlarging the choir, retained the
same principal features.

Together with the cathedral of Canterbury, the work
of Rochester and London went on, and there is little
doubt that the same plan was followed. We have also
an account of the building of the cathedral at York by
Paulinus, c. A.D. 630.

We may, however, take Canterbury as the type of
the plan of the English Cathedrals up to the eleventh
century, and also the alterations and extensions there
made during that century, as the type of what was done
in the other cathedrals.

Of the new cathedral, begun by Lanfranc, and continued by successive Archbishops, we learn, partly from
what has been recorded by Gervase (who saw the church
of Anselm), and partly from the existing remains, sufficient not only to form a tolerable estimate of the plan
and extent of the cathedral, but also to gain some idea
of the general aspect. This has been worked out by
Professor Willis [a].

The original plan of these cathedrals, i.e. those erected
by the close of the eleventh or beginning of the twelfth
centuries, as most of our cathedrals were, has been much
obscured by the frequent alterations, and, as a rule, considerable extension, which has taken place either towards
the end of that century or in centuries succeeding. The
most frequent extension has been eastwards — scarcely
ever westwards. This eastward extension, arising from
a desire to increase the number of altars, has in most
cases assumed the character of a Lady-chapel. In Canterbury, the small Trinity Chapel which was at the east
end of the choir, gave place in A.D. 1180 to a considerable extension of the choir itself, and this again was
made to end in the chapel called "Becket's Crown,"

[a] "The Architectural History of Canterbury Cathedral, by Professor Willis,
M.A., F.R.S., &c." (Oxford, 1845.)

thereby adding in all some eighty feet additional length to the cathedral in this direction.

At York, the cathedral as completed *circa* 1150, had the choir more than doubled in length, and tripled in width, *circa* 1200; while in 1370 the choir was again considerably extended to the eastward, till the site of the original cathedral, as compared with the present one, looks most diminutive in the plan [b].

At Winchester, the cathedral as completed by Bishop Walkelin, *c.* A.D. 1093, was considerably enlarged at the eastern end, *c.* A.D. 1200, by Bishop Godfrey de Lucy; while in the fifteenth century, when the nave was so far re-constructed that the aspect was totally different, a still further extension eastward was made.

Durham choir, the work of Bishop Carileph (A.D. 1093 —1104) remains, with the nave and aisles added by his successor, the notorious Bishop Flambard (A.D. 1104—33); while the western porch, or Galilee, was added by Bishop Pudsey, *c.* 1190, and the eastern chapel by Bishop Poore, *c.* 1250.

Lincoln has preserved the west front as erected by the founder, Bishop Remigius, A.D. 1087—92, while the glorious choir is due to Bishop Hugh, A.D. 1190—1200, the nave being the work of Hugh de Wells, *c.* 1230.

Exeter has preserved only the two towers (forming the two transepts), of the work of Bishop Warelwast, A.D. 1107—36. Under successive bishops, beginning *c.* A.D. 1280, and up to *c.* 1350, so that the work is wholly of the Decorated style, the choir and nave were completed as we now find them, the western front being added by Bishop Brantingham, *c.* 1380.

The above summaries are typical of the general history of nearly all our cathedrals.

Salisbury is the only example of a cathedral now existing as erected complete from the foundation. It was built between A.D. 1220 and 1258.

In the mediæval cathedrals the Lady-chapel has thus frequently been built on the lines of the original apse, and the *Bishop's seat* or throne has become a distinct

---

[b] See the series of Comparative Plans given in the "Architectural History of York Cathedral, by Robert Willis, M.A." (Oxford, 1849.)

piece of furniture, usually of wood, and placed on the south side of the nave, eastward of the stalls for the canons. The choir is also enclosed in its own solid screen, with a space between the east end of the screen and the Lady-chapel.

In England, Wells affords the most perfect example of a Cathedral with all its parts and appurtenances. Both nave and choir and presbytery have aisles. There is a second transept eastward of the altar between that and the Lady-chapel. The chapter-house is on the north side of the choir, and joins on to the eastern corner of the north transept, its vestibule being parallel to that transept on the east side of it. This is perhaps the most usual position, though there appears to be no strict rule for the place of the chapter-house. The two transepts have each two chapels on the east side, and an aisle on the west; the aisle communicates at the south end with the cloister, which is on the south side of the nave, and has the library over it on the east side, and the singing-school on the west. The nave has aisles on both sides, and another transept at the west end, with towers at the extremities; there is also a central tower and a north porch.

Wells was a cathedral proper, and independent of any monastic foundation, but with a separate house for each of its officers, either in the Close or in the Liberty adjoining to it. The Bishop's palace was enclosed by a separate moat and fortified, being on the south side of the cloister, from which it is separated by the moat; the houses for the Dean and for the Archdeacon are on the north side of the Close, with some of the canons' houses; the organist's house is at the west end, adjoining to the singing-school and the cloister; the precentor's house is at the east end, near the Lady-chapel. The vicars choral have a close of their own joining to the north-east corner of the canons' close, with a bridge across through the gate-house into the north transept; they were a collegiate body, with their own chapel, library, and hall, but were chiefly laymen.

A *plan* of Wells Cathedral is given as the frontispiece to this volume.

Caulicoli, small volutes under the flowers on the sides
of the abacus in the Corinthian
capital, representing the curled tops
of the acanthus stalks. Also, like
the large volutes, continued in the
Norman style, and may even be
traced, though much modified in
form, in later styles.

Cavetto, a concave
moulding of one quarter
of a circle, used in the
Grecian and other styles
of architecture. [See
Column.]

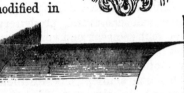

Cavetto, Theatre of Marcellus, Rome.

Ceiling, the under covering of a roof, floor, &c., con-
cealing the timbers from the room below; now usually
formed of plaster, but formerly most commonly of boarding; also the under surface of the vaulting in vaulted
rooms and buildings. During the middle ages, the ceilings were generally enriched with gilding and colouring
of the most brilliant kind, traces of which may often
still be found in churches, though in a faded and di-
lapidated condition; plaster and wood ceilings under
roofs are often made flat, as at Peterborough Cathedral
and St. Alban's Abbey, both of which are Norman with
old painting, but they frequently follow the line of the
timbers of the roof, which are sometimes arranged so as
to give the shape of a barrel-vault, especially in Early
English and Decorated work.

In the Perpendicular style they are more common than
in any other, and are usually either flat or canted, and
divided by ribs into square panels. [See *Rib.*]

The ceiling in churches immediately over the altar, and
occasionally also that over the roodloft, is sometimes richly
ornamented, while the remainder is plain, as at Ilfracombe.

Cell, (1) the naos or enclosed space within the walls of
an ancient temple; (2) also applied to various apartments
in the Roman houses; (3) to the sleeping apartments in
monastic establishments; and (4) the term is used for
a dependency of some larger monastery: e.g. Iffley and
Stukeley were cells to Kenilworth.

Cemetery. The early Christians used the subterraneous quarries or excavations beneath the hills in the neighbourhood of Rome, chiefly for the purpose of burial. At the entrance, chapels were erected, and hence the cemetery-chapel was spoken of under the name of *cemeterium.* The vaults containing the coffins were called *catacombs,* and besides being used as burial-places, were possibly during times of persecution, though rarely, used by the early Christians for worship. In after times, when persecution ceased, access to them was frequent, in consequence of so many saints and martyrs reposing there, and prayers at their tombs were considered more efficacious than elsewhere. It is most probable that they gave rise to the introduction of *crypts* beneath our own churches, where saints only were buried, or to which their remains were moved sometimes years after their burial. At their tombs the faithful of all ages have worshipped as at an *altar.* In mediæval times the cemetery for the faithful was simply the ground adjoining the church, which was enclosed as church-yards are now, and was often called Paradise. At times, as at Canterbury to A.D. 750, it was forbidden to bury within towns, and in that case a cemetery was provided outside the town with its church or chapel, as in our own times.

Centering, or Centre, the temporary support placed under vaults and arches to sustain them while they are in building, usually a frame of woodwork. In Norman architecture, in which the vaulting is constructed with rough unhewn stones, the center-ing was covered with a thick layer of mortar, in which the stones were imbedded, so that when the

Centering of a round-headed arch.

centering was removed it remained adhering to the under surface of the vault, and exhibiting an exact impression of the boards on which it was spread. In Ireland hurdles were used instead of boards over the centering, and their impression frequently remains on the plaster.

CENOTAPH (Gr.), an empty tomb, or a monument elsewhere than over the grave.

CENTRY-GARTH, a corruption of Cemetery.

Chalice (Lat. *Calix*), the cup used for the wine at the celebration of the Eucharist. In early ages the chalice was sometimes made of glass or wood, more often of gold or silver, with a representation frequently of the Good Shepherd carrying the lost sheep on His back. Especial care was taken that the brim of the chalice should not turn down.

Corpus College, Oxford, c. 1500.

Chamber, a room, or apartment, distinguished from the hall, chapel, &c. The *great chamber* usually adjoined, or was contiguous to the hall, and answered to the modern drawing-room, or *withdrawing* room. The *camera* of an abbot or prior means his suite of lodgings in the establishment. The *guest-chamber* in monasteries was sometimes a separate building. The great distinction between the bed-chambers and the reception-chambers did not exist in medieval houses as it does now in England.

Chamfer, Champfer (Gr. *Kampto*); an *arris* or angle which is slightly pared off is said to be chamfered: a chamfer resembles a *splay*, but is much smaller, and is usually taken off equally on the two sides; it applies to woodwork as well as stone. In the Early English and Decorated styles, more especially in the former, chamfers have frequently ornamental terminations of several kinds, some of which are sufficiently marked to be characteristic of the date of the architecture, and they are

Abbey Barn, Glastonbury, c. 1410.

Warmington, Northants, c. 1250.

more varied and produce a stronger effect than might be expected in such minute features. The angles of Early English buttresses are very commonly chamfered.

Chancel, (from the Latin *cancellus* = a screen,) the choir or eastern part of a church appropriated to the use of those who officiate in the performance of the services, and separated from the nave and other portions in which the congregation assemble by the screen from which the name is derived. The term is now generally confined to the eastern division of parish churches, and such as have no aisle or chapels round the choir. In some churches, in addition to the principal chancel, there are others at the end of the aisles, &c. [See *Choir* and *Cathedral.*]

Chantry (from the Fr. *Chanter*), an ecclesiastical benefice or endowment to provide for the chanting of masses; it was very commonly a testamentary bequest, the testator also directing a chapel to be built over the spot where he was buried, in which the masses were to be celebrated for the especial benefit of the souls of himself and others named in his will; hence the term has come to be sometimes applied to the chapel itself. Many of the aisles to our churches are chantry chapels, one chapel after another having been added.

Chapel (Lat. *Capella*). There are many varieties of chapels used for various purposes, partly of a private character and partly public. The earliest Christian chapels are probably the *cubicula*, or small burial-chapels in the catacombs at Rome, and the larger burial-chapels at the entrances of the catacombs for families, or for official persons such as the bishops and popes; and some of these chapels are in the catacombs themselves, not merely round the entrances. After the time of Constantine, family chapels were attached to the churches, and some remained in the houses where they had been previously established. In France burial-chapels in the cemeteries are very usual throughout the Middle Ages as separate and detached buildings, in addition to the very numerous chapels attached to the churches, and dedicated in honour of particular saints: these latter are usually between the buttresses. In England detached chapels are comparatively rare, and when in churches they are usually built as part of the aisles, or enclosed with screens and called Parcloses. Domestic chapels were also made in rooms of a castle or house, more frequently than erected as separate buildings. In Ireland the ancient Roman practice of having many small family chapels in the same cemetery was continued to quite a late period.

Chapter-house (Lat. *Capitulum*), the place of assembly for the dean and canons in a cathedral body for the transaction of business. It was customary to ornament them in a very rich manner, especially in England: the sort of independence belonging to the assembled chapter had something congenial to the English character, and our chapter-houses are very superior to those of our neighbours. The usual form in England is polygonal, with a rich vault resting on a central pillar, e.g. at Wells. This form is almost peculiar to England, but it was never exclusive; the simple parallelogram is found of all periods: of the twelfth century at Worcester, of the thirteenth at Chester and Oxford, of the fourteenth and fifteenth in several places both in England and on the Continent.

Chest. Among our ancestors chests appear to have been very import-ant pieces of furniture, serv-ing as recep-tacles for every kind of goods that required to be kept with any degree of care; they were also placed in churches for keeping the

Graveney, Kent, c. 1280.

CHAMP, the field or ground on which carving is raised.

CHAPITER (of a column), the Capital.

CHAR or CHARE, to hew or work, e.g. Charred stone = hewn stone.

CHARNEL-HOUSE, a chamber in the neighbourhood of a church-yard to receive the human bones disinterred by the grave-digger.

CHASSE, Fr. for Reliquary.

CHASUBLE (priests' robe). See illustrations to *Brass*.

holy vessels, vestments, &c., and many of them still remain. Large chests were called standards, and were used for packing the furniture when the family moved from one manor-house to another. The oldest chests known to exist are of Early English date. Some of the old chests found in this country are evidently of foreign workmanship, and "Flanders chests" are frequently mentioned in ancient documents. As Gothic architecture lost its purity, chests gradually degenerated into the plain boxes which are now placed in our churches to receive the registers; however, for a considerable time they continued to retain a certain degree of ornament, and were occasionally highly enriched, though in no very chaste style, while in houses they were superseded by more convenient articles of furniture.

Chimney (Fr.) This term was not originally restricted to the shaft of the chimney, but included the fireplace. There does not appear to be any evidence of the use of chimney-shafts in England prior to the twelfth century. In the part of Rochester Castle which is of the date probably of 1130, there are complete fireplaces with semicircular backs, and a shaft in each jamb supporting a semicircular arch over the opening, which is enriched with the zigzag moulding; some of these project slightly from the wall; the flues, however, go only a few feet up in the thickness of the wall, and are then turned out at the back, the apertures being small oblong holes. A few years later, the improvement of carrying the flue up through the whole height of the wall appears. The early chimney-shafts are of considerable height, and circular; afterwards they assumed a great variety of forms, and during the fourteenth century they are frequently very short. Previous to the

Burford, Oxon.

CHEVET (Fr.), the apse or eastern termination of a church.

CHEVRON or ZIGZAG. See *Moulding.*

sixteenth century the shaft is often short and not unfrequently terminated by a spire or pinnacle, usually of rather low proportions, having apertures of various forms under, and sometimes in it, for the escape of the smoke. There are also taller shafts of various forms, square, octangular, or circular, surmounted with a cornice, forming a sort of capital, the smoke issuing from the top. In the fifteenth century the most common form of chimney-shafts is octangular, though they are sometimes square: the smoke

Chepstow Castle, c. 1320.

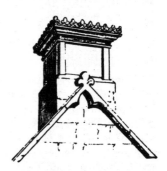

Sherborne, Dorset, c. 1320.

issues from the top, unless, as is sometimes the case, they terminate in a spire. Clustered chimney-shafts do not appear until rather late in the fifteenth century; afterwards they became very common, and were frequently highly ornamented, especially when of brick.

Choir, or Quire (Lat. *chorus*), literally a place for the singers, but usually that part of the church, eastward of the nave, in which the services were celebrated, and which was appropriated to the priest and canons and others assisting in the services: it was separated from the other parts of the building in which the congregation assemble, by a screen, which was usually of open-work. In large churches there are generally aisles at the sides of the choir, sometimes continued across the east end of the building so as to surround it, especially in churches which have polygonal or semicircular terminations, like many of the continental cathedrals: it is usually raised at least one step above the nave, and in strictness does not extend further eastward than the steps leading up to the altar where the *presbytery* or *sanctuary* begins, but this distinction is by no means adhered to, and the term choir is very generally applied to the whole space set apart for the celebration of the services of the church, including the presbytery. In parochial churches it forms the *Chancel*. [See also *Basilica, Cathedral,* and *Church.*]

Church; the place for Christians "to assemble themselves together" for the worship of God according to the apostolic injunction. Churches are built on many different plans, and have been so at all periods; one plan has no more authority than another, it is entirely a matter of convenience and decent order. The earliest churches were chambers in the houses of the more wealthy Christians, who allowed their poorer brethren to assemble in their houses, usually in the hall or the largest room; in the east, in the upper rooms of the house, as mentioned in the book of the Acts of the Apostles: at Rome, in the chambers below the level of the street which were usual in the houses or palaces of the Roman nobility. Several of these subterranean churches remain, as St. Pudentiana, and St. Sylvester. In these cases other chambers appear to have been built above them for churches after the peace of the Church in the time of Constantine.

The name of basilica was derived from this early use of the hall which was also a Court of Justice, [see *Basilica*]; and in the case of the cathedral of Treves the actual hall of a Roman house remains to this day, converted into a church, while there is another basilica or Law Court near to it also converted into a church in more recent times. At Rome the seven great churches made by Constantine, which still retain the name of basilica in an especial manner, were probably all originally law courts, and so preserved their old arrangements, which served as types for others, and came to be considered the usual arrangement of a church.

The church of Santa Croce was the Prætorium or Law Court of a different kind, in the Sessorium or palace of the Empress Helena, and had an apse added to it by Con-

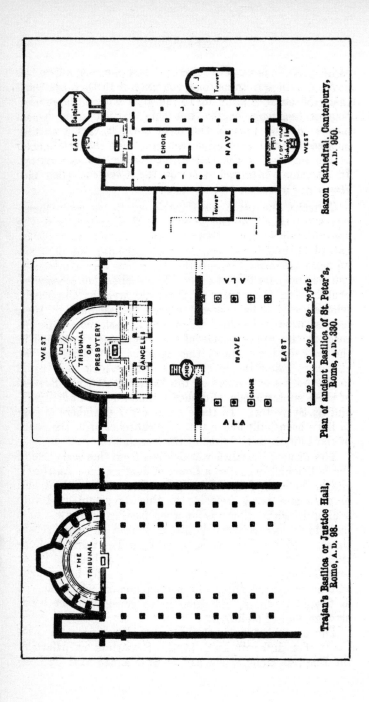

Saxon Cathedral, Canterbury, A.D. 950.

Plan of ancient Basilica of St. Peter's, Rome, A.D. 330.

Trajan's Basilica or Justice Hall, Rome, A.D. 98.

stantine as a necessary part of the arrangement. That of St. John Lateran, which was the first that he made into a church, was originally one of the halls in the great palace of the Lateran family. Those of St. Lorenzo and St. Agnes were originally two of the small burial-chapels at the entrance of their respective catacombs, and other chapels in the Catacombs are called Basilicas by some writers, though they seldom held more than fifty persons, and the largest not more than eighty; these are evidently burial-chapels only, and afford no guidance for the arrangement of a church. St. Clement's is usually appealed to as the primitive type; the original church, which now forms a crypt to the present one, is considerably wider. When the upper part of the church was rebuilt in the twelfth century, the old nave of the upper church was found inconveniently wide, and one of the aisles of this underground church is now outside the wall of the upper church, the width of the nave having been divided into a nave and aisle. The marble screen was brought up from the lower church and re-arranged to suit the smaller one. This church therefore affords no certain type of primitive arrangement. That of Torcello, at Venice, is more perfect and unaltered, but is probably also of the twelfth century. There is no example of primitive arrangement remaining, excepting perhaps at St. Agnes outside of the walls of Rome; but it is certain that the plan of the Roman court of justice was closely followed, and all the names of the different parts were retained.

When the art of building in stone was revived in Western Europe in the eleventh century, the apse seems at first to have been considered an essential feature, as at Canterbury, which we are told followed the plan of the original church of St. Peter's at Rome; and in such cases the altar was probably placed on the chord of the apse, as at Rome, but this practice was soon abandoned, and from the twelfth century in England the square east end became almost universal, and the altar was placed against the east wall, often resting partly upon corbels in the wall. The chorus or choir, which in Italy is sometimes in one part of the church and sometimes another, and in Spain and the south of France is usually in the middle, was in England and France almost universally in the eastern limb of the church, and enclosed by a screen called originally *Cancelli*, from which the name of chancel and choir became synonymous, but usage now generally confines the name of choir to the cathedrals or large churches. [See *Chancel* and *Choir*.] When there are aisles to the eastern part of a church the central division of it is generally called the choir. Although no general rule can be laid down, the most usual plan of our English mediæval church may be said to be,— 1. A chancel without aisles; 2. A nave with aisles; 3. A western tower; 4. A south porch.

Garsington Church, Oxfordshire, affords a good example of the simplest plan of a parish church unaltered.

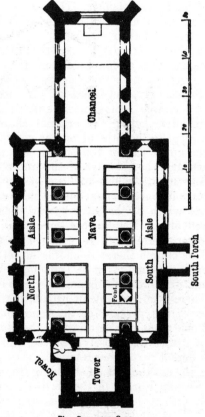

Plan, Garsington, Oxon.

Ciborium (Gr. = a cup) is applied in several ways: 1. To the portion of ceiling over an altar. 2. To the ceiling of, and so to the whole of the canopy over the altar, which was usually erected on four pillars, also called the *Baldaquin*. It is used also (3.) in the sense of the arch over the place where the altar stood.

CHYMOL, a hinge.
CILL = Sill.

CIMATIUM. See *Cymatium*.
CIMBIA, a fillet, band, or *Cincture*.

Clear-story, or Clere-story, an upper story, or row of windows in a Gothic church rising well above the ad-

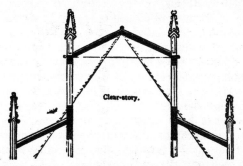

Clear-story.

joining parts of the building (in contradistinction to the *Blindstory*, often called the *Triforium*). In churches it appears to have been adopted as a means of obtaining an increase of light in the body of the building; but the windows are not unfrequently so small that they serve this purpose very imperfectly. Numerous churches exist both

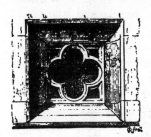

Witney, c. 1450.

Stanton St. John's, c. 1350.

in the Norman and in each of the later styles of Gothic architecture, in which the clear-story is an original feature; but many more instances occur in which it is evidently a subsequent addition to the original design, especially when the high-pitched roofs (which frequently included the body and aisles in a single span) have given way to flat ones, the walls having been raised over the arches of the nave to receive the clear-story windows. [See illustration under *Triforium*.]

CINCTURE, a ring, or fillet, or band, on the top and bottom of the shaft of a column.

CINQUE-FOIL. See *Foil*.

Cloister, a covered way round a quadrangle in a monastic or collegiate establishment. Of its four sides one was usually bounded by the church or chapel, and the others by different buildings, or by a high wall. The cloisters were appropriated for the recreation of the inmates of the establishment, who also sometimes used them as places of study, for which purpose they occasionally had cells or stalls on one side, as at Gloucester and at Durham, called *Carols;* the cloisters likewise served as passages of communication between the different buildings, and they appear to have been often used as places of sepulture; they are sometimes covered with rich stone vaulting, and there is frequently a lavatory in them, and a stone bench along the wall opposite to the windows. The term cloister is also sometimes used as a general name for a monastery.

Cob-wall, a wall built of unburnt clay, mixed with straw. This material is still used in some parts of the country for cottages and outbuildings, and was formerly employed for houses of a better description: it is supposed also to be the material of which the domestic edifices of the ancients, including even the Greeks and Romans in their most civilized period, were chiefly built.

Coffin (prob. from Saxon *Cofa* = a cave). The slight wooden case in which bodies are now interred appears to be of comparatively recent origin; in earlier ages the graves were sometimes lined with slabs of stone, but usually a stone coffin formed of a single block was used, and the body placed in it, either enveloped in grave-clothes or

Bishop Ralph, 1123, Chichester Cathedral.

Cippus, a small pillar or column used by the Romans for milestones or boundary stones.

Clamp-irons, Cramp irons.

Classical Orders of Architecture. See *Orders.*

Clavis (Lat.), the key-stone of an arch.

Clicket, a key probably resembling a "latch-key."

Clocher (Fr.), a bell, hence the bell-tower or steeple.

Clustered Column, a pier consisting of several shafts clustered together.

Cochlea (Lat.), a small *newel* staircase.

Coffer, 1. A deep panel in a ceiling = Caisson; 2. A small chest.

clad in some particular dress; ecclesiastics were generally buried in the habit of the order to which they belonged, the dignitaries of the Church frequently in their official robes and accompanied with the ensigns of their office, and sovereigns in their robes of state. Numerous stone coffins exist in this country which appear to be as old as the eleventh and twelfth centuries; they are formed of a single block of stone hollowed out to receive the body, with a small circular cavity at one end to fit the head, and they are usually rather wider at this end than at the other; there are generally one or more small holes in the bottom to drain off moisture; these coffins were never buried deeply in the ground; very frequently they were placed close to the surface, so that the lid was visible, and when within a church, formed part of the paving; sometimes, in churches, they were placed entirely above the ground. [See *Tomb*.]

Compass-roof, an open-timber roof: it is more commonly called a *Span-roof*, meaning that the roof extends from one wall to the other, with a ridge in the centre, as distinguished from a *lean-to*, &c.

Console is strictly the French term for a bracket, or for the *ancones*, but it is commonly used by English authors also for a bracket or corbel of any kind in Classical architecture.

Console, Palace of Diocletian.

Construction of Walls. There are many different methods of constructing the walls of a building, which vary according to the materials employed, and also according to the date and the country. At first sight it may be thought that the best and cheapest mode of employing any given material would be soon discovered, and con-

COILLON or COIN, the angle of a building, *Quoin*.

COLLARINO, the cylindrical part of the column between the annulets and under the ovolo and the astragal.

COLONNADE, in Classical architecture, answers to the arcade in Gothic: the former has an entablature, the latter arches.

COLUMBARIA, Dove-cots, hence also similar places for urns at Rome, and sometimes the holes left in the walls for the timbers.

COLURA. See *Tester*.

COMPASS WINDOW, a bay-window or oriel.

COMPLUVIUM. See *Atrium*.

COMPOSITE. See *Order*.

tinued ever after in the same district; and this is true
to a certain extent: nevertheless, it is certain that the
mode of construction is often a very useful guide to the
age of a building.

The earliest buildings of which we have any record
are the Tower of Babel and the walls of Babylon; these
were built of sun-dried bricks, cemented with bitumen;
they have nothing to correspond with them in Europe.

The next in order of date are probably the Pyramids
of Egypt. These are built of enormous masses of stone
in the form of a parallelogram, and the stones are split
off the rocks, not cut, and are put together without
cement of any kind, arranged in alternate courses, being
thrown in cross-wise, and supported by their own enormous weight only. This kind of construction is called
Cyclopean masonry, and is used in all early buildings in
the East, where such rocks are found as admit of the stone
being split in this manner, such as tufa and sandstone. The
walls of the Etruscan cities are built in the same manner,
wherever the same materials are found. The later buildings have the stones of smaller size, but the change is
very gradual, and in the later buildings of this class
the stones are cut, not merely split, and the joints are
then extremely fine. The early temples of Greece are
for the most part built in this manner, as are the temples
at Pæstum.

In Rome the wall earliest in character is that of Roma
Quadrata, usually called the wall of Romulus, this belongs
to the earlier class of Etruscan or Cyclopean masonry.
The next class are the walls of the *later* kings. These
are of more regular character than the wall of Romulus,
and agree pretty nearly with the temples of Pæstum.
Simultaneously with these, in other districts, where the
material is a hard stone that will not split, and cannot
be easily cut into square blocks, such as the hill limestone,
basaltic stones, and lava, we find a different kind of construction, popularly called Phœnician, and probably used
by that people. In this the stones are sometimes much
smaller, and often polygonal; these are closely fitted together, but without cement, and when the stones cannot be
made to fit closely, small chippings of stone are wedged in

Opus Quadratum. Wall of Roma Quadrata, on the Palatine, B.C. 750.

Polygonal, B.C. 500.

Opus Incertum. Concrete. The Emporium, B.C. 175.

Opus Reticulatum. Net-work,
Palace of the Cæsars, A.D. 10.

Opus Lateritium. Brick-work,
Arches of Nero, A.D. 60.

Opera Della Decadenza. The Decadence.
Circus of Maxentius, A.D. 310.

Opera Saracenesca. Work of the Saracens.
Palace of the Savelli, A.D. 1200.

MODES OF ANCIENT ROMAN CONSTRUCTION.

between the joints to make all firm. This construction being the easiest and cheapest with these materials, is also continued at all periods, even to our own day.

The next class is where *lime mortar* is used. The art of burning stone into lime and making mortar does not appear to have been invented, or at least brought into use by the Romans, until about three centuries before the Christian era. It is not found in the temples of Greece, nor at Pæstum. The earliest dated example is the Emporium on the bank of the Tiber, about two centuries before the Christian era. When men understood the advantages of lime mortar, it was used in profusion and even excess, and from that time forwards the body of a Roman wall was almost universally built of concrete or rough stone (*rubble*), well joined together with lime mortar, the lime being always burnt on the spot, and used quite fresh, before the cooling and crystallization had taken place. These massive concrete walls were faced in various ways, at first with small pieces of tufa, diamond-shaped on the surface, and wedge-shaped behind, which were fixed into the concrete mass while it was wet, and held so firmly by the crystallization of the lime that it is almost impossible to separate the ornamental smooth surface of a Roman wall, from the mass of rough concrete behind it. This mode of facing the wall occurs first in buildings of the time of Sylla the dictator.

Bricks burnt in kilns probably came in about that period. In the time of Augustus brick is generally used sparingly in layers of thin bricks, separating the tufa surface, called *opus reticulatum*, into panels, and this fashion is continued to the time of Hadrian. In the time of Tiberius the walls are frequently faced entirely with the excellent brick-work called *opus lateritium*, and this style was imitated in Rome for many centuries. In the earlier brick-work, that is, in the first century of the Christian era, the bricks are better than at any other period; they are large, flat, and thin, commonly two feet square and one inch thick, what we call *Roman tiles*, but used for building walls, and not merely for roofing or pavement. The facing tiles are commonly triangular, with the broad side outwards. The bricks gradually became thicker and smaller, until in the fourth century they are often only four to a foot on the surface of the wall, as in modern walls. Simultaneously with these brick walls (that is, walls *faced* with brick), stone walls continued to be used, and these are frequently built of the large blocks of stone, like the walls of the Kings, but the material is travertine, that of the early walls in Rome is tufa only, and they either have mortar, or are wedged together with wooden wedges, or clamped with metal. In the arcade of the Aqueduct of Claudius the arches are built of very large stones, which extend right through the width of the arcade from one side to the other, about fifteen feet. These large stones are well cut, and fitted closely, and held together by wooden tenons of the dove-tail form, let into hollows cut for them in the surface of each stone. From the first century to the tenth there is a gradual decay in the art of building, until in the tenth century, in the monastery of S. Croce, it is as bad as it well could be to stand at all.

In the eleventh century the great revival of the art of building began. The buildings of this century in France and England are generally very massive, and built of large stones where they could be had, with wide joints of mortar, which are generally characteristic of this period. These walls being built with good fresh lime, like those of the earliest Roman, are equally lasting, and were commonly suffered to remain as what is called *the gross construction* of the building, even when the whole ornamentation of the building was entirely altered according to the fashion of the later periods, when it was required to adapt it to the fashion of the day. This change of outward appearance mainly took place in the twelfth century. In the great abbey church of St. Stephen at Caen the walls are chiefly of the eleventh century, the vaults and the ornamentation of the twelfth. This is also the case at St. Remi at Rheims, at Jumiège in Normandy, in Winchester Cathedral, and in numerous other instances.

See also *Ashlar, Bonders, Brick, Cob-wall, Free-mason, Free-stone, Garreting, Herring-bone-work, Rag-stone, Roman Architecture, Romanesque Style, Rubble, Rustic-work, Saxon, Tiles.*

Column, a round pillar; the term includes the base, shaft, and capital: in Grecian and Roman architecture. Tho column is so important a feature that the exact proportions of its several parts are settled, and vary according to the Order.

In the Illustration which is given here the chief features are shewn, with the nomenclature of the details commonly employed. Under the Composite Order [vide *Order*] will be found additional nomenclature. [See also the words *Corona* and *Cymatium*, and the illustrations given under *Astragal, Cavetto, Cyma, Ogee, Ovolo, Pedestal, Portico, Scotia.*]

The term is also sometimes applied to the pillars or piers in Norman and Gothic architecture.

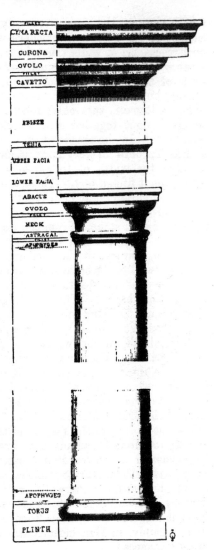

Compound Arch, a term applied to signify a *Recessed* arch.

Compound Pier, a clustered column.

Concha (Lat.), name applied to the apse from the shell-like shape of the vault.

Conduit, properly a watercourse (or *Specus*), applied also to the structure forming the reservoir for water.

Coping, or capping, the covering course of a wall or parapet, either flat, or sloping on the upper surface, to throw off water; it often presents characteristic mouldings attesting the age. The stones also along the ridge of a roof are called coping-stones.

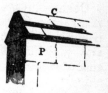

C. Coping. P. Parapet.

Corbel (Lat. *Corbis* = a basket), a term denoting a projecting stone or piece of timber which supports a superincumbent weight. Corbels are used in a great

Broadwater, Sussex, c. 1250.

St. Benedict's Church, Lincoln, c. 1350.

variety of situations, and are carved and moulded in various ways according to the taste of the age in which they are executed; the form of a head was very frequently given to them in each of the styles, from Norman to late Perpendicular, especially when used under the ends of the weather-mouldings of doors and windows, and in other similar situations. Sometimes also *masks* were introduced.

Corbel-table, a row of corbels supporting a parapet or cornice, usually having small arcs between them. [See *Cornice.*]

Corbie-steps, a Scotch term for the steps up the sides of a gable : they are frequently found on old houses, particularly in Flanders, Holland, and Germany, and produce a very picturesque effect. The top stone is termed the crow-stone.

Cornice, (from Ital. and that from Lat. *Corona*), the horizontal moulded projection encircling the top of a building, or the component parts of a building, and generally beneath the eaves of the roof. In Classic architecture each of the Orders has its peculiar cornice.

In the *Norman* style of architecture, a plain face of parapet, slightly projecting from the wall, is frequently used as a cornice, and a row of blocks is often placed under it, sometimes plain, some-
times moulded or
carved into heads
and other orna-
ments, when it is
called a *corbel-ta-
ble :* these blocks
very commonly

Norman Corbel-table, St. Peter's, Oxford.

have a range of small arches over them ; a small plain string is also sometimes used as a cornice.

In the *Early English* style, the corbel-table continued in use as a cornice, but it is generally more ornamented than in the Norman, and the arches are commonly trefoils and well moulded ; the blocks, also, are more delicately carved, either with a head or some other ornament characteristic of the style, and if there are no arches above them they often support a suite of horizontal mouldings ; sometimes there is a range of horizontal mouldings above the arches of the corbel-table, and sometimes the cornice con-

---

Confessio, 1. The Confessio*nary,* i.e. the under part of an altar, or a crypt, or structure under an altar to contain the relics of a martyr, used in this sense chiefly in the early Italian churches. 2. The con-fessio*nal,* i.e. the recess or seat in which the priest sits to hear the confession of penitents.

Cops, a name sometimes applied to the *Merlons* of a battlement.

Corinthian. See *Order.*

sists of mouldings only, without any corbel-table. The
hollow mouldings
of the cornice are
generally plain,
seldom containing
flowers or carv-
ings, except the
toothed orna-
ment.

Early English Cornice, Stanwick, Northants.

In the *Deco-
rated* style, the cornice is usually very regular; and
though in some large buildings it has several mouldings,
it principally consists of a slope above, and a deep sunk
hollow, with an astragal under it; in these hollows,
flowers at regu-
lar distances are
often placed, and
in some large
buildings, and in
towers, &c., there
are frequently
heads, and the

Decorated Cornice, Irchester, c. 1350.

cornice almost filled with them; other varieties of cornice
may also be occasionally met with in this style.

In the *Perpendicular* style, the cornice is often composed of several small mouldings, sometimes divided by
one or two considerable hollows, not very deep: in plain
buildings, the cornice-mouldings of the preceding style
are much adhered to;
but it is more often
ornamented in the
hollow with flowers,
&c., and sometimes
with figures and gro-
tesque animals. In
the latter end of this

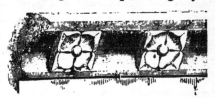

Perpendicular Cornice, Ensham, c. 1450.

style, something very analogous to an ornamented frieze
is perceived, of which the canopies to the niches in various
works are examples; and the angels so profusely introduced in the later rich works are a sort of cornice ornaments.

Corona (Lat.) the lower member, or drip, of the projecting part of a Classic cornice: the horizontal under-surface of it is called the soffit. [See *Column*.]

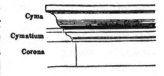

Cyma

Cymatium

Corona

Course, Cors, a continuous range of stones or bricks of uniform height in the wall of a building.

Credence (Ital. *Credenza*, a side table), the small table at the side of the altar, or communion-table, on which the bread and wine were placed before they were consecrated. This was a very early custom in the Church. In many instances in this country the place of the credence - table is found supplied by a shelf across the piscina: this shelf was either of wood or stone. The word in its literal sense signifies simply a buffet or sideboard.

Woodford, c. 1350.

Crenelle (or old Eng. Kernel). This term appears sometimes to signify a battlement, but it usually means the embrasures of a battlement, or loopholes and other openings in the walls of a fortress through which arrows and other missiles might be discharged against assailants; the adjective 'crenellated,' when applied to a building, signified fortified or provided with crenelles as a means of defence. A licence from the Crown (*quod possit kernellare*) was required in mediæval times before a subject could build a castle or fortify his existing house.

CORKSCREW-STAIRS. See *Newel*, *Step*, and *Vise*.

CORONA (Lat.), 1. Part of a Classic cornice, as above; 2. The apse, hence the name "Becket's Crown" at Canterbury; 3. A circle of lights or chandelier.

Crest (Lat. *Crista*), the ornamental finishing which surmounts a screen, canopy, or other similar subordinate portion of a building, whether a battlement, open carved work, or other enrichment: a row of Tudor - flowers is very often used in late Perpendicular work. The coping stones on the parapet and other similar parts of a Gothic building, likewise called the capping or coping.

Exeter Cathedral.

The finials of gables and pinnacles are also sometimes called crests. *Crest-tiles* were formerly sometimes made with a row of ornaments, resembling small battlements or Tudor-flowers, on the top, and glazed, and still are so occasionally, but in general they are quite plain. Sometimes these ornaments were formed in lead when the ridge of the roof was covered with that material, as at Exeter Cathedral.

Crockets (Fr. *Croc* = a hook), projecting leaves, flowers, or bunches of foliage, used in Gothic architecture to decorate the angles of spires, canopies, pinnacles, &c.; they are also frequently found on gables, and on the weather-mouldings of doors and windows, and in other similar situations: occasionally they are used among vertical mouldings, as at Lincoln Cathedral, where they run up the mullions of the windows of the tower, and the sides of some of the arches, but they are not employed in horizontal situations. They are used in suites, and are placed at equal distances apart: the varieties are innumerable. The earliest crockets are to be found

COUPLE CLOSE. See *Roof.*
COUTES (in armour). See illustrations to *Brass.*
COVIE, COVEY, a pantry.
CRADLE-VAULT. See *Cylindrical Vault.*

CRAMP-IRON, iron bent at each end for fastening stones together in a building.
CRESSET, an open frame for a lantern to serve as a beacon.

in the *Early English* style; they usually consist either
of small leaves or rather long stalks, or bunches of leaves

Hereford Cathedral, c. 1250.

Kidlington, Oxfordshire, c. 1350.

curled back something like the head of a bishop's pastoral
crook; but they were not used till late in this style.

Choir, Lincoln Cathedral, c. 1200.

Litcham, Norfolk, c. 1450.

Decorated crockets vary considerably; the most usual form is that of a broad leaf with the edges attached to the moulding on which it is placed, and the middle part and point raised.

In the *Perpendicular* style this is the most prevalent form, but they are not unfrequently made like flat square leaves, which are united with the mouldings by the stalk and one edge only. In a few instances, animals and figures are used in place of crockets, as in Henry the Seventh's chapel.

Southwell Minster, A.D. 1330.

Cross (Lat. *Crux*), the usual symbol of the Christian religion. The difference between the Latin and Greek type is, that in the Roman cross the foot is longer than the upper part or the branches; or, in other words, the shaft or upright portion is longer than the horizontal bar which crosses it, giving as it were the form of a man standing with arms extended. In the Eastern form, on the other hand, the limbs or arms are all equal. The Latin cross is supposed to resemble the actual cross of Christ, but the form of the Greek cross is considered ideal.

As an architectural ornament in churches and religious edifices it was almost always placed upon the points of the gables, the form varying considerably according to the style of the architecture and the character of the building; many of these crosses are extremely elegant and ornamental, and considering the animosity displayed by the Puritans against the representations of the sacred symbol, more gable crosses are

Warmington, Northants. A.D. 1350.

CROOK. See *Knee.*
CROPE, old word used for a finial.

CROSS OF CONSTANTINE. See *Labarum.*

remaining than might be expected. It was also very frequently carved on gravestones, and was introduced in various ways among the decorations of churches.

A small cross (which was often a *crucifix*) was placed upon the altar, and was usually of a costly material: crosses were also carried in religious processions upon long staves.

Merton College Chapel, A.D. 1450.

A large cross with the figure attached, called the rood, was placed over the main entrance of the chancel in every church.

It was formerly the custom in this kingdom, as it still is in foreign countries, to erect crosses in cemeteries, by the road-side, and in the market-places and open spaces in towns and villages; of such, numerous examples remain, though with the exception of the market crosses most of them are greatly defaced: those in cemeteries and by the way-side were generally simple structures, raised on a few steps, consisting of a tall shaft, with sometimes a few mouldings to form a base, and a cross on the top; in some instances they had small niches or other ornaments round the top of the shaft below the cross: the village crosses appear generally to have been of the same simple description, but sometimes they were more important erections. Market crosses were usually polygonal buildings with an open archway on each of the sides, and vaulted within, large enough to afford shelter to a considerable number of persons; of these good examples remain at Malmesbury, Salisbury, Chichester, Glastonbury, &c. Crosses were

CROSSES. There are several forms, to which technical names have been applied by the heralds. A cross *of Calvary* is when it is mounted on steps. Of *Jerusalem* or Cross *Potent*, when the end of the arms have a bar across like a crutch ✠. *Trefflée*, with the arms ending in a trefoil. *Patonce* and *Fleury*, when terminated in three leaves or points, but the latter when the leaves are curved, the former when straight. *Pattée*, when the sides of the arms are curved inwards ✠. If they nearly meet in the centre, and the ends are notched so as to produce eight prominent points it is a *Maltese* cross ✠. The *Tau* cross (or *St. Antony's*) having three arms only. *St. Andrew's* cross, when in the form of the letter X.

also erected in commemoration of remarkable occurrences; and of them Queen Eleanor's crosses are beautiful ex-amples, erected as they were as memo-rials wherever the corpse was rested on its journey to West-minster, for inter-ment, [see illustra-tion under *Canopy*]. Of this type of cross is the one erected at Oxford to commemo-rate the deaths of Cranmer, Ridley, and Latimer.

The cross was a favourite form for the plan of churches; while the Western churches mostly fol-lowed the Latin form of cross, the By-zantine churches fol-lowed the Greek form, i.e. with the chancel, nave, and two transepts all of equal length.

Churchyard Cross, Waterperry, c. 1320.

Crozier (Low Lat. *Crocia*), the *pastoral staff* of a bishop or mitred abbot, which has the head curled round some-thing in the manner of a shepherd's crook. The crozier of an archbishop was surmounted by a cross, after the twelfth century.

CROSS-SPRINGERS, the trans-verse ribs of a groined roof.

CROSSE, word used to signify the transept. A cross church means a cruciform church.

CROUDS or SHROUDS, the crypt of a church.

CROW-STONE. See *Corbie Steps*.

CULLIS (Fr.), a groove, as in Port-cullis, Machi-coulis: also written Killesse.

CURSTABLE, a course of stones with mouldings cut on them to form a string-course.

Crypt (Gr. *Krupto* = to bury), a vault beneath a building, either entirely or partly under ground. Crypts are frequent under churches: they do not in general extend beyond the limits of the choir or chancel and its aisles, and are often of very much smaller dimensions, under the altar only; they are carefully constructed and well finished, though in a plainer style than the upper parts of the building, and were formerly in this country, as they still are abroad, used as chapels, and provided with altars and other fittings requisite for the celebration of religious services; they were also used as places of sepulture. [See *Cemetery*.]

Cupola (Ital.), a concave ceiling, either hemispherical or of any other curve, covering a circular or polygonal area; also a roof, the exterior of which is of either of these forms, more usually called a dome, and in Latin *tholus*.

Cusps (Lat. = a spear-point), are the projecting points forming the featherings or foliations in Gothic tracery, arches, panels, &c.; they came into use during the latter part of the Early English style, at which period they were sometimes worked with a small leaf, usually a trefoil, on the end. When first introduced, the cusps sprang from the flat under-surface or soffit of the arch, entirely independent of the mouldings, and this method was sometimes followed in Decorated structures; but they very soon began to be formed from the inner moulding next the soffit (usually either a splay or a

Crosby Hall.

Screen, Lincoln Cathedral.

Curtain-wall, a wall between two towers, especially in military architecture.

hollow,) and this moulding continued on the cusp. The general practice was to cusp the upper part of the lights of all windows, and this was followed until the expiration of Gothic architecture. Some of the richest examples may be found in Lincoln Cathedral, an illustration from which will be found under *Panel.*

In the *Decorated* and *Perpendicular* styles, they were frequently ornamented at the ends, either with heads, leaves, or flowers, and occasionally with animals. [See also *Foils.*]

Cyma (Gr.), an undulated moulding, of which there are two kinds: cyma recta, which is hollow in the upper part, and round in the lower; and cyma reversa, called also the ogee, which is hollow in the lower part, and round in the upper. The term cyma, without an adjective, is always considered to mean a cyma recta. It is usually the upper member of Grecian and Roman entablatures, excepting in the Tuscan

Cyma recta.   Theatre of Marcellus, Rome.

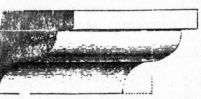

Cyma reversa or Ogee.   Temple of Antoninus and Faustinus, Rome.

and Doric orders, and in Classical architecture is very rarely used in any but a horizontal position, except over pediments. In the Norman style this moulding is not very often met with, but in Gothic architecture it is frequent, especially in doorways, windows, archways, &c., but the proportions are generally very different from those given to it by the ancients, and it is called an ogee. An example of a *quirked* cyma is given beneath *Ogee.* [See also *Column.*]

CYCLAS (in costume). See illustration to *Brass.*

CYLINDRICAL VAULT. See *Vault.*

Cymatium: this is not easy to define, but it may be called a capping moulding to certain parts and subdivisions of the orders in Classic architecture: the projecting mouldings on the upper part of the architrave, (except in the Doric order, where it is denominated *tenia*,) the corresponding moulding over the frieze, and the small mould- ing between the corona and cyma of the cornice, are each called by this name; the small moulding, also, which runs round the upper part of the modillons of a cornice is their cymatium: and the upper

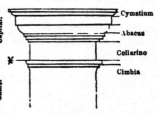

moulding of the abacus of the Roman Doric capital is likewise so called; the upper mouldings which serve as a cornice to pedestals, have occasionally the same name.

Dado, the solid block or cube forming the body of a pedestal in Classical architecture, between the base- mouldings and cornice: an architectural arrangement of mouldings, &c., round the lower part of the walls of a room, resembling a continuous pedestal. [See *Pedestal*.]

Dais (Old Fr. = a canopy) is applied first to the chief seat at the "high board," or principal table, in a baro- nial hall, secondly to the principal table itself, and thirdly to the raised part of the floor on which it was placed; this raised space extended all across the upper end of the hall, and was usually but one step above the rest of the floor; at one end was a large bay window; the high table thus stood across the hall, the chief seat being in the middle of it, on the upper side next the wall, which was usually covered with hangings of tapestry or carpeting; but in the hall of the Archbishop of Canterbury's palace, at Mayfield, Sussex, are the remains of the chief seat in stonework, the back of which is covered with diapering; these seats generally no doubt had a canopy over them. The hall being the apartment used during the Middle Ages on occasions of state and ceremony, the term dais became general for a seat of dignity or judgment.

Decorated Style of Gothic Architecture. This style exhibits the most complete and perfect development of Gothic architecture, which in the Early English style was not fully matured, and in the Perpendicular began to decline. The name was given by Rickman to signify that in this style the decoration or ornament becomes more essentially a part of the style, entering more into the construction, and not merely applied. The most prominent characteristic of this style is to be found in the *Windows*, the

Tracery, &c., Higham Ferrers.

tracery of which is always either of geometrical figures, circles, quatrefoils, &c., as in the earlier instances, or flowing in wavy lines, as in the later examples. [See *Window* and *Tracery*.] The doorways of this style have frequently a close resemblance in form to those of the Early English, and are chiefly distinguished by the ornaments and mouldings. A weather-moulding, or dripstone, is generally used over the heads of doorways, windows, niches, &c., the ends of which are supported on *corbel* heads, or bosses of foliage, or are returned in various

---

DAYS, the lights of a window, or spaces between the mullions.

DEALBATOR, DAUBOR (med. Lat.), a whitewasher.

DEAMBULATORY=*Ambulatory.*

DEARN or DERN, a door-post or threshold.

ways: this is not unfrequently formed into an ogee and
crocketed, and surmounted with a finial so as to become
a canopy, [see illustration from Walpole St. Andrew's,
under *Tabernacle*]. The pillars in rich buildings are either
of clustered shafts, or moulded; in plainer buildings they
are usually either octagonal or circular; when of clustered
shafts the plan of the pillar very frequently partakes of
the form of a lozenge:
the capitals are either
plain or enriched with
foliage, which, like most
of the ornaments in this
style, is usually very
well executed. Niches
are very freely used,
either singly, as on but-
tresses, &c., or in ranges,
so as to have the effect
of a series of deeply
sunk panels, and both
are usually surmounted
by crocketed canopies.

The *Mouldings* of the
Decorated style gene-
rally consist of rounds
and hollows separated
by small fillets, and are
almost always extremely
effective, and arranged
so as to produce a very
pleasing contrast of light

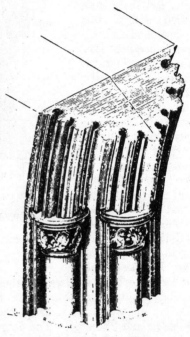

Yarmouth, Norfolk, c. 1351.

and shade; the hollows are frequently enriched with
running foliage, or with flowers at intervals, particularly
the *ball*-flower, and a flower of *four leaves*, which succeeded
the toothed ornament of the preceding style. Examples
of the four-leaved flower in use will be found under
Canopy, *Doorway*, and *Tabernacle*.

The Decorated style prevailed throughout the greater
part of the fourteenth century; it was first introduced in
the reign of Edward I., some of the earliest examples
being the celebrated crosses erected to the memory of

Queen Eleanor, who died in 1290, [see example under *Canopy*]; but it was in the reigns of his successors, Edward II. and III., that this style was in general use.

A few of the chief examples of Decorated work of which *the date is tolerably well ascertained* may be mentioned:—

EDW. I., 1272—1307.

Howden, Yorkshire—Choir.
Norwich—St. Ethelbert's Gate.
    „   Cathedral Vaulting.
Hereford—Chapter-house.
    „   Part of Cloisters.
Stoke Golding, Leicestershire.
Merton Chapel, Oxford.
Exeter Cathedral—Nave, &c.
    „   „   Part of Choir.
Acton Burnel, Salop—Castle.
    „   „   Part of Church.
Dorchester, Oxon.—Choir.
Queen Eleanor Crosses at Northampton, Geddington, Waltham.
Westminster Abbey—Tomb of Queen Eleanor.
York Cathedral—Nave.
Wycombe, Buckinghamshire.
Wells—Chapter-house.
Norwich—Cloisters.
Lichfield—Chapter-house.
Tideswell Church, Derbyshire.
Oxford, St. Mary's—Tower and Spire.

EDW. II., 1307—1327.

Bristol Cathedral—Choir.
Trinity Church, Hull.

Gloucester Cath.—South Aisle.
Oxford, Magdalen Church—South Aisle.
Ely Cathedral—Lady-chapel.
    „   „   Central Lantern.

EDW. III., 1327—1377.

Gloucester Cath.—Tomb of Edward II.
Exeter Cathedral—Nave.
Shottesbroke Church, Berkshire.
York Cathedral—Nave.
    „   „   West Window.
    „ Parapet of Chapter-house.
Battle, Sussex—Abbey Gate.
Durham Cath.—West Window.
Oxford Cath.—Latin Chapel.
    „ St. Aldate's—South Aisle.
Windsor Castle—King's Cloister.
    „   „   Round Tower.
York Cathedral—Presbytery.
Ely—Holy Cross Church on the north side of cathedral.
Ely Cathedral — Windows of Presbytery.
Wells—The Vicar's Close and part of the Hall
Westminster Abbey—Tomb of Queen Philippa.

Dentels (Lat. *Denticulus* = a little tooth), ornaments resembling teeth, used in the bed-moulding of Ionic, Corinthian, and Composite cornices.

DECASTYLE, a portico of ten columns in front.
DEGREES, steps or stairs.
DIAZOMATA (Gr.), the passages encircling the seats in a theatre.

DIE (Old Fr. *Dé*) = Ital. *Dado.*
DIPTERAL (Gr.), a temple having a double range of columns all round.

Diaper-work, or Diapering, an ornament of flowers applied to a plain surface, whether carved or painted; if carved, the flowers are entirely sunk into the work below the general surface; they are usually square, and placed

close to each other, but occasionally other forms are used, as in the choir-screen of Canterbury; this kind of decoration was first introduced in the Early English style, when it was sometimes applied to large spaces, as in Westminster Abbey and Chichester Cathedral; in the Decorated style it was also extensively used. An example of its use will be seen in the illustration of part of one of the Eleanor Crosses given under *Canopy.* In the Perpendicular style diapering was used only as a painted ornament, and as no attention has been paid to the preservation of such decorations, but few specimens remain. The name is derived from a kind of cloth then very commonly

Monument of Wilham de Valence, Westminster.

used, which was worked in square patterns, and which was called "Dyaper," i.e. D'Ypres, from the chief manufactory being at "Ypres," in Belgium. In the later styles, *Panelling, Pargetting,* and the like, took the place of this class of ornamentation.

Diastyle, an arrangement of columns in Grecian and Roman architecture in which the inter-columniation or space between them is equal to three, or according to some, four diameters of the shaft.

DIPTYCHS, shutters or folding-doors, especially over an altar. See *Leaves.* The Roman diptychs were a pair of covers usually handsomely carved in ivory.

DISCHARGING ARCH, called also Relieving Arch, and Arch of Construction; an arch formed in the substance of a wall, to relieve the part which is below it from the superincumbent weight; they are frequently used over lintels and flat-headed openings.

DOG-TOOTH MOULDING. See *Moulding* and *Tooth-ornament.*

DOGS = Andirons.

Dome, a cupola; the term is derived from the Italian, *duomo*, a cathedral, the custom of erecting cupolas on those buildings having been so prevalent that the name dome has, in the French and English languages, been transferred from the church to this kind of roof. [See *Cupola.*]

Domestic Architecture. Beyond the foundations of the walls and the hypocausts under the bath-rooms we have little to guide us as to the chief domestic buildings of the Romans in this country. From their departure to the time of the revival of building in the eleventh and twelfth centuries, we have no remains whatever. The habitations were without doubt built mainly of wood, and whatever stone constructions may have existed were of probably so slight and rude a character that they have never been preserved. In the twelfth century we have several remains of manor houses, and they appear to have been usually of two stories, and built in the form of a parallelogram; the lower story being vaulted, and the upper approached by a staircase on the outside. Remains of town houses of this century are rare, the Jew's House at Lincoln perhaps being the best. It is, however, difficult if not impossible to distinguish between what is properly the house and what the castle; all houses of importance being, from the state of the times, necessarily fortified. Thus perhaps the most perfect house of the next century (the thirteenth), shewing all the offices, and remaining perfect with its fortifications, is Aydon Castle in Northumberland. And in the same or in the fourteenth century Markenfield Hall is a good example, though less fortified. Towards the end of that century the military aspect of the house gave way to the domestic. At Warwick Castle, though the fortifications are most complete, the domestic part assumes a much greater importance both as to extent and number of the rooms, in other cases there is a separate building standing within the fortifications. The great hall dividing the family apartments from the servants' offices, was the chief feature which remained throughout to the end of the fifteenth century, and indeed, in some cases, to the time of Elizabeth, but our modern arrangement of the house gradually grew up; the bed-chambers were made more numerous, sitting and private rooms also were added, and these generally resulting in the diminution of the size of the hall.

The several plans of mediæval houses, which are very numerous, are treated of in a separate work on the subject [c].

The architectural details, it may be added, were the same as in the churches, and the error of the last generation in putting every Gothic window down to a church or chapel has been exploded. The Gothic style was the national style of the country, and it was just the same for cathedrals, castles, churches, monasteries, public buildings, houses, or the meanest cottage, which could boast of stonework.

Donjon (Old Fr.), the *Keep* of a castle: the term is Norman-French, but is extensively used by English writers. In the Roman castles there does not appear to have been any principal tower corresponding to the keep of a mediæval castle, which seems rather to have been derived from the Celtic earthworks, in which there was always a keep. These earthworks were originally occupied by wooden buildings only, and stone castles with keep towers do not appear to have been commonly used during the interval between the fall of the Romans and the eleventh century. The earliest Norman keep known is the tower called St. Leonard's tower, at Malling, in Kent, built by Bishop Gundulph about 1080. No traces of Early Norman masonry can be found on the sites of the castles in Normandy of the barons who came over to England with William the Conqueror, although fine earthworks remain in all cases.

Donjon, Conisborough Castle, Yorkshire.

[c] The work is entitled "Domestic Architecture of the Middle Ages," Oxford, 4 vols., 8vo.

Door. In the times of the Romans the doors were of wood or metal, and occasionally of marble, panelled, and turning on pivots working in sockets, and this custom continued in some countries to a late period, as in Ireland.

In this country a few original Norman doors exist; they are devoid of ornaments except the hinges and iron scrollwork on the front, and large projecting nail-heads. In the thirteenth century also they were dependent upon the ironwork for ornamentation, this consisting not only of the ornamental hinges and nail-heads, but also of escutcheons, round the locks and handles. Examples occur of the ornamentation of the door in the inside as well as on the out, but rarely. In the fourteenth century panels were introduced on the woodwork and other ornamentation, though the ironwork of the preceding century was not lost sight

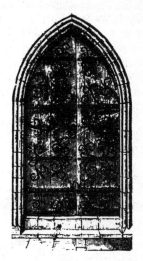

Door, Uffington, Berkshire, c. 1250.

of. In the fifteenth century the panelling was the chief ornamentation of the doors, the panels being cusped and elaborately worked.

Doorway. The stone framework in which the door hangs, or the entrance into a building, or into an apartment of a building. Among the ancients, doorways were usually rectangular in form, though occasionally the opening diminished towards the top, until architecture became corrupted in the latter times of the Roman empire, when they were sometimes arched; when not arched they generally had a suite of mouldings, called an architrave, running round them, and there were often additional mouldings over the top, supported by a large console or truss at each end.

In the architecture of the Middle Ages doorways are striking and important features, and afford in the character of their mouldings and ornaments clear evidence of the styles to which they belong. In the style mentioned in this Glossary as perhaps being *Saxon*, they are always plain, with very little, if any, moulding, excepting in some instances a rude impost, and even that is frequently a plain stone slightly projecting from the face of the wall: the arches are semicircular, and (like all the rest of the work) rudely constructed, but in some instances the head of the opening is formed by two straight pieces of stone placed upon their ends on the impost, and leaning together at the top so as to produce the form of a triangle.

In the *Norman* style doorways became more ornamental, though at its commencement very little decoration was used. In the earliest examples the jambs and archivolt were merely cut into square recesses, or angles without mouldings, with a simple impost at the springing of the arch; but as the style advanced, mouldings and other enrichments were introduced, and continued to be applied in increasing numbers until they sometimes nearly or quite equalled the breadth of the

Weston Favell, Northants, c. 1100.

opening of the doorway, fine examples of which remain at Lincoln Cathedral: the ornaments were used almost entirely on the outside, the inside usually being (as in all the styles of Gothic architecture) perfectly plain. The arch is commonly semicircular, though occasionally segmental or horse-shoe: the mouldings and enrichments are very various, but are generally bold, and, though not so well worked as those of the later styles, they very often equal and sometimes surpass them in richness and effect. The outer moulding of the arch in some cases stops upon the impost, producing the effect

Middleton Stoney, c. 1160.

of a weather-moulding, although it does not project from the face of the wall; weather-mouldings also are very frequently used, and they either stop upon the impost or terminate in carved corbels. Shafts are often, but not always, used in the jambs; they are generally circular, but occasionally octagonal, and are sometimes ornamented with zigzags or spiral mouldings. The capitals are usually in some degree enriched, and are often carved with figures and a rude kind of foliage. The impost-moulding above the caps generally runs through the whole jamb, and is frequently continued along the wall as a string. Some of the most usual ornaments in Norman doorways are zigzags of various kinds, several of which will be found engraved under *Mouldings*, and series of grotesque heads, set in a hollow moulding, with projecting tongues or beaks, (see *Beak-heads*,) overlapping a large torus or bead; small figures and animals are also frequently used, and occasionally the signs of the zodiac. The actual opening of the doorway is often flat at the top, and rises no higher than the springing of the arch, (see illustration under *Tympanum*); the tympanum, or space between the top of the opening and the arch, is sometimes left plain, but is generally ornamented, and frequently sculptured with a rude representation of some scriptural or legendary subject.

Early English doorways generally have pointed arches, though a few have semi-circular, and occasionally the top of the opening is flat. In doorways of large size the mouldings are very numerous, and the jambs contain several small shafts which usually stand quite free, and are often of Purbeck or Forest marble, or some fine stone of a different kind from the rest of the work; the jamb is generally cut into recesses to receive these shafts, with a small suite of mouldings between each of them. In

Paul's Cray, Kent, c. 1220.

small doorways there is often but one shaft in each jamb, and sometimes none. The capitals are generally enriched with delicate leaves, but they often consist of plain mouldings. The archivolt, and the spaces between the shafts in the jambs, are frequently enriched with the toothed-ornament, or with leaves and other decorations characteristic of the style, but in some very good examples they have only plain mouldings. The opening of the doorway is sometimes divided into two by a single shaft, or a clustered column,

Cloisters, Salisbury Cathedral, c. 1230.

with a quatrefoil or other ornament above it, and instances of this are found in the early part of the Decorated style also. There is almost invariably a weather moulding over the arch, which is generally supported on a head at each end. In many instances the inner mouldings of the head are formed into a trefoil or cinquefoil arch, the points of which generally terminate in small flowers or leaves, and in some small doorways the whole of the mouldings follow these forms.

Decorated doorways are not in general so deeply recessed as those of the last style, but they very much resemble them in the mouldings and shafts in the jambs. There are a few examples, early in the style, in which the opening is divided into two, as at York Minster and Lichfield, but it is not the usual arrangement. The shafts in the jambs are usually of slighter proportions than in the Early English

Dorchester, Oxon., c. 1320.

style, and instead of being worked separate, form part of the general suite of mouldings; the capitals consist either of plain mouldings, or are enriched with leaves of different kinds characteristic of the style. Many small doorways have no shafts in the jambs, but the mouldings of the arch are continued down to the plinth, where they stop upon a slope. The arch in large doorways is almost invariably pointed; in smaller it is frequently an ogee and rarely segmental. The mouldings are commonly very rich; the most prevalent ornament, as usual in all work of the style, being the ball-flower and four-leaved flower: occasionally a series of small niches, with statues in them, like a hollow moulding, are carried up the jambs and round the arch; and sometimes doubly feathered tracery, hanging quite free from some of the outer mouldings, is used in the arch, and has a very rich effect: small buttresses or niches are sometimes placed at the sides of the doorways. A weather-moulding is almost universally used; it is generally supported at each end on a boss of foliage, or a corbel, which is frequently a head, but it sometimes terminates in a curl or a short return: for illustration see *Dripstone*. The weather-mould is seldom continuous along the wall; occasionally it is crocketed and surmounted at the top by a finial, especially when in the form of an ogee, or it has a finial and no crockets. In rich examples canopies are common over Decorated Doorways; they are either triangular, or ogees with crockets and finials, the space

Crick, Northants., c. 1350.

between them and the mouldings of the arch being filled with tracery-panels, foliage, or sculpture.

In plain buildings the doorways of this style are frequently quite plain, and the head is often of the form called the *shoulder-arch:* the name of *Decorated* applies more especially to the window tracery, and although some doorways are much enriched in this style, as a rule they are *plain* when compared with those of other styles.

In the *Perpendicular* style a very considerable change took place in the appearance of the doorways, from the outer mouldings being constantly formed into a square over the arch, with the spandrels feathered, or filled with ornaments, either tracery, foliage, or sculpture; this square head, however, is not uni-

versal. Shafts are often, though by no means always, used in the jambs; they are generally small, and are always worked on the jamb with the other mouldings, and frequently are not clearly defined, except by the capital and base, the other mouldings uniting with them without a fillet, or even an angle to mark the separation; the capitals usually consist of plain mouldings, but in some instances they are enriched with foliage or flowers. There are generally one or more large hollows in the jambs, sometimes filled with niches for statues, but more often left plain : these large hollows are characteristics of the Perpendicular style.

St. Erasmus' Chapel, Westminster.

In this style the four-centred arch was brought into general use, and became the most prevalent for doorways as well as other openings; many, however, have two-centred arches, and in small doorways ogees are sometimes used; a very few have elliptical arches.

DORIC ORDER. See *Order.*

DORMANT-TREE, DORMOND, a large beam lying across a room: a joist or sleeper.

DORSER, a cushion, especially for the back of the seat. Dorsers and Bankers are frequently mentioned together in inventories.

DOSEL (or *Dorsal*), the hangings on the walls of a hall, especially behind the dais; or in a church, behind the altar.

Dormer, a window pierced through a sloping roof and placed in a small gable which rises on the side of the roof. There do not appear to be any dormers now existing of an earlier date than the middle of the fourteenth century. It was usually the window of the sleeping - apartments; hence the name Dormer, from

Chapel Cleeve, Somerset, c. 1350.

Dormitory (Lat.), a sleeping apartment; the term is generally used with reference to the sleeping-room of the inmates of monasteries and religious establishments, which was of considerable size, and sometimes had a range of cells parted off on each side, as in the Bede-house at Higham Ferrars, Northants., at St. Mary's Hospital, Chichester, at Durham, and at Gloucester.

Dressings, (1.) The mouldings and sculptured decorations of all kinds which are used on the walls and ceilings of a building for the purpose of ornament; (2.) Applied to a square opening in the stonework or mouldings which surround it like a frame, such as a brick building with stone dressings.

Dripstone, called also Label, Weather-moulding, Watertable, and Hoodmould; a projecting tablet or moulding over the heads of doorways, windows, archways, niches, &c., in Norman and Gothic architecture, to throw off the rain, or in some instances for ornament, as it is used both in internal and external work. It is not in general carried below the level of the springing of the arch, except over windows in which the tracery extends below that level, when it is usually continued to the bottom of the

DOWELS, pieces of wood or iron, used at the edges of boards in laying floors.

DRAGON-PIECE. See *Roof.*

DRIP, the projecting edge of a moulding, channelled beneath so that the rain will drip from it: the corona of the Italian architects.

tracery; occasionally it descends the whole length of the jamb.

In the Norman style the dripstone does not in general project much from the face of the wall, and it usually consists of a few very simple mouldings, often of a flat fillet with a splay or slight hollow on the lower side, and it is in some cases enriched with billets or other small ornaments; sometimes it is continued horizontally on the wall as a string, level with the springing of the arch, but it oftener stops upon a corbel or on the impost-moulding, which is prolonged far enough to receive it.

Malmesbury Abbey, Wilts.
(Norman.)

In the Early English style, the dripstone is generally rather small, but clearly defined, with a deep hollow on the lower side; it varies however considerably in mouldings and proportion: it usually terminates with a small *corbel* (called a *dripstone termination*) consisting of a head, or a boss of foliage, sometimes with a short horizontal *return*, and sometimes it is carried along the wall as a string.

In the two preceding styles the dripstone follows the general shape of the arch, but in the Decorated it frequently takes the form of an ogee, while the arch is of a simple curve, and in such cases it is very commonly surmounted by a finial and is often crocketed, when it is sometimes called a canopy, (see illustration, p. 104): it is very rarely continued along the wall, but terminates with a short return, or on a corbel-head, a boss of foliage, or some other sculptured ornament; or the end is turned up or curled in

Rushden, Northants.

St. Martin's, Canterbury.

several ways, which are characteristic of the style, as at Chippenham.

In the *Perpendicular* style, whenever the outer mouldings of the doorways and other openings, &c., are arranged in a square over the arch, the drip stone follows the same form; in other cases it

All Souls College, Oxford, c. 1460.

follows the curve of the arch or is changed to an ogee, and has sometimes a finial and crockets on it, as in the Decorated style; it is not unfrequently continued horizontally along the wall as a string, but this is not the most usual arrangement; it very commonly terminates with a head, an animal, or other sculptured ornament, sometimes with a shield or an heraldic device. Several engravings illustrating the various dripstones will be found under *Doorway*.

Chippenham Church, c. 1480.

Early English, the first of the pointed or Gothic styles of architecture used in this country; it succeeded the Norman towards the end of the twelfth century and gradually merged into the Decorated at the end of the thirteenth. At its first appearance it partook somewhat of the heaviness of the preceding style, but all resemblance to the Norman was speedily effaced by the

West Door, Shere Church, Surrey, c. 1220.

development of its own peculiar and beautiful characteristics. The mouldings, in general, consist of alternate rounds and deeply-cut hollows, with a small admixture of

---

DUNGEON. See *Donjon*. The word however came to be used | for a prison in or beneath any tower.

fillets, producing a strong effect of light and shadow. The
arches are usually equilateral
or lancet-shaped, although the
drop arches are often met
with, and sometimes pointed
segmental arches; trefoil and
cinquefoil arches are also often
used in small openings and
panellings. The doorways of
this style, in large buildings,
are often divided into two by
a single shaft or small pier,
with a quatrefoil or other ornament above it, as the west
end of St. Cross Church, Hants;
they are generally very deeply recessed, with numerous
mouldings in the arch and
small shafts in the jambs,
which are usually entirely detached from the wall; these
shafts are also very freely
used in the jambs of windows,
niches, panellings, &c., and
are not unfrequently encircled
at intervals by continuous
bands of mouldings.

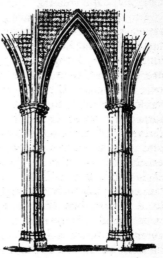

Westminster Abbey, c. 1250.

The windows are almost
universally of long and narrow
proportions, and, except late
in the style, are without featherings; they are either used
singly, or in combinations of
two, three, five, and seven;
when thus combined the space
between them sometimes but
little exceeds the width of
the mullions of the later
styles; occasionally they are

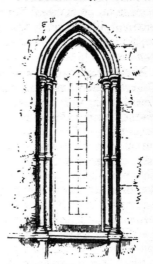

Jesus College Chapel, Cambridge, c. 1250.

surmounted by a large arch, embracing the whole group
of windows, and the space left between this arch and

the tops of the windows is often pierced with circles,
trefoils, quatrefoils, &c., thus
forming the commencement of
tracery. Circular windows were
more used in England during the
prevalence of this style than in
either the Decorated or Perpendicular, and fine specimens remain
at York and Lincoln Cathedrals, and
Beverley Minster. Groined ceilings are very common in this style;
in general they have only cross
springers and diagonal ribs, with
sometimes longitudinal and trans-
verse ribs at the apex of the vaults,
and good bosses of foliage at the

Hargrave, c. 1260.

intersections. The *pillars* usually consist of small shafts
arranged round a larger circular pier, but others of different kinds are to be found, and a plain octagonal or
circular pillar is common in country churches. The *capitals*
consist of plain mouldings, or are enriched with foliage
and sculpture characteristic of the
style. The most prevalent *base*
has very close resemblance to
the Attic base of the ancients,
though the proportions are different and the lower torus is
worked with a considerably larger
projection. The *buttresses* are
often very bold and prominent,
and are frequently carried up to

Chapter House, Southwell, c. 1220.

the top of the building with but little diminution, and
terminate in acutely-pointed pediments which, when raised
above the parapet, produce in some degree the effect of
pinnacles. Flying buttresses were first introduced in
this style. The roofs appear always to have been high
pitched.

The ornaments used in this style are by no means so
various as in either of the others; occasionally small roses
or other flowers, and bunches of foliage, are carved at
intervals in the hollow mouldings, but by far the most

common and characteristic is the dog-tooth ornament, which is often introduced in great profusion, and the hollows entirely filled with it. The foliage is very remarkable for boldness of effect, and it is often so much undercut as to be connected with the mouldings only by the stalks, and edges of the leaves; there is frequently considerable stiffness in the mode in which it is combined, but the effect is almost always good: the prevailing leaf is a trefoil. Towards the latter part of the style crockets were first introduced.

The style may be said to begin in the later half of Richard the First's reign, about which time St. Hugh began his choir at Lincoln. During the reign of King John the style had obtained the complete mastery; but the reign of Henry III. was the great period of the Early English style, which had now obtained perfection. The most perfect example of the style is undoubtedly Salisbury Cathedral. Towards the end of the reign we have examples, such as the presbytery of Lincoln and the chapter-house of Salisbury, of what may be almost called the Decorated Style, though the mouldings and many of the details are pure Early English. The work is in fact transitional from this style to the next.

RICH. I., 1189—1199.
Clee Church, Lincolnshire—The choir, A.D. 1198.
Lincoln Cathedral, built by St. Hugh, 1192—1200.
Oxford, St. Giles' Church.
Rochester Cathedral—Parts of the choir and transept.
Winchester Cath.—Lady-chapel.
„ „ Presbytery.
St. Alban's Abbey — Western part of nave.
Ely Cathedral—Galilee.

JOHN, 1199—1216.
Worcester Cathedral—Choir.
„ „ Presbytery.
Beaulieu, Hants.—Refectory.
Fountains Abbey, Yorkshire.
Hales Owen Abbey.

HEN. III., 1216—1272.
Salisbury Cathedral. (The spire added a century later.)
Worcester—Part of cathedral.

Wells Cathedral—West front.
„ „ Nave and transepts.
„ „ Western part of choir.
„ Bishop's palace.
Rochester Cathedral—Parts of choir and transepts.
Lincoln Cathedral—Nave.
„ St. Mary-le-Wigford Ch.
Ely Cathedral—Presbytery.
Ashbourne Church, Derbyshire —Choir and transepts.
Abington Church, Northants.
Peterborough Cath.—West front.
Temple Church, London—Choir.
Durham—Chapel of the Nine Altars.
Westminster Abbey—Choir and transepts.
Chetwood, Bucks.—Chancel.
Skelton Church, Yorkshire.
Wells Cathedral—Lady-chapel.
York, St. Mary's Abbey.
Lincoln Cathedral—Presbytery.
Salisbury—Chapter-house.

Echinus (Lat.), the egg-and-anchor, or egg-and-tongue ornament, very frequently carved on the ovolo in Classical architecture: the term is also applied to the ovolo moulding, but in strictness it belongs to it only when thus enriched.

Embrasure (Old Fr. *Ebraser* = to widen), the crenelles or intervals between the *merlons* of a battlement.

Embroidery (Fr. *Broder*) **and Tapestry** (which although closely resembling each other in many instances, are not the same, one being the work of the needle the other of the loom), were both extensively used in the Middle Ages, for convenience and for ornament; the existing remains of the houses, and even of churches of that period, often appear poor and bald for want of the necessary furniture, which the architect always calculated upon being in its proper place. Every doorway had a piece of tapestry or embroidery hanging over it, (as is still the fashion in Italy); the walls were hung with tapestry; the cushions were covered with rich embroidery, both in houses and churches; the back of the high seat in the hall and of the stalls in the churches were hung with embroidery or tapestry. The carved and painted diaper patterns which we so often find are only an imitation of the original tapestry or embroidery, of which Ypres was the principal seat of manufacture from a period as early as the fourth century, or earlier, as according to the local history the Romans found it established there. Allowing this to be doubtful, it is certain that in the eleventh century Queen Matilda and her maidens, or the nuns of Bayeux on her foundation, were employed in working the embroidery which still exists and is now carefully preserved in the museum there. Before that time the English women were celebrated for their skill in embroidery or needlework, as the men were for working in the precious metals. The *Opus Anglicanum*, or needlework, was celebrated and eagerly sought for even at Rome and at Byzantium.

EARTH-TABLE = *Ground-table.*

ELBOWS, the projections on the side of stalls; also applied by joiners to panels or sides of windows.

ELE, ELING (old Engl.) = Aisle.

Entablature (Fr. from Lat. *in tabula*), the superstructure which lies horizontally upon the columns in Classic architecture: it is divided into *architrave*, the part immediately above the column; *frieze*, the central space; and *cornice*, the upper projecting mouldings. Each of the orders has its appropriate entablature, of which both the general height and the subdivisions are regulated by a scale of proportion derived from the diameter of the column. [See *Column* and *Order*.]

Escutcheon or Scutcheon (Fr. *Escusson*, dim. of *escn* =Lat. *scutum*, a shield), (1.) A shield charged with armorial bearings. Escutcheons are abundantly used in Gothic architecture as ornaments to perpetuate the memory of benefactors, or as tokens of the influence of particular families or individuals; they are frequently carved on the bosses of ceilings and at the ends of weather-mouldings, particularly in the Perpendicular style, and in the spandrels of doorways, panels, &c. The armorial bearings are either cut on the stone or painted on the surface, and sometimes the shields are perfectly plain; when found on tombs they are charged with the arms of the deceased, and often also with those of his family connections. Sometimes, instead of armorial bearings, escutcheons have the instruments of the Crucifixion, or other devices, carved on them. More frequent also than in stone, these coats of arms appeared in the windows, very many specimens of which are remaining, as the heraldic devices were less a prey to Puritan zeal, than the figures of Saints.

(2.) This term is also applied to the iron plate on a door, &c., from the centre of which the handle is sus-

ENTAIL, now obsolete, but applied by old writers to delicate sculpture or ornamentation.

ENTASIS, the swelling in the middle of a balustre or shaft of a column.

ENTERCLOSE, the passage between two rooms in a house.

ENTRESOL (Fr.), same as Mezanine. See *Story*.

EPISTLE side of an altar. See note under *Altar*.

EPISTYLIUM, the Architrave.

EPITITHYDES, upper member of the cornice of an entablature.

ESCAPE, term used sometimes for the Apophyge.

ESCOINSON or Scoinson (old Fr.), interior edge of the window side or jamb. In mediæval windows this is often ornamented with a shaft carrying an arched rib.

pended, and to the plate which surrounds the keyhole:
these are made of various shapes,
and are sometimes highly ornamented: the escutcheons of door-
handles are sometimes raised in
the centre like a boss, and some
of these appear to be of Decorated
or Early English date. [See *Ironwork*.]

Headington, Oxon.

(3.) The boss in the centre of
a vaulted ceiling appears occasionally to have been called by
this name, but perhaps only in consequence of its being
frequently in the fifteenth century ornamented with an
escutcheon.

Exedra or Exhedra (Gr.), (1.) The portico of the palæstra or gymnasium, in which disputations of the learned
were held among the ancients: also, in private houses, the
pastas, or vestibule, used for conversation. (2.) The term
also signifies an apse, with ranges of seats for viewing
the games in the *Circus* or *Stadium*. On the Palatine in
Rome are remains of three of them, also a recess or large
niche in a wall, and is sometimes applied to a porch or
chapel which projects from a larger building. (3.) It is
also used as synonymous with Cathedra, for a throne or
seat of any kind; for a small private chamber; the space
within an oriel window; and the small chapels between
the buttresses of a large church or cathedral. The word,
however, is not frequently met with.

Extrados (Fr. from Lat. *Extra, dorsum*), the exterior
curve of an arch, measured on the top of the voussoirs,
as opposed to the soffit or intrados.

ESTRADE (Fr.), a platform raised a few inches above the floor
of a chamber, e.g. for a bed, or
for the dais.

EUSTYLE, the fifth order of
temples, according to Vitruvius,
who considered it as the most
elegant; having a space equal to
two diameters and a quarter between the columns.

EWERY, an office or place for
keeping the ewers or bowls for
washing, as the Scutellerie, or
Scullery, was for the plates and
dishes.

Faldstool (or *Folding-stool*), a portable seat made to fold up in the manner of a camp-stool: it was made either of metal or wood, and sometimes was covered with rich silk. Formerly, when a bishop was required to officiate in any but his own cathedral church where his throne was erected, a faldstool was placed for him in the choir, and he frequently carried one with him in his journeys. They are not unfrequently represented in the illuminations of early manuscripts.

This term is also frequently applied to the Litany-stool, or small low desk at which the Litany is enjoined to be sung or said. This is generally placed in the middle of the choir, or near the steps of the altar.

Fan-tracery Vaulting, a kind of vaulting peculiar to English Gothic, and used chiefly in late Perpendicular work, in which all the ribs that rise from the springing of the vault have the same curve, and diverge equally in every direction, producing an effect something like that of the bones of a fan. This kind of vaulting admits of considerable variety in the subordinate parts, but the general effect of the leading features is more nearly uniform. It is very  frequently used over tombs, chantry chapels, and other small erections, and fine examples on a larger scale exist at Henry the Seventh's Chapel, St. George's Chapel, Windsor, King's College Chapel, Cambridge, &c.

Fascia, or *Facia* (Lat. *Facies* = a face), a broad fillet, band, or face, used in Classical architecture, sometimes by itself but usually in combination with mouldings. Architraves are frequently divided into two or three faciæ, each of which projects slightly beyond that which is below it.

FAÇADE (Fr.), exterior face of a building.

FANE or VANE, a weathercock. The fane is found existing throughout the Middle Ages, and assumes a variety of shapes. See *Vane*.

Fenestral (Lat.), a window-blind, or a casement closed with paper or cloth instead of glass. Perhaps, also, the term was applied to the shutters or *leaves* with which many, if not most, of the windows in dwellings were closed during the Middle Ages, instead of glass; these shutters were generally plain, and turned on hinges at the side, and were fastened by a bolt within, but sometimes they were made with panels with delicate tracery on the front, and the panels hung on hinges to open inwards, so that when they were turned back the tracery became a kind of lattice-work. This term appears to be sometimes used for the window which is closed with a fenestral.

Feretory (Lat. *Feretrum*), a bier, or coffin; tomb, or shrine. This term seems more properly to belong to the *portable shrines* in which the relics of saints were carried about in processions, but was also applied to the *fixed shrines*, or tombs, in which their bodies were deposited.

Fillet, or Felet (Fr. *Filet*, Lat. *Filum*), a small flat face or band used principally between mouldings, to sepa-

Stanton St. John.

Stanton, Bucks.

Brackley.

rate them from each other, in Classical architecture; in Gothic architecture it is also employed for the same purpose, and in the Early English and Decorated styles it is frequently worked upon larger mouldings and shafts; in these situations it is not always flat, but is sometimes cut into two or more narrow faces with sharp edges between them. When this appendage is placed upon the front of a moulding, as at A, it has been termed the *keel* of the moulding by Professor Willis, and when attached to the sides, as at B, its *wings*.

FEATHERING or FOLIATION. See *Foil*.

FEMERELL or FUMERELL. See *Louvre*.

FENESTELLA, same as *Piscina*.

FERETER, a bier; sometimes a tomb or shrine.

FISH. See *Vesica*.

FLAG, stone used for paving.

Finial (Lat. *Finis* = the end): by old writers this term is frequently applied to a pinnacle, but it is now usually confined to the bunch of foliage which terminates pinnacles, canopies, pediments. &c., in Gothic architecture. The intro- duction of finials was contemporary with that of *crockets*, to which they bear a close affinity, the leaves of which they are composed almost al- ways having a resemblance to them; and sometimes they are formed by uniting four or more crockets to- gether. They were especially used in the Decorated style; the example from

King's College, Cambridge.

Walpole St. Andrew, given under *Tabernacle*, shews the ap- plication to a niche in the wall, and that from Crick to a *Door- way.* Spires when perfect are often surmounted with finials.

Fireplace. Although the usual custom in houses was to have a brazier in the middle of the hall and the smoke to escape through the louvre at the top, in the other chambers fireplaces were in- troduced. They are not uncommon in the Norman keeps (though most have been altered at some subsequent period), and down to the thirteenth, four- teenth, and fifteenth centuries numerous examples may be found. In the thir-

Aydon Castle, Northumberland, c. 1270.

teenth and fourteenth centuries they were usually somewhat plainer, the ornamentation being chiefly the carved corbel on either side of the projecting hood. In the Perpendicular style the system of panelling having been introduced, this was applied profusely to the ornamentation of the fireplace or *Cheminé*.

Flamboyant (Fr. *Flambeau* = a torch), a term applied by the antiquaries of France to the style of architecture which was contemporary in that country with the Perpendicular of England, from the flame-like wavings of its tracery. It ought perhaps to be regarded as a vitiated Decorated rather than a distinct style, though some of its characteristics are peculiar, and it seldom possesses the purity or boldness of earlier ages; in rich works the intricacy and redundancy of the ornaments are sometimes truly surprising. One of the most striking and universal features is the waving arrangement of the tracery of the windows, panels, &c. The mouldings are often very ill combined, the suites consisting of large hollows separated by disproportionately small members of other kinds with but a slight admixture of fillets; the mouldings either running into each other without any line of separation, or being divided only by an arris, which

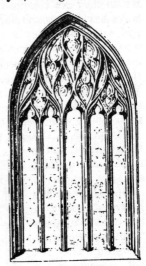

St Ouen, Rouen.

produces a very tame effect: there are, however, many examples in which the mouldings are bold and good, but they are the exceptions, not the rule. The centre or principal moulding in mullions of windows, &c., and in ribs of vaulting, is often made to project very prominently, so as to

Rib, Villequier.

produce an appearance of weakness. In jambs, pillars, &c.,

the mouldings have frequently bases and no capitals, and these are often arranged at different levels to the different members, like those of the Perpendicular style. The pillars sometimes consist of good mouldings, but they are often circular, either perfectly plain or with a few only of the more prominent mouldings of the arches continued down them, and in either of these cases the mouldings of the arches which abut against the pillars die into them without any kind of impost or capital; this arrangement is very common in Flamboyant work, and although occasionally to be found in buildings of earlier date, it may be considered characteristic of the style. It is by no means uncommon for mouldings that meet each other, instead of one or both of them stopping, to interpenetrate and both to run on and terminate in some more prominent member. The arches are usually two-centred, but sometimes the semicircle is employed, and late in the style the ellipse, and occasionally, in small openings, the ogee; sometimes also a flat head, with the angles rounded off, is used over doors and windows. The canopies in this style, from their size and shapes, are striking; in the earlier styles they are either simple triangles or ogees, but in Flamboyant work they are sometimes made of other and far more complicated forms. The foliage used for enrichments is generally well carved, but its effect is seldom so good as that of the Decorated, from its minuteness and intricacy.

Harfleur, Normandy.

Flower, Four-leaved, a very favourite ornament in the *Decorated* and *Perpendicular* styles.

St. Alban's.

Flutings, or Flutes (Lat. *Fluo*), the hollows or channels cut perpendicularly in the shafts of columns, &c., in Classical architecture; they are used in all the orders except the

Grecian Doric, Parthenon.

Tuscan; in the Doric they are twenty in number, and are separated by a sharp edge or arris; in the Ionic, Corinthian,

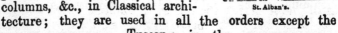

Grecian Ionic, Erectheum.

and Composite, their number is twenty-four, and they are

separated by a small fillet. They are sometimes (except in the Doric order) partly filled with a round convex moulding or bead, when they are said to be *cabled;* this does not in general extend higher than one-third of the shaft. Occasionally channellings, in some degree resembling flutes, are cut in Norman pillars, a remarkable instance of which occurs in the crypt of Canterbury Cathedral. Precisely the same kind of

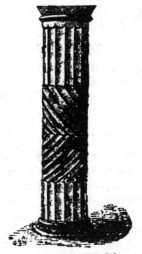

Crypt, Canterbury Cathedral.

ornament occurs frequently in Germany, as in the crypt of Roda Rolduc, near Aix-la-Chapelle, which might be a copy from Canterbury, and it occurs in many buildings of the twelfth century in other parts of the Continent.

The flutings are sometimes carried diagonally across the columns, as in the pillars in Durham, Waltham, &c., and later in the style this ornamentation became developed into a rich cable-ornament.

Foils (Lat. *Folium* = a leaf). The *feathering* or *foliation* consists of the *cusps*, which are the projecting portions, and the *foils*, which are technically the spaces between the cusps. Most usually the curves of the featherings spring from some one of the mouldings of an arch, &c., but there are numerous instances, especially in the Early English style, in which the whole suite of mouldings follows the same form; the arch is then said to be *foiled*. Feathering was first introduced towards the close of the early style, and continued universally prevalent until the revival of Classic architecture. The varieties of foliation

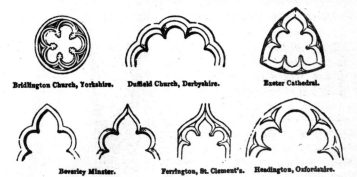

Bridlington Church, Yorkshire.   Duffield Church, Derbyshire.   Exeter Cathedral.

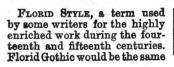

Beverley Minster.   Ferrington, St. Clement's.   Headington, Oxfordshire.

are very numerous. Sometimes the upper foil (as there are usually either three or five foils) is an ogee, sometimes round, specimens of which are given. When a *trefoil*, *quatrefoil* or *cinquefoil* are spoken of, it generally means an opening pierced with three, four, or five foils respectively. These are not only very fre-

FLORID STYLE, a term used by some writers for the highly enriched work during the fourteenth and fifteenth centuries. Florid Gothic would be the same as late Gothic.

FLUSH, used by builders to signify that the surfaces are on the same plane.

quent in tracery, but are found in several places as

Quarter from the tomb of R. Earl of Warwick.

a means of ornamentation. The quatrefoil is especially used for the surface ornamentation, or panelling, and is sometimes called a *quarter*. The *cinquefoil* is rarely used in the French Gothic. [For illustrations, see under *Band, Cusp, Clearstory, Doorway*.]

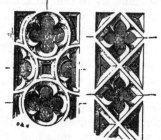

King's College Chapel, Cambridge.

Font (Lat. *Fons* = a spring), the vessel which contains the consecrated water to be used in baptism. Ancient fonts were always large enough to allow of the immersion of infants, the hollow basin usually being about a foot or rather more in depth, and from one and a-half to two feet in diameter. There are a few fonts of Norman date made of lead, but with these exceptions the common material for them is stone lined with lead, having a hole in the bottom

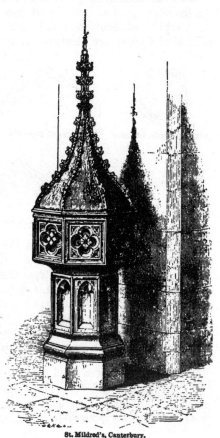

St. Mildred's, Canterbury.

of the basin through which the water can be allowed to escape. By a constitution of Edmund, Archbishop of Canterbury (A.D. 1236), fonts were required to be covered and locked; at that period the covers are likely, in general, to have been little more than flat moveable lids, but they were afterwards often highly ornamented, and were sometimes carried up to a very considerable height in the form of spires, and enriched with a variety of little buttresses, pinnacles, and other decorations. The forms of fonts varied considerably in different ages, and in the same age in different districts; in many instances, when the fonts in neighbouring churches are of the same date, there is such close resemblance between them as to lead to the conviction that they are all the work of the same hand.

Freemason. The term Freemason appears formerly to have signified no more than the present name of mason, a stone-cutter who worked with a chisel, as distinguished from one who could only dress stone with an axe or hammer, and build walls, in which sense it is still used in some parts of the kingdom: it is not improbably a contraction of Freestone-mason. During the Middle Ages the craftsmen of almost every trade formed themselves into societies or guilds, and prescribed rules for their governance which were recognised by the higher powers, who also sometimes conferred particular privileges upon them. The masons in some parts of Europe were early united in an association of this kind, for they are found to have been established as a free guild or corporation in Lombardy in the tenth century; but whether this society was descended from the Dionysiasts of antiquity, or originated in a later age, has not been ascertained: in Nor-

FOOTING of a wall, projecting course of stones at base for giving stability.

FOOT-PACE, the raised part of a hall for the dais, or in a church for the altar, also the landing-place on a staircase. See *Step*.

FOOTSTALL, English word for pedestal.

FOREYN, a drain or cesspool.

FORMA (Lat.), channel for water, aqueduct.

FORMPIECES or FRAMEPIECES, pieces of stone which form the tracery of the window.

FOSSE (Lat.), the artificial trench or ditch round castles. It was, with the mound, the chief defence in the British camps on the hill-tops. In mediæval times the fosse round the outer wall was usually filled with water.

mandy they appear to have become associated in 1145. When, as in the Middle Ages, architects, as distinct practitioners, were scarcely known, and but little more than the general forms and arrangement of a building were prescribed by those who superintended its erection, much of its beauty must have depended on the skill of the workmen to whose control the subordinate parts were entrusted; the masons therefore must have had the power of largely influencing the appearance of the structures on which they were employed : hence it might be expected, that at a time when the greatest architectural splendour was sought for in ecclesiastical edifices, the artificers on whom so much depended should have been especially patronized by the dignitaries and friends of the Church, and this is found to have been the case; some Popes are recorded to have issued bulls conferring especial privileges upon them. Although the guilds of most other trades have been abrogated, the society of Freemasons has preserved its existence, in name at least, to the present day, and in modern times has been spread over the greater part of the civilized portion of the world; but it has no connection with the practice of the art from which its name is derived, and its laws are recognised only by its own members.

Freestone, building stone which may be cut into blocks and worked with a chisel. The term is applied to stone of very different qualities in different districts, but always to such as may be worked with freedom in comparison with others of the neighbourhood.

Fret (Lat. *Fretum* = a strait), an ornament used in Classical architecture, formed by small fillets intersecting each other at right angles; the varieties are very numerous.

FRESCO (Ital.), a mode of painting in colours on stucco or plaster while it is *fresh*, and so wet, by which the colour is absorbed.

FRIARY (Fr. *Frère*, Lat. *Frater*), the community, or the building for the community, of certain orders of religious men. See *Monastery*.

Frieze, or Frize, the middle division of an entablature, which lies between the architrave and the cornice. In the Tuscan order it is always plain: in the Doric it has slight projections at intervals, on which are cut three angular flutes, called triglyphs; the intervals between these are called metopes, and are frequently enriched with sculpture: in the Ionic it is occasionally enriched with sculpture, and is sometimes made to swell out in the middle, when it is said to be cushioned or pulvinated: in the Corinthian and Composite it is ornamented in a variety of ways, but usually either with figures or foliage.

Frithstool, or Freedstool, literally 'the seat of peace.' A seat or chair placed near the altar in some churches, the last and most sacred refuge for those who claimed the privilege of sanctuary within them, and for the violation of which the severest punishment was decreed. They were frequently, if not always, of stone: according to Spelman that at Beverley had this inscription: "Hæc sedes lapidea *freedstoll* dicitur i.e. pacis cathedra, ad quam reus fugiendo perveniens omnimodam habet securitatem." Frithstools still exist in the church at Hexham, and Beverley Minster, both in the north aisle of the chancel: the former of these has the seat hollowed out in a semicircular form, and is slightly ornamented with patterns of Norman character; that at Beverley is very rude and plain.

Beverley Minster.

FRONT: with ancient writers this means the façade at the east end of the church; with later writers, the *west* end.

FRONTAL, the hanging with which the front of the altar is covered.

FUMERELL (Lat. *Fumus* = smoke). See *Louvre*.

FURRINGS, short pieces attached to the feet of the rafters of a roof for carrying the eaves beyond the line of the wall.

FUST, Fr. (1) of a column = shaft; (2) of a house, the ridge of the roof, (a Devonshire expression).

Gable. This term was formerly sometimes applied to the entire end wall of a building, the top of which conforms to the slope of the roof which abuts against it, but is now applied only to the upper part of such a wall, above the level of the eaves. In reference to the former sense, the large end window of a building, such as the east window of a church, was not unfrequently called a gable-window. The term is not used in Classical architecture, as the ends of roofs, when made in this way, are formed into *pediments*. Their proportions are regulated by the slope of the roof, and vary considerably; in the Norman style, the angle of the apex is seldom much more acute than a right angle; in the Early English they are usually about equilateral triangles; in the Decorated and Perpendicular they have sometimes about the same proportions, but are often much lower. Norman gables appear to have been usually finished with a plain flat coping up the sides and an ornament on the top, which on churches was a cross; Early English gables also, on plain buildings, have often flat copings, but in rich works they are moulded, and have sometimes an additional set of mouldings below them. In the Perpendicular style, and

Gable, East End, Stanton Harcourt, c. 1250.

subsequently, gables sometimes have a series of steps up the sides.

Galilee: a porch or chapel at the entrance of a church; the term also appears sometimes to be applied to the nave, or at least to the western portion of it, and in some churches there are indications of the west end of the nave having been parted off from the rest, either by a step in

GABLETS, small ornamental gables or canopies formed over buttresses, niches, &c.

the floor, a division in the architecture, or some other line
of demarcation: it was considered to be somewhat less
sacred than the other portions of the building. The
galilee at Lincoln Cathedral is a porch on the west side
of the south transept: at Ely Cathedral it is a porch at
the west end of the nave: at Durham it is a large chapel
at the west end of the nave, which was built for the use
of the women, who were not allowed to advance further
into the church than the second pillar of the nave, and
was dedicated to the Blessed Virgin; it was also used as
the Bishop's consistory court: St. Stephen's Chapel at
Westminster formerly had a galilee, forming a kind of
vestibule or ante-chapel, at the west end.

Gallery. (1.) An apartment of great length in proportion to its width, either used as a passage, or serving as
a place of resort for dancing or other amusements; a gallery of this kind was always to be found in large houses
built during the reign of Queen Elizabeth, and very frequently in those of earlier date: it was often in the upper
story. (2.) Also a raised floor or stage erected within an
apartment, either for the purpose of affording additional
room, or of accommodating musicians and spectators, frequently called a loft; a gallery of this kind was commonly formed at the lower end of the great hall in the
mansions of our forefathers, and called the *Minstrels' Gallery*. (3.) Ancient galleries in the sense of lofts are not
unfrequently to be met with in churches; over the entrances of chancels they were formerly most abundant;
in this situation they are constructed of wood, and are
called *Rood-lofts*, from their having supported the large
cross or rood which, previous to the Reformation, was
always set up over the entrance of the chancel. (4.) In
other situations the existing examples are generally of
stone, and vaulted beneath: they are to be found of Norman date at the end of the north transept of Winchester
Cathedral, but are much more common abroad. In many
parts of France a western gallery of stone forms part of
the original plan and construction of a church: this is
still more frequently the case in Germany. The lower
triforium gallery over the aisles is also there usually con-

structed so as to be used for service, and is in many places still commonly so used. Such galleries as parts of the original construction are not confined to any one period; they were perhaps more common in work of the twelfth

Gallery, Exeter Cathedral, c. 1300

century, but they are used at all periods. There is a very good example of this, and very conveniently arranged, at Frankfort. Several instances occur of a western gallery of the fifteenth century in small churches.

(5.) Most of the screens between the nave and choir in the cathedrals in this country are surmounted by galleries, in which the organs are placed. (6.) A triforium or passage-way in the thickness of a wall, and a passage-way supported on corbels or other projections from the face of a wall, are sometimes called galleries. (7.) Projections occur also from the triforium, such as the Minstrels' Gallery in the nave of Exeter Cathedral, of the fourteenth century. The modern style of wooden galleries in churches, cutting off the arches of the nave, was introduced subsequently to the Reformation, and appears to have originated with the Puritans; they were frequently called *Scaffolds*.

Gargoyle, or Gurgoyle, a projecting spout used in Gothic architecture to throw the water from the gutter of a building off the wall. Sometimes they are perfectly plain, but are oftener carved into figures or animals, which are frequently grotesque; these are very commonly represented with open mouths, from which the water issues, but in many cases it is conveyed through a leaden spout, either above or below the

Merton College Chapel, Oxford.

stone figure. Gargoyles appear to have been first introduced with the Early English style, during the prevalence of which they were usually made with a very considerable projection: subsequently they were often much less prominent. Their most usual situation is in the cornice, but they are sometimes, especially in Early English and Decorated buildings, placed on the fronts of the buttresses.

Garreting, small splinters of stone, inserted in the joints of coarse masonry; they are stuck in after the work is built. Flint walls are very frequently garreted.

GAMBOISON. See Illustrations to *Brass*.

GARLAND. A term used by William of Worcester for the band of ornamental work surrounding the spire of Redcliffe Church, Bristol.

GARNETT, a kind of hinge.

Gateway. The gatehouses or gateways of the Middle Ages are often large and imposing structures; they were erected over the principal entrances of the precincts of religious establishments, colleges, &c., and sometimes also of the courts of houses, as well as castles and other fortifications. In military edifices the entrance usually consists of a single archway, large enough to admit carriages, with a strong door, and *portcullis* at each end, and a vaulted ceiling pierced with holes through which missiles could be cast upon an enemy: the sides of the gateway are generally flanked with large projecting towers pierced with loopholes, and the upper part terminates with a series of *machicolations* and battlemented *parapet.* In civil edifices there is

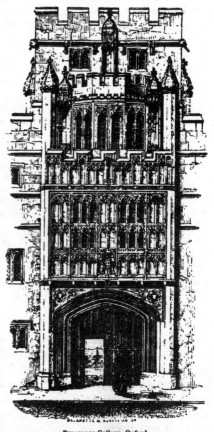

Brasenose College, Oxford.

much greater diversity in the forms and architectural arrangements of gatehouses: sometimes they resemble plain square towers of rather low proportions, with a single turret containing a staircase, or with a turret at each of the front angles, and occasionally at all the four angles: but in this case those on the front are generally the largest and the most ornamental; sometimes they are extended to a considerable breadth, as at Battle Abbey, Sussex, and the

College, Maidstone, Kent; and sometimes they are plain buildings without any particular architectural character. The entrance most commonly consists of a large archway for horses and carriages, and a smaller one by the side of it for foot passengers, with strong doors at one or both ends. The ceiling is commonly vaulted, and sometimes pierced with holes like those of military works. When the building is of sufficient height to allow of it, there is generally a room over the archway, with one or more large windows (not unfrequently an oriel window) next the front. The gateways of religious establishments had frequently a chapel attached to them. Examples of ancient gateways are to be met with in most of our cathedral towns, bounding the close or cathedral precincts; at Oxford and Cambridge, as entrances to the colleges; among the ruins of many of our abbeys and castles, and at numerous ancient houses, as at Canterbury, (especially that of St. Augustine's Abbey). The city gateways are also not to be passed over In many towns traces, if not in actual buildings at least in name, can be found of the gate, e.g. Bishopsgate, Aldersgate, &c., in London, and in other places, Northgate, Southgate, Littlegate, &c.

Girder, a main beam which sustains the joists of a floor when the distance between the walls renders it necessary to give them additional support.

Glazing. During the Middle Ages the use of coloured glass in windows was almost universal. [See *Stained Glass.*] The use of Quarries, i.e. diamond-shaped pieces of glass, with a pattern of a flower or some device lightly burnt upon it, were common at the latter part of the fourteenth century, and during the fifteenth. It is not till very late work that we find any geometrical patterns produced by the mere arrangement of the leadwork round plain glass. In the sixteenth and seventeenth centuries, very effective patterns are produced by the leading only.

GENOUILLERES. See illustrations to *Brass.*

GENTEN, a word used by William of Worcester for the cusps of a doorway.

GETEE (Fr.) See *Jettie.*

GEOMETRICAL STAIRS. See *Steps.*

GEOMETRICAL TRACERY. See *Tracery.*

GIMMER and GEMELL. Ancient name for Chymol or Hinge.

Gothic Architecture. This term was originally applied to the mediæval styles at the time of the Renaissance of the Pagan orders : some say it was first given by Sir Christopher Wren, but it is now believed to be older than his time. In any case it was given as a term of reproach and contempt at a time when it was also the fashion to write Latin, and to expect it to become the universal language. But the different nations of modern Europe have retained their respective languages in spite of the efforts of the pedants of the sixteenth century, and have now generally returned to their national styles of architecture also. The one seems to follow naturally from the other : if the Roman language could neither be preserved everywhere, nor effectually revived, so also the permanent establishment of the Roman architecture was not to be expected. The marvel is that modern Europe submitted so long to its trammels.

Groin. The angle formed by an intersection of vaults. Most of the vaulted ceilings of the buildings of the Middle Ages are groined, and therefore called groined vaults, or *Groined Ceilings.* During the early part of the Norman style the groins were left perfectly plain, but afterwards they were invariably covered with ribs.

Grotesque, a name given to the light and fanciful ornaments used by the ancients in the decoration of the walls and some of the subordinate parts of their buildings : so called from their having been long buried, the Italians calling any subterranean apartment by the name of Grotto. This kind of ornament is also called Arabesque, and the Spanish writers call it Pluteresque. A very similar kind of decoration is found in Arabian architecture ; it was also used extensively about the period of the Renaissance. This name is also applied to the ornaments commonly used in grottoes in the seventeenth and eighteenth centuries, made to resemble moss or stalactites, or the dripping of water.

GIRDER. The main beam supporting the joists of the floor.

GLYPHS. The perpendicular flutings or channels under the Doric frieze.

GOLA, or GULA. An Italian name for the *Cyma.*

GRANGE. A farming establishment, especially such as belonged to a monastery. Many grange houses and barns exist dating from the thirteenth century.

Ground-table-stones, the projecting course of stones in a wall, immediately above the surface of the ground; now called the plinth.

Guilloche, an ornament used in Classical architecture, formed by two or more intertwining bands. The term is adopted from the French.

Guttæ, small ornaments resembling drops, used in the Doric entablature on the under side of the mutules of the cornice, and beneath the tænia of the architrave, under the triglyphs.

Hall. The chief apartment in a mediæval house, a monastery, or a college, where meals were had. In the large mediæval houses it also served for other purposes. Justice was administered there, entertainments given, and at night oftentimes the floor was strewed with rushes, and many of the servants slept there. [See *Domestic Architecture, Fireplace, &c.*]

Halpace, or Halfpace (probably Fr. *Haute-pace*), a raised floor in a bay window, before a fireplace, or in similar situations: the floors in such places are often a step higher than the rest in old English houses: the dais in a hall: also a raised stage or platform, and a landing in a flight of stairs. [See *Footpace* and *Dais.*]

GRAVESTONE. See *Tombstone.*

GRECIAN ARCHITECTURE. See Doric, Ionic, and Corinthian Orders: also Column.

GREES = steps, or a staircase.

GRILLE. Literally a grating of iron, but applied to open ironwork generally.

GROUT. Thin semi-liquid mortar poured into the internal joints of masonry or rubble-work.

GUEST-CHAMBER. See *Chamber.*

GURGOYLE. See *Gargoyle.*

GYNECÆUM. That part of a Greek house appropriated to the women.

HABITACLE, an old word for a dwelling, but applied also to a niche for a statue. See *Tabernacle.*

HAGIOSCOPE (Gr.), name given by ecclesiologists to Squint, q.v.

HALF-TIMBER HOUSES. Vide *Timber Houses.*

HALLYNGS, the hangings of a hall.

Hammer-beam, a beam very frequently used in the principals of Gothic roofs to strengthen the framing and to diminish the lateral pressure that falls upon the walls. Each principal has two hammer-beams, which occupy the situation of a tie-beam, and in some degree serve the same purpose, but they do not extend across the whole width of the roof, as *a, a.* The ends of hammer-beams are often ornamented with heads, shields, or foliage, and sometimes with figures; those of the roof of Westminster Hall are carved with large angels holding shields; sometimes there are pendants under them, as at the halls of Eltham Palace, and Christ Church, Oxford, &c.

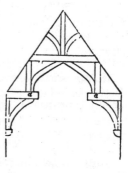

Herring-bone Work, masonry in which the stones are laid aslant instead of being bedded flat; it is very commonly found in rough walling, and occasionally, in the Norman style, in ashlar work. Square tiles are sometimes arranged in the same fashion, especially in the backs of fireplaces, e.g. at Corfe Castle. This

Tamworth Castle.

masonry is not to be relied upon as evidence of the date of a building, though it is frequently of the eleventh cen-

---

HAND-IRON == Andiron.

HANSE, or HAUNCH of an arch: that part between the vertex and the springing.

HATCH, or HATCHED ORNAMENT. See *Moulding.*

HAUBERK. See illustrations to *Brass.*

HEADER, a brick or stone, of which the longest dimension is in the thickness of the wall.

HEAUME. See illustrations to *Brass.*

HELE == Aisle, *Heil,* 'to cover.'

HELIX and HELICES: used to signify the caulicoli, from their snail-like shape.

HELYING, (1) a covering, (2) used corruptly for Aisle.

tury. It is sometimes found introduced in the walls in bands, apparently for ornament, but it has often been manifestly adopted for convenience, in order to enable the workmen to level off the work at each course, which could not well be done in any other way with stones of irregular shapes and sizes: in herring-bone work, by vary-ing the inclination of the stones, it is

easy to preserve a level. The interior, or backing, of Roman walls, is often of irregular herring-bone work, formed this way.

Herse, (1.) a portcullis, so called from its resemblance to a framework termed *hercia*, fashioned like a harrow, whereon lighted candles were placed on the obsequies of distinguished persons. The entrance gateways of many castles were defended by two portcullises, as at Warwick Castle, where one of them is at this time lowered every night, for greater security. (2.) Also a frame set over the coffin of a person deceased, and covered with a pall; it was usually of light woodwork, and appears in many instances to have been part of the furniture of the church, to be used when occasion required There is a brass frame of a similar kind over the effigy of Richard, Earl of Warwick, in the Beauchamp Chapel at Warwick, which is called

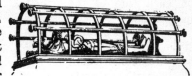

a *herse* in the contract for the tomb; there is also one of iron over an ancient tomb in Bedell Church, Yorkshire.

Hinge, the joints on which doors, gates, &c., turn. During the Middle Ages, even at an early period, they were frequently made very conspicuous, and were orna-mented with scrolls : several of the illuminations of Cæd-mon's metrical Paraphrase of Scripture History, which is considered to have been written soon after the year 1000, exhibit doors with ornamental hinges, and another is represented in an illumination in a Pontifical at Rouen, written at a rather earlier period.

No existing hinges can be assigned to an earlier date than the close of the twelfth century, and they are not often met with so old; at this period they have not in general much scrollwork attached to them, and the turns are often very stiff; the principal branches at the head of the hinge frequently represent the letter C.

Warborough, Oxon.

In the Early English style, the hinges were often ornamented with most elaborate scrollwork, nearly covering the door, and this was sometimes further enriched with leaves, and occasionally with animals' heads; the nails also were made ornamental, and the main bands were stamped with various minute patterns; at other times they were devoid of all ornament, or had the ends terminating in simple curls, with a few small branches on each side of the main band.

In the Decorated style they continued to be occasionally used of the same elaborate kind, with little if any

Faringdon, Berks.

variation, except occasionally in the character of the leaves on the scrolls; but were not so common as in the Early English, the increased use of wood panellings and tracery having in great measure superseded such kind of decorations. In the Perpendicular style they are rarely ornamented, except on plain doors, and then have usually only a fleur-de-lis or some similar decoration, at the ends of the strap.

Hip. The external angle formed by the meeting of the sloping sides of a roof, which have their wall-plates running in different directions: thus, when a roof has the end sloped back, instead of finishing with a gable, the pieces of timber in these angles are called hip-rafters, and the tiles with which they are covered are called hip-tiles. The internal angles formed by the meeting of the sides are termed

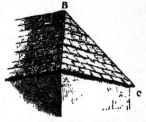

The angles AB, BC, are the hips.

the *valleys*, whether the latter be horizontal or sloping, and the piece of timber that supports a sloping valley is termed the *Valley Rafter*.

Hip-Knob: a pinnacle, finial, or other similar ornament, placed on the top of the hips of a roof, or on the point of a gable. On ecclesiastical edifices, previous to the Reformation, crosses were usually fixed in these situations, but on other buildings ornaments of various kinds were used; when applied to gables with barge-boards, the lower part of the hip-knob frequently terminated in a pendant. They are, however, rather characteristic of sixteenth and seventeenth century work.

Friar Gate, Derby.

The Holy-water Stone, or **Stock,** was the stone basin for holding the holy water placed near the entrances of churches, so that each person as he came in or went out might sprinkle himself with it. They are generally of very plain workmanship, though sometimes they have a simple moulding carried round them. [See *Stoup.*]

HEXASTYLE, a portico having six columns in front.

HIGH-TOMB: used by Leland for Altar-tomb.

HISTORIA. See *Story*.

HOLLOW. See *Cavetto*.

HOOD-MOULDING. The Label-moulding. See *Dripstone*.

HOSTRIE, HOSTELRIE (Fr. *Hotellerie*), an inn, or house of entertainment for travellers. See *Inn*.

Hour-glass Stand. A bracket or frame of iron for receiving the hour-glass, which was often placed near the pulpit, subsequent to the Reformation, and especially during the Commonwealth. Specimens are not unfrequently met with in country churches, as at Wolvercot and Beckley, Oxfordshire, and Leigh Church, Kent. They are common in some districts, but rare in others.

Leigh Church, Kent.

Hourd, Hoard, Hoarding, boarding used for protection: it is a term in common use in London for the boarding round a scaffolding to keep off the people from the workmen. It is also a term in military architecture for the wooden gallery, protected by boarding in front, which was thrown out from the surface of the wall in time of war, to enable the defenders to protect the foot of the wall. There are sometimes corbels provided for them, more frequently put-log holes in the wall only, in Roman work as well as Mediæval.

Image, this term was formerly applied to paintings as well as statues; and a sculptor, and sometimes also a painter, was called an Imageour. Both sculpture and painting were extensively employed in the architecture of the Middle Ages, especially in churches; and although much was destroyed and more injured in this country at the Reformation, a considerable quantity still remains. Examples of sculpture are too numerous to require to be

HOUSING, a tabernacle or niche for a statue.

HOVEL, sometimes used in the sense of tabernacles for images.

HUTCH, a chest or locker in which sacred utensils were kept.

HYPAETHRAL (Gr.), a name given to temples having part of the cell open to the sky.

HYPERTHERUM (Gr.), project-ing cornice forming upper part of the dressings of a door, above the architrave.

HYPOCAUST, the heating-flues, &c., beneath the floors of the bath-chambers in Roman houses.

HYPOGEUM, any subterranean construction.

HYPOTRACHELIUM, the neck or frieze of the capital in some Classical columns.

pointed out. The image of the Virgin and Child (as at King's Sutton) was the most frequent, though of course the greater number have been destroyed. Ancient paintings exist in various churches, but most of them are in a mutilated condition. The statues in the insides of buildings were probably often painted to imitate life, the costume being painted and gilded very brightly.

King's Sutton, Northamptonshire, c. 1400

Impost (Lat. *Impositus*), the horizontal mouldings or capitals *on the top* of a pilaster, pillar, or pier, or corbel, from which an arch springs; in Classical architecture the form varies in the several orders; sometimes the entablature of an order serves for the impost of an arch. In Mediæval architecture the imposts vary according to the style; on pillars and the small shafts in the jambs of doorways, windows, &c., they are usually complete *capitals*, and will therefore be

Barton Seagrave, c. 1160.

found described under that head. When shafts are used
in the jambs of archways, it is very usual in the Norman
style for the abacus of the capitals to be continued through
the whole suite of mouldings, and it is sometimes carried
along the walls as a string; this arrangement also is occasionally used in the Early English. In the Decorated
and Perpendicular styles it is not common to find any
impost-mouldings in the jambs of archways, except the
capitals of the small shafts.

Incised or **Engraved Slabs:** stone or alabaster slabs,
with figures engraved on them, used as sepulchral memorials. It would be difficult to attribute confidently the
priority of date to the use of these memorials, or to that
of sepulchral brasses, and it is most probable that both
were introduced about the same period, namely, in the
middle of the thirteenth century, that both were the
works of the same artificers, and used indifferently as
suited the taste or fortune of individuals; the sepulchral
brass being, as it would appear, the more costly, as well
as more durable memorial. In England, incised slabs do
not appear ever to have existed in great number, the prevalent fashion being to use the brass, shaped to the form
of the figure, and imbedded in a cavity in the slab,
whereby the cost of the tomb was much less than that of
the Flemish brasses, which usually were formed of large
sheets of metal, covering the entire surface of the slab.
In France brasses are very rare, in many districts quite unknown; but the incised slabs of stone, marble or alabaster
are often very fine, much finer than any known in England.

Inn, or **Hostel.** These terms were formerly employed
as synonymous with any house used as a lodging-house,
and not confined to taverns as at present. For example,
the inns or halls which were so numerous in Oxford and
Cambridge, before the erection of colleges, were merely
lodging-houses for the scholars, subject to certain regu-
lations; the Inns of court in London were of a similar
character for the use of the law-students. There are yet
remaining in some old towns, buildings of considerable

IMPLUVIUM. See *Atrium.*
INCERTUM OPUS (Vitruvius), a
term for masonry used by the
Romans, similar to our "ran-
dom or rubble-work."

antiquity originally built for public inns, and some of them are still used for that purpose, though for the most part they have been considerably altered, as at Rochester, Salisbury, Glastonbury, Sherborne, Malmesbury, Fotheringhay, Ludlow, Grantham, York.

Intercolumniation, the clear space between two columns; it varies considerably in width, and from its proportions the porticoes of the ancients are divided into the following orders: *pycnostyle*, in which the intercolumniation is equal to one diameter and a half of the shaft of the column; *systyle*, in which the intercolumniation is equal to two diameters; *eustyle*, two and a quarter diameters; *diastyle*, three diameters; *aræostyle*, four diameters.

Ironwork. Of the ironwork of the Middle Ages, connected with architecture, we have not very numerous specimens remaining in this country, although sufficient to shew the care that was bestowed upon it: some of the earliest and most ornamental kind is exhibited in the hinges and scrollwork on doors, illustrations of which will be found described under *Hinge* and *Scroll*. In the making of these, considerable skill as well as elegance is displayed, and the junctions of the subordinate branches of the patterns with the larger stems are formed with the greatest neatness and precision; the minute ornaments also which are frequently introduced on them, such as animals' heads, leaves, flowers, &c., are often finished with more care and accuracy than might be

Henry VII.'s Chapel, Westminster.

expected in such materials; the *heads* of the *nails* (vide *Nail-head*) assume a great variety of forms, some projecting

INSERTUM OPUS (Vitruvius), regular bonded masonry.

INSULA, used by Leland for aisle.

INTERSTITIUM, a name applied to the central space beneath the tower in a cruciform church.

INTRADOS, the soffit or under surface of an arch, as opposed to *extrados*.

like a spike, others rounded, others flat. The *Handles*
and *Knockers* on doors are also made ornamental. The
former, especially when of simple character, are usually in
the shape of rings with a spindle going through the centre
of a circular escutcheon, but sometimes they are of other
forms. Those of Early English and Decorated date are
almost always rings, and they have seldom any ornament
about them beyond occasionally a few spiral lines arising
from their being made of a square bar of iron twisted, and
sometimes a small flower or animal's head on each side
of the end of the spindle to keep them in their places:

when not made in the form of rings, the
handles are ornamented in various ways,
frequently with minute patterns of tracery. The *Escutcheons* are occasionally
made with a projecting boss or umbo in
the centre, and sometimes have a few
branches of foliage under them, but they
are more usually ornamented with minute
tracery, or with holes pierced through
them in various patterns. Sometimes the
whole escutcheon is cut into leaves: the
end of the spindle is not unfrequently
formed into a head. Besides these handles. others in the

form of a bow are also
used ; they are fre-
quently, if not usually,
made angular, and are
placed upright on the
doors ; sometimes they
are fixed, but are oftener
made to turn in a small
eye or staple at each
end. The pendant han-
dles are in general suf-
ficiently ponderous to
serve for knockers, and
they were evidently often
intended to be used as
such, for there is a large-
headed nail fixed in the

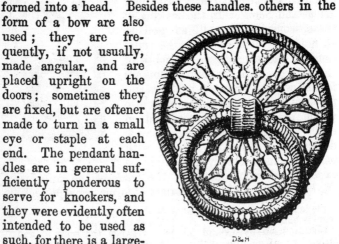

Stogumber, Somersetshire.

door for them to strike upon; but sometimes the knocker
is distinct from the handle, and is made equally, if not
more ornamental. In the sixteenth and seventeenth centuries, *Knockers* partake very much of the form of a hammer; are frequently fixed on an ornamental escutcheon,
and usually strike upon a large-headed nail. *Locks*, especially when placed on the outside of doors, are very commonly ornamented with patterns of tracery, and studs
formed by the heads of nails, and sometimes also with
small mouldings; when placed on the inside of the doors
there are frequently enriched escutcheons over the key-
holes, which are often in the form of shields.

Throughout the period in which Gothic architecture
flourished, the appearance of the ironwork that was exposed to view seems to have been duly regarded, and in
enriched buildings usually to have been made proportion-
ably ornamental: the heads of the stancheons in windows,
and in the openings of screens, are often enriched with
flowers or other decorations. Monuments are not unfre-

Eyworth Church, Bedfordshire.   Crick Church, Northants.   Eyworth Church, Bedfordshire.

quently surrounded with iron railings, in the details of
which the characteristics of the style of architecture
which prevailed at the period of their erection are to be
detected. Several ancient *doors of iron* also remain, consisting of small flat bars crossing each other, and riveted
together after the fashion of *grilles*. One of the most
elaborate specimens of the ironwork of the Middle Ages is

the tomb of Edward IV., in St. George's Chapel, Windsor; it consists of rich open screenwork, with a variety of buttresses, pinnacles, crockets, tabernacles, tracery, and other ornaments, which are introduced in great profusion. [See *Escutcheon*, *Hinge*, and *Nail-head*.]

Jamb (Fr.), the side of a window, door, chimney, &c.

Jesse, or Tree of Jesse, a representation of the genealogy of Christ, in which the different persons forming the descent are placed on scrolls of foliage branching out of each other, intended to represent a tree; it was by no means an uncommon subject for sculpture, painting, and embroidery. At Dorchester Church, Oxfordshire, it is curiously formed in the stonework of one of the chancel windows; at Christ Church, Hampshire, and in the chapel of All Souls' College, Oxford, it is cut in stone on the reredos of the altar; it is often made the subject of the stained glass in an eastern window. It was likewise wrought into a branched candlestick, thence called a Jesse, not an unusual piece of furniture in ancient churches.

Jettie (Fr.), or Jutty, a part of a building that projects beyond the rest, and overhangs the wall below, as the upper stories of timber houses, bay windows, penthouses, small turrets at the corners, &c. (2.) Also used as a pier projecting into the water.

Joggle. A term peculiar to masons, who use it in various senses relating to the fitting of stones together; almost every sort of jointing, in which one piece of stone is let or fitted into another, is called

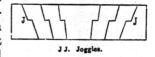

J J. Joggles.

a joggle; what a carpenter would call a rebate is also a joggle in stone.

Isodomum, masonry in which the courses are of equal thickness.

Jack-rafter, a short rafter fixed to the hips of a roof; a piece of timber in a frame cut short of its usual length often receives the name of *Jack*.

Jawe-piece, an ancient term in carpentry, somewhat obscure, but probably applied to struts and braces in a roof.

Jerkin-head Roof, a roof the end of which is fashioned into a shape intermediate between a gable and a hip.

Joint: the interstices between the stones or bricks in masonry and brickwork are called joints. A *straight* joint shews an addition made to the work after it was complete

Joists (Fr.), the horizontal timbers in a floor, on which the flooring is laid: also the small timbers which sustain a ceiling. In floors constructed without girders there is usually but one thickness of joists, to the underside of which the ceiling is attached, but when girders are used they are often double, (the upper row carrying the flooring, and the lower the ceiling,) with a series of larger timbers between them, called *binding joists;* when this kind of construction is used the upper joists are called *bridging joists.*

Jubé, the *Rood-loft,* or gallery, over the entrance into the choir, is called in France and sometimes in England the Jubé, from the words, *Jube, Domine, benedicere,* which were pronounced from it immediately before certain lessons in the Roman Catholic service, which were sometimes chanted from this gallery, when the dean, abbot, or other superior of the choir, gave his benediction; a custom still continued in some of the foreign churches, as at Bayeux Cathedral. This name was also applied to the *Ambo* for the same reason.

Key-stone, the central stone, or voussoir, at the top of an arch; the last which is placed in its position to complete the construction of an arch. The *Bosses* in vaulted ceilings are sometimes called Keys. See *Voussoir.*

Killesse, also Cullis, Coulisse (Fr.), a gutter, groove, or channel; whence the term Port-coulisse or Port-cullie, a gate sliding down in a groove. This term is in some districts corruptly applied to a hipped roof by country carpenters, who speak of a *killessed* or *cullidged* roof. A dormer window is also sometimes called a *killesse* or *cullidge* window.

JOPY, probably the same as Jawe-piece.

JYMEWE = a hinge.

KAGK or CAGK, sometimes applied to chantry chapels enclosed with lattice-work.

KEEP, the chief tower or *donjon* of a castle.

KERNEL. See *Crenelle.*

KIRK, a church; still in use in Scotland.

King-post, the middle or *chief* post of a roof, standing on the tie-beam and reaching up to the ridge; it is often formed into an octagonal column with capital and base, and small struts or braces, which are usually slightly curved, spreading from it above the capital to some of the other timbers. [For illustration, see *Roof.*]

Kitchen. Although in the Bayeux Tapestry the cooking is shewn as taking place in the open air, still there is no doubt that from the earliest Norman times there was a chamber in all large houses set apart for the kitchen. It is mentioned by Necham, and some of the large fireplaces which we find remaining in twelfth-century buildings were no doubt employed for this purpose. In the Middle Ages the kitchen became an important building in all castles, monasteries, and large houses; often it was a building almost detached from the main structure, such as at Glastonbury or Stanton Harcourt. Its usual position was at the end of the hall, with an entrance to it by a short passage from the screens; the buttery and pantry were generally on the two sides of the passage. In fact the plan which we still find in many of the collegiate buildings of the Universities is the usual plan which was adopted in the Middle Ages in all large establishments.

Knee, a term used in some parts of the west of England for the return of the dripstone at the spring of the arch. (2.) Also a crooked piece of wood or iron fixed in the manner of a corbel under the ends of a beam.

Labarum, properly the standard bearing the cross of Constantine, as it is called, and not the cross itself. This consists of the combination of the two Greek initial letters of the name of CHRIST, x.p. In the Catacombs it is frequently found, and continued in the Eastern Church. In the Western Church it seems to have been eventually supplanted by the monogram IHS. being the Greek initials of the name of IHΣOYΣ (Jesus).

KNEE-RAFTER, a rafter in the principal truss of a roof, the lower end or foot of which is crooked downwards so that it may rest more firmly on the walls.

KNEE-TIMBER, in carpentry a bent piece of wood formed out of a tree which has grown crooked, so that the fibres of the wood follow the curve.

KNOCKER. See *Ironwork.*

Lacunar, or Lequear, a ceiling, and also sometimes used for panels or coffers in ceilings, or in the soffits of cornices, &c.

Lady-chapel, a chapel dedicated to the Blessed Virgin, called Our Lady, which was attached to large churches. It was usually placed eastward of the high altar, often forming a projection from the main building.

Lantern, in Italian or modern architecture a small structure on the top of a dome, or in other similar situations, for the purpose of admitting light, promoting ventilation, or for ornament, of which those on the top of St. Paul's Cathedral, and the Radcliffe Library at Oxford, may be referred to as Palladian examples. In Gothic architecture the term is applied to *louvres* on the roofs of halls, &c., but it usually signifies a tower which has the whole height, or a considerable portion of the interior, open to view from the ground, and is lighted by an upper tier of windows: lantern-towers

St. Helen's, York.

KNOT, KNOP, KNOPPE, a bunch of leaves or flowers forming a boss; or the foliage on a capital.

LABEL, or LABEL-MOULDING, a square or horizontal dripstone.

LANCET, a term applied sometimes to the form of an *arch*, and especially to that over *windows*.

of this kind are common over the centre of cross churches, as at York Minster, Ely Cathedral, &c. The same name is also given to the light open erections often placed on the tops of towers, as at Boston, Lincolnshire, and Lowick, Northamptonshire; these sometimes have spires rising from them, but in such cases they are less perforated with windows, as at St. Michael's Church, Coventry.

Lanternes des Morts occur in the churchyards on the Continent, chiefly in Poitou; they were simply pillars with a place for a light on the top, similar to small light-houses, and it is not improbable that something of the kind was adopted in the early Roman cemeteries. Some of the Irish round towers have been supposed to be of this nature.

Lavatory (Lat.), a cistern or trough to wash in. There was usually a lavatory in the cloisters of mo-nastic establishments, at which the inmates washed their hands and faces, also the sur-plices and other vest-ments; some of these still remain, as at Gloucester and Wor-cester. The name is also given to the pis-cina. In the south of Germany the lavatory is an important fea-ture resembling a bap-tistery; it is a sepa-rate chamber, square or octagonal, standing on one side of the cloister-court with a reservoir of water or

Selby, Yorkshire.

a fountain in the middle, and water-troughs for washing at, round them. There is a very fine one of the thirteenth century at the royal monastery of Holy Cross, near Vienna.

Latten (Old Eng. spelt Laten, Lattin, Laton), a mixed metal resembling brass, but apparently not considered the same, for Lydgate, in his "Boke of Troye," uses the expression "of brasse, of coper, and laton." In the will of Henry VII. this kind of metal is spoken of as copper, by which name it is directed to be used about his tomb, but in other ancient documents it is almost invariably called latten, as in the contract for the tomb of Richard, Earl of Warwick; the monumental brasses so common in our churches are referred to as being of latten. No rules can be laid down for its exact composition, as it varies in different examples which have been tested.

Leaves, a term formerly applied to window-shutters, the folding-doors of closets, &c., especially to those of the almeries and the repositories of reliques, formerly so numerous in churches: some pieces of sacred sculpture and paintings also were protected by light folding-doors or leaves, particularly those over altars, and the insides of the leaves themselves were often painted, so that when turned back they formed part of the general subject. These are usually called Diptychs or Triptychs, according to the number of the folds. The term is occasionally applied to the folding-doors of buildings.

Lectern or Lettern (Lat. *Lego*), the desk or stand on which the larger books used in the services of the Roman Catholic Church are placed. In this country they are usually employed to hold the Bible only. The principal lectern stood in the middle of the choir, but there were sometimes others in different places. They were occasionally made of stone or marble, and fixed, but were usually of

LAORDOSE (Fr. *La Reredos*), a screen at the back of a seat behind an altar.

LARMIER (Fr.), the corona.

LEANING-PLACE OF A WINDOW, the thin wall frequently placed below the sill of a window on the inside.

LEAN TO. See *To-fall.*

LEDGEMENT, a string-course, or horizontal suite of mouldings.

LEDGER, a large flat stone such as is frequently laid over a tomb, &c. Some of the horizontal timbers of scaffolding are called ledgers.

LEVECEL, a projecting roof over a door, the same as Penthouse.

LEVYS (Old Eng.) =Leaves.

LEWIS, a machine for raising large stones by means of a dovetail.

wood or brass, and moveable; they were also often covered with costly hangings embroidered
in the same man-
ner as the hang-
ings of the altar.
At Debtling is one
of Decorated date;
it is made with a
desk for a book on
four sides, and is
more ornamented
than any of the
others; they are
usually made with
desks on two sides
only. The speci-
mens of brass lec-
terns are not so
numerous as those
of wood. A com-
mon form for brass
lecterns, and one
which is some-
times given to
those of wood, is
that of an eagle or
pelican with the
wings expanded to
receive the book,
but they are also
often made with
two flat sloping
sides, or desks, for
books.

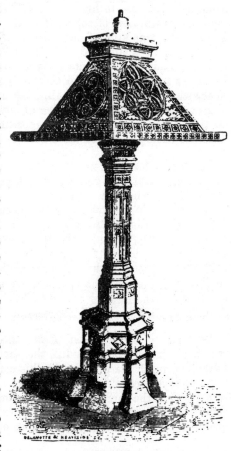

Debtling, Kent.

Library, a room or suite of rooms attached to collegiate
and monastic establishments for the keeping of the books.
No evidence remains of the fittings further than it is probable the few books and rolls possessed were kept in chests.
In early wills the books are generally mentioned among
the particular bequests.

Lich-gate, or Corpse-gate (*Lich*, Ang.-Saxon, = corpse), a shed over the entrance of a churchyard, beneath which the bearers generally paused when bringing a corpse for interment. The term is also used in some parts of the country for the path by which a corpse is usually conveyed to the church. In Herefordshire it is called a Scallage.

Garsington, Oxfordshire.

Lock. Several kinds of locks were formerly used; that most common on large doors was a *stock-lock*, the works of which were let into a block of wood which was fixed on the inside of the door; locks of this kind are now often to be seen on church doors. Another kind was entirely of metal with one side made ornamental, which, when fixed, was exposed to view, the works being let into the door: this sort of lock does not appear to be older than the fifteenth century; various specimens remain, but principally on internal doors. A lock of very similar description to this last-mentioned is also frequently found

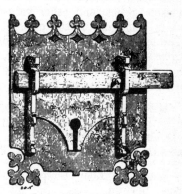

Winchester Cathedral.

LIERNE-RIB, in a vault a cross rib that does not rise from the impost and is not a ridge-rib.

LIGHTS, the openings between the mullions of a window, screen, &c.

LINEN PATTERN. Vide *Panel*.

LINTEL, a piece of timber or stone placed horizontally over a doorway, window, or other opening through a wall to support the superincumbent weight.

LIST, a *fillet*.

LOBE (Fr.), in an arch = *foil*, i.e. Trilobe = *trefoil*.

on chests, but with a hasp which shuts into it to receive
the bolt. Ingenious contrivances were sometimes resorted
to in order to add to the security of locks; a door on the
tower staircase at Snodland Church, Kent, has a lock the
principal keyhole of which is covered by a plate of iron
shutting over it as a hasp, which is secured by a second
key. In the sixteenth century they were frequently very
elaborate and complicated pieces of mechanism, and when
fixed on ornamental works were often very conspicuous.
In addition to these kinds, *pad-locks* or *hang-locks* were
also frequently used. [See further illustrations under
Ironwork.]

Locker, a small closet or cupboard frequently found in
churches, especially on the north
side of the sites of altars; they
are now usually open, but were
formerly closed with doors, and
were used to contain the sacred
vessels, relics, and other valuables belonging to the church.
The locker is usually considered
to be smaller than the *Aumbry,*
but the terms are frequently
used synonymously.

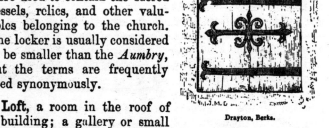

Drayton, Berks.

Loft, a room in the roof of
a building; a gallery or small
chamber, raised within a larger apartment, or in a church,
as a music-loft, a singing-loft, a rood-loft, &c.

Loop-hole, Loop, Loup, narrow openings, used in the
fortifications of the Middle
Ages, through which arrows
and other missiles might be
discharged upon assailants,
hence called *Balistraria* or
Arbalisteria; they were most
especially placed in situations
to command the approaches,

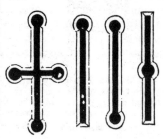

LOCKBAND, in masonry, a course of bond-stone.

and sometimes were introduced in the merlons of the battlements. These apertures seem to have come into use in the thirteenth century. They are occasionally in the form of a cross; and of this last-mentioned shape they are sometimes found as ornaments in the battlements of ecclesiastical buildings.

Long-and-Short Work, a kind of masonry considered by many as a mark of the eleventh-century work, though it occurs in later times. It consists of the quoins being placed alternately flat and upright, the main wall being of rubble masonry. The illustration shews its character, and others will be found under *Saxon.*

Louvre (Fr. *L' Ouverture*), a turret, or small lantern, placed on the roofs of ancient halls, kitchens, &c., to allow of the escape of smoke, or to promote ventilation; originally they were entirely open at the sides, or closed only with narrow boards, placed horizontally and sloping, and at a little distance apart, so as to exclude rain and snow without impeding the passage of the smoke. When, as was formerly by no means uncommon, fires were made on open hearths, without flues for the conveyance of the smoke, louvres were indispensable, and when not required for use they were very frequently

Lincoln College, Oxford.

LOGGIA, a term applied in Italian architecture to any covered space of which one or more sides are open to the air.

erected for ornament, but in the latter case were usually glazed, and many which once were open have been glazed in later times; examples may be seen still on some of the college halls at Oxford and Cambridge. Similar in structure to lanterns, they were used only for allowing the smoke to escape (whence the name *Fumerell* was applied), while the lantern was especially for admitting light.

Low-side Windows, a peculiar opening or window, usually on the south side of the chancel, and *lower* than the other windows, for the purpose of affording communication between a person on the outside and a priest within. The best explanation is that they were for lepers, or for any one so afflicted as to be inconvenient for him to join the congregation, though several theories have been put forward; one, viz. that a light might be seen burning, suggested the name of *Lychnoscope.* Most examples have traces of being closed by a shutter.

Machicolations, and Machicoulis (Fr.), openings formed for the purpose of defence at the tops of castles and fortifications, by setting the parapet out on corbels, so as to project beyond the face of the wall, the intervals between the corbels being left open to allow of missiles being thrown down on the heads of assailants; they are more especially found over the gateways and entrances, but are also common in other situations.

They took the place of the *Hourds* of an earlier period. Parapets are sometimes set out on projecting corbels, so as to have a similar appearance when there are no machicolations behind them. [See also illustration given under *Alure.*]

LORYMER = Larmier.

LOZENGE-MOULDING. See *Moulding.*

LUCARNE, a dormer or garret window.

LUFFER-BOARDS (i.q. Louvre-boards), the series of sloping boards in unglazed windows to keep out the weather; often seen in tower-windows.

Mask, or Notch-head, a kind of corbel, the shadow of
which bears a close resemblance
to that of the human face; it is
common in some districts in work
of the thirteenth and fourteenth
centuries, and is usually carved
under the eaves as a *corbel-table.*
[See illustration from Stanwick,
Northants.] A good example occurs in Portsmouth Church, where
it is mixed with the tooth-ornament. It is a favourite ornament
in Northamptonshire in the cornices of the tower under a broach
spire, and under the parapet of
the chancel; but it is by no
means confined to any particular
district.

Corbel, West Clandon, Surrey.

Member, a moulding; as a cornice of five members,
a base of three members. The term is also sometimes
applied to the subordinate parts of a building.

Metal-work. Besides *Ironwork,* the Middle Ages have
left to us several examples of the great skill of workers in
gold and silver, as well as in brass and less costly metal.
[See illustration under *Chalice, Paten, Pyx,* &c.]

Metope, or Metopse (Gr.), the space between the triglyphs in the frieze of the Doric order: in some of

MAILLES, COIF DE. See illustrations to *Brass.*

MANIPLE, part of the priest's
dress. See illustrations to *Brass.*

MANSE, the parsonage-house;
chiefly a north-country word.

MANTLE-TREE, i.q. mantel-
piece over a fireplace.

MARQUETRY (Fr.), a kind of
mosaic or inlaid woodwork.

MASONRY. See *Construction
of Walls.*

MERLON, the solid part of an
embattled parapet between the

embrasures. See *Battlement.*

MEROS, the plain surface between the channels of a triglyph.

MESTLING, MASTLIN, yellow
metal, brass. Sacred ornaments
or utensils are described as made
thereof; in the Inventory taken
at Wolverhampton, 1541, there
are enumerated great basins,
censers, vessels, and two great
candlesticks of "mastlin,"
weighing 120 lbs. It is called
also *Latten.*

the Greek examples they are quite plain, and in others
ornamented with sculpture; in
Roman buildings they are usually carved with ox-sculls, but
sometimes with pateras, shields,
or other devices, and are rarely
left plain. According to the
Roman method of working the
Doric order, it is indispensable
that the metopes should all be
exact squares, but in the Grecian Doric this is not necessary.

Minster, the church of a monastery, or one to which
a monastery has been attached: the name is also occasionally applied to a cathedral.

Miserere, the projecting bracket on the under side of
the seats of stalls in churches; these, where perfect, are
fixed with hinges so that they may be turned up, and
when this is done the projection of the miserere is sufficient, without actually forming a seat, to afford very considerable rest to any one leaning upon it. They were
allowed in the Roman Catholic Church as a relief to the
infirm during
the long ser-
vices that were
required to be
performed by
the ecclesiastics
in a standing
posture. They
are always more
or less ornamen-
ted with carv-
ings of leaves,

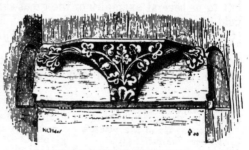

Henry the Seventh's Chapel, Westminster.

foliage, small figures, animals, &c., which are generally
very boldly cut. Examples are to be found in almost all
churches which retain any of the ancient stalls; perhaps
the oldest remaining is in Henry the Seventh's Chapel at
Westminster, where there is one in the style of the
thirteenth century.

Mitre, the line formed by the meeting of mouldings or other surfaces, which intersect or intercept each other at an angle, as A B.

Module (Lat.), a measure of proportion by which the parts of an order or of a building are regulated in Classical architecture; it has been generally considered as the diameter, or semi-diameter, of the lower end of the shaft of the column, but different architects have taken it from different parts and subdivided it in various ways. [See also *Minute*.]

Modillion (Fr.), projecting brackets under the corona of the Corinthian and Composite, and occasionally also of the Roman Ionic orders.

Monastery, a habitation for monks, but commonly used for any other religious house: a *convent*, or *nunnery*, or *friary* was considered only as a subdivision of the general term; an *abbey* was a monastery governed by an abbot, and a *priory* was one governed by a prior, in some cases subordinate to another house; an *alien* priory was a cell to a foreign monastery.

1. The *Benedictine* order. The most famous and ancient order of monks followed the rule of St. Benedict, and were established in Rome prior to the sending of Augustine into England by Gregory the Great. The Benedictines were afterwards divided into different orders, but their buildings were arranged on the same plan. All the older monasteries in England belonged to the Benedictines, and these were generally the largest and most wealthy. Their usual plan consists of a square cloister

MEZZANINE (Ital.), a low intermediate storey between two higher ones, = French, *Entresole*. See *Storey*.

MEZZO RELIEVO (Ital.) See *Bas-relief*.

MINUTE, a proportionate measure by which the parts of the Classical orders are regulated; the sixtieth part of the lower diameter of the shaft of a column.

with the buildings grouped round it; the nave of a cruciform church forming one side, and this usually had aisles; the transept formed a part of the east side, with the chapter-house beyond, separated from the transept by a narrow passage called the slype: but there is no fixed place for the chapter-house; it is often on one side of the choir. The refectory is usually parallel with the nave on the opposite side of the cloister, with store-rooms under it, and the dormitory forms the western side with a staircase down from it into the nave of the church for the night services. All the mitred abbeys in England belonged to the Benedictine order, and their head establishment was at Canterbury.

2. The *Cluniac* order was founded by Odo, Abbot of Cluny, in 912, but was not introduced into England until 1077; their first establishment was at Lewes, in Sussex, and this order was much in fashion during the last quarter of the eleventh century, very few being founded after that time. Their plan differs slightly from the Benedictine.

3. The *Cistercians* were founded by the Abbot of Cisteaux, in Burgundy, in 1098, and introduced into England in 1128, at Waverly Abbey, Surrey; and during the remainder of the twelfth century they were so much in vogue that there were often two or three establishments founded in a single year, but after the end of that century the fashion again changed, and we have very few founded after 1200. Their plan differs considerably from the Benedictine: the nave is divided into three parts, either by screens, walls, or steps, and has no aisles; the choir is short and the transepts also short. The other buildings are also arranged in a different order.

4. The *Augustinian Canons* or Canons Regular, were canons who lived according to rule, which the secular canons did not. Their rule differed very little practically from that of the Benedictines: they had a common dormitory and refectory, whilst the secular canons lived each in his own house. They were introduced into England by Henry I., in 1105, at Colchester, and their establishments were very numerous.

5. The *Premonstratensian* order of regular canons, was instituted by Norbert, Archbishop of Magdeburg, and the

head establishment was at Pratum Monstratum or Præmonstratum (Premontré), in Picardy; it was introduced into England in 1140, at New-house, in Lincolnshire. Their dress was white; they were reformed Augustinians.

6. The *Carthusians* were another reformed branch of the Benedictines, their founder was St. Bruno, of Cologne, and their head establishment the Grande Chartreuse, in the diocese of Grenoble, founded about 1080. Their monasteries were called Charter-houses; their first house in England was at Witham, in Somersetshire, founded by Henry II., in 1180, the first prior being St. Hugh, afterwards Bishop of Lincoln, who was brought over from the Grande Chartreuse by the King. Their plan is different from the Benedictine abbeys; instead of having the choir of a large church for the monks and the nave for the people, they built two smaller churches, one for the monks, the other for the people: the latter having become a parish church has often been preserved where the monastery has entirely disappeared, as in the case at Witham. These brethren lived each in a separate cottage of three rooms, with a small garden to it; this was called his cell; they were arranged round a cloister. Many of these establishments remain unaltered and are still in use in Italy.

These were the chief divisions of orders of monks, but there were several subordinate ones of minor importance.

The chief *Military* orders were the Templars and the Hospitallers. The *Templars* were established in 1118, for the defence of the Temple at Jerusalem, and of pilgrims to it, the *Hospitallers* for that of the Hospital of St. John, also at Jerusalem, but after Jerusalem was abandoned by the Crusaders, they settled at Rhodes and afterwards at Malta, and their order is not quite extinct. The Templars were suppressed in the fourteenth century, and their establishments were then given up to other purposes or destroyed.

At a later period the *Friars* were more popular than either the Monks or the Knights, and most of the foundations of the fifteenth century are of Friaries: but they had no estates; their churches are generally plain, and without aisles, but often large, and well calculated for preaching. There were three principal orders:—

1. The *Dominicans*, or Black Friars, called also the Preaching Friars, established by St. Dominic about 1170, first introduced into England in 1221.

2. The *Franciscans*, or Grey Friars, called also Minorites, from their head establishment in the Minories, London. Instituted by St. Francis, at Assisi in Italy, A.D. 1209, established in England at Canterbury in 1224.

3. The *Carmelites*, or White Friars, who were driven out from Mount Carmel by the Saracens, in 1098; established in England, at Alnwick, in 1240.

4. The *Austin Friars*, or Hermits, introduced into England in 1250. Their usual dress in public was black.

5. *Friars of the Holy Trinity*, or Maturines, established for the redemption of captives; instituted by St. John de Matha in 1197. Their head establishment was at St. Maturine's Chapel, Paris; they were introduced into England in 1224, at Mottenden, Kent. Dress white, with red and blue crosses on the breast.

6. *Crutched* or *Crouched Friars*, instituted at Bologna in 1169, and established in England, at Colchester, in 1244. Their dress was blue with a red cross; originally they carried a cross on a staff, and crouched before it.

There were seven more orders of friars, but of less importance and with few establishments, and there were nuns of nearly all the orders of which there were monks.

The Jesuits first came into England in 1538; their object was to crush the Reformation, and they were introduced immediately after the dissolution of the monasteries.

Mosaic-work (Lat. *Opus Musivum*), ornamental work formed by inlaying small pieces, usually cubes, of glass,

MODINATURE, the general distribution, profiles, and arrangement of the mouldings of an order, a building, or any architectural member.

MONOPTERAL, a circular form of *Temple*, consisting of a roof supported on columns without any cell.

MONOSTYLE, an epithet applied by some French writers to the piers of mediæval architecture when they consist of a single shaft.

MONOTRIGLYPH, the intercolumniation in the Doric order which embraces one triglyph and two metopes in the entablature.

MONSTRANCE, the glass vessel in which the consecrated wafer or Host was placed when the congregation were blessed with it.

MONUMENT. See *Tomb*.

MONYAL or Monion. See *Mullion*.

MORTICE. See illustration under *Tenon*.

stone, &c. It was much used by the Romans in floors, and on the walls of houses, and many specimens which have been discovered are exceedingly beautiful from the introduction of different-coloured materials, and represent a variety of subjects with figures of animals, or often simply patterns such as frets, guilloches, foliage, &c.

In the Middle Ages this kind of work continued to be used in Italy and some other parts of the Continent, and was applied to pictures on the walls and vaults of churches as well as to pavements. The favourite pattern in the mediæval pavements is called *Opus Alexandrinum;* this was used chiefly in the twelfth and thirteenth centuries. In England it was never extensively employed, though used in some parts of the shrine of Edward the Confessor, on the tomb of Henry III., and in the paving of the choir at Westminster Abbey, and Becket's crown at Canterbury, where curious patterns may be seen. Mosaic-work is still executed with great skill by the Italians, and at a distance the work has all the appearance of oil-paintings.

Mould, or **Mold,** the model or pattern used by workmen, especially by masons, as a guide in working mouldings, and ornaments: it consists of a thin board or plate of metal cut to represent the exact section of the mouldings, &c., to be worked from it.

Moulding, or **Molding,** a term applied to all the varieties of outline or contour given to the angles of the various subordinate parts and features of buildings, whether projections or cavities, such as cornices, capitals, bases, door and window jambs and heads, &c. The regular mouldings of *Classical* architecture are the *Fillet,* or *list;* the *Astragal,* or *bead;* the *Cyma reversa,* or *Ogee;* the *Cyma recta,* or *cyma;* the *Cavetto;* the *Ovolo;* the *Scotia,* or *trochilus;* and the *Torus;* each of these admits of some variety of form, and there is considerable difference in the manner of working them between the Greeks and Romans. [See those terms.] The mouldings in Classical architecture are frequently enriched by being cut into leaves, eggs, and tongues, or other ornaments, and sometimes the larger members have running patterns of foliage carved on them in low relief; the upper moulding of cornices is occasionally ornamented with a series of projecting lions' heads.

In mediæval architecture, the diversities in the proportions and arrangements of the mouldings are very great, and it is scarcely possible to do more than point out a few of the leading and most characteristic varieties.

In the *Norman* style the plain mouldings consist simply of squares, rounds, and hollows, variously combined, with an admixture of splays, and a few fillets. The rich mouldings, however, are very various, one of the most marked being the constant recurrence of the *Zigzag* or *Chevron* moulding: it has not been very clearly

Binham, Norfolk.

Norwich Cathedral.

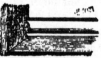

Peterborough Cathedral.

Peterborough Cathedral.

ascertained at what period this kind of decoration was first introduced, but it was certainly not till some considerable time after the commencement of the style; when once adopted, it became more common than any other ornament. A series of grotesque heads placed in a hollow moulding, called *Beak-heads*, with their tongues or beaks lapping over a large bead or torus, was also very common.

The *Hatched* moulding is also not uncommon, and is found early in the style, as it can be cut conveniently without the aid of elaborate tools.

Westminster Hall, A.D. 1097.

The other favourite mouldings of the Norman style are the *Billet* mouldings, both square and round, the *Lozenge*, the *Nail-head*, the *Pellet*, the *Chain*, the *Cable*, and the *Rose*, of all which illustrations are given on the plate in the next page. There may also be mentioned the *Star*, the *Billeted Cable*, the *Nebule*, the *Studded*, the *Indented*, the *Scolloped*, the *Fir Cone*, the *Double Cone*, the *Dovetail*, the *Embattled*, the *Open Heart*, and the *Antique*.

Lozenge.—Tickencote, Rutland.

Square Billet.—St. Augustine's, Canterbury.

Round Billet.—Blnham Priory, Norfolk.

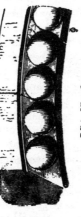

Billet.—Iffley, Oxon.

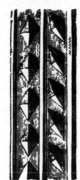

Nailhead.—Ely Cathedral.

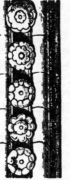

Rose.—Iffley Church, Oxfordshire.

Cable.—Romsey, Hants.

Chain.—St. William's Chapel, York.

In the *Early English* style, the plain mouldings become lighter, and are more boldly cut than in the Norman; the varieties are not very great, and in arches, jambs of doors, windows, &c., they are very commonly so arranged that if they are circumscribed by a line drawn to touch the most prominent points of their contour it will be found to form a succession of rectangular recesses. [See illustration under *Templet.*] They gene-rally consist of alternate rounds and hollows, the latter very deeply cut, and a few small fillets; sometimes also splays are used: there is considerable inequality in the sizes of the round

Salisbury Cathedral.

mouldings, and the larger ones are very usually placed at such a distance apart as to admit of several smaller between them; these large rounds have frequently one or more narrow fillets worked on them, or are brought to a sharp edge in the middle (as may be seen in the illustrations from Stanton and Brackley, under *Fillet;*) the smaller rounds are often undercut with a deep cavity on one side (*e e*), and the round and hollow members constantly unite with each other without any parting fillet or angle.

The ornamental mouldings in this style are not numerous, and they are almost invariably placed in the hollows; the commonest and most characteristic is that which is known by the name of the *Dog-tooth ornament*, which usually consists of four small plain leaves united so as to form a pyramid, (in French, *vio-lettes;*) these ornaments are commonly placed close together, and sometimes in series: the other enrichments consist chiefly of single leaves and flowers, or of running patterns of the foliage pecu-liar to the style. [See illustrations under *Doorway, Tooth-ornament,* &c.]

Peterborough Cathedral.

The plain mouldings in the *Decorated* style are more
diversified than in the Early English, though in large suites
rounds and hollows continue for the most part to prevail;
the hollows are often very deeply cut, but in many instances,
especially towards the end of the style, they become shallower and broader; ovolos are not very uncommon and ogees
are frequent; splays also
are often used, either by
themselves or with other
mouldings; fillets placed
upon larger members are
abundant, especially in the
early part of the style, and
around moulding called the
Roll-moulding (or *Scroll-
moulding*), like a roll of
parchment, with a sharp
projecting edge on it, aris-

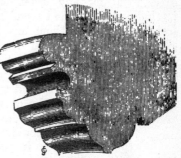

Door, Kiddington, Oxon.

ing from one half being formed from a smaller curve than
the other, is frequently used, and is characteristic of Decorated work; when used horizontally the larger curve is
placed uppermost: there is also another moulding, convex
in the middle and concave at each extrem-
ity, which, though sometimes found in the
Perpendicular style, may be considered as
generally characteristic of the Decorated.
Fillets are very frequently used to separate other members, but the rounds and
hollows often run together, as in the

Early English style. The enrichments consist of leaves
and flowers, either set separately or in running patterns,
figures, heads, and animals, all of which are generally
carved with greater
truth than at any other
period; but the *ball-
flower*, which belongs
especially to this style,
and a variety of the
four-leaved flower, are

Ball-flower, Kiddington, Oxon.

the commonest. [See illustrations under *Ball-flower*, *Niche*,
Rib, *Window*, *Canopy*, *Doorway*, and *Tabernacle*.]

In the *Perpendicular* style, the mouldings are generally flatter and less effective than at an earlier period. One of the most striking characteristics is the prevalence of very large, and often shallow hollows; these sometimes occupied so large a space as to leave but little room for any other mouldings: the hollows and round members not un-

Balliol College, Oxford.

frequently unite without any line of separation, but the other members are parted either by quirks or fillets. The most prevalent moulding is the ogee, but rounds, which are often so small as to be only beads, are very abundant, and it is very usual to find two ogees in close contact, with the convex sides next each other. There is also an un-dulating moulding, which is common in the abacus and dripstones, peculiar to

Deddington Church, Oxon.

the Perpendicular style, especially the lat-ter part of it; and another indicative of the same date, which is concave in the middle and round at each extremity, is occasionally used in door-jambs, &c. In Perpendicular work, small fillets are not placed upon larger members, as in Decorated and Early English; splays also are much less frequent. The ornaments used in the mouldings are running patterns of foliage and flowers; detached leaves, flowers, and bunches of foliage; heads, animals, and figures, usually grotesque; shields, and vari-ous heraldic and fanciful devices: the large hollow mould-ings, when used in arches or the jambs of doors and win-dows, sometimes contain statues with canopies over them.

Mullion (or *Monion*, or *Monial*), the division between the lights of windows, screens, &c., in Gothic architecture; the styles, or upright divisions, in wainscoting are also some-times called by the same name. Mullions are scarcely ever found of earlier date than the Early English style, for though windows are not unfrequently used in couplets, and sometimes in triplets, in Norman work, they are almost invariably separated by small shafts, or by piers, too massive to be called mullions; Early English windows

also are often separated by piers; but in numerous instances they are placed so close together, that the divisions
become real mullions, and from the date of the introduction of tracery they are
universal. In unglazed
windows, such as those in
belfries, single shafts are
sometimes used in place
of mullions in the Early
English style, and per-
haps occasionally in the
Decorated; in open screen-
work they appear to pre-
vail in both these styles,
and examples of Decorated
date are by no means un-
common. The mouldings
of mullions are extremely
various, but they always
partake of the character-

Decorated.

Oxford Cathedral.

Perpendicular.

Westminster Hall.

istics of the prevailing style of architecture; in rich Early
English and Decorated work they have frequently one or
more small shafts attached to them which terminate at the
level of the springing of the arch,
and the mouldings in the tracery
(where tracery is used) over the
capitals of the shafts are generally
different from those below; but in
very numerous instances, mullions,
in both these styles, have plain
splays only, and no mouldings,
and many of Decorated date have
shallow hollows instead of splays at
the sides; in Perpendicular work
a plain mullion of this last-mentioned kind is extremely common.
After the introduction of the Perpendicular style, shafts are rarely
found on mullions, though bases are
sometimes worked at the bottoms of the principal mouldings, an arrangement which is also occasionally found in

Early plain Mullion. Late plain Mullion.

Duffield, Derbyshire. Headington, Oxon.

earlier work, and most abundantly in the Flamboyant style of France.

Mutule (Lat.), a projecting block worked under the corona of the Doric cornice, in the same situation as the modillions in the Corinthian and Composite orders; it is often made to slope downward towards the most prominent part, and has usually a number of small guttæ, or drops, worked on the underside.

Nail-heads. In middle-age architecture the heads of the nails were very frequently

made ornamental, and varied to some extent during the prevalence of the

Nail-heads, Compton, Berks.

different styles. They were used not only in fastening the metalwork to the door, but the door was often studded with them. They are sometimes very elaborate, being made of three or four pieces.

Nail-head on a wooden quatrefoil, Coleshill, Warwickshire.

Nave (Lat. *Navis* = a ship), the part of a church westward of the choir, in which the general congregation assemble; in large buildings it consists of a central division, or body, with two or more aisles, and there is sometimes a series of small chapels at the sides beyond the aisles; in smaller buildings it is often without aisles, but has sometimes two, or more, and sometimes one. In *Cathedral* and

MULTIFOIL, a foil-arch of which the *foils* are so numerous that it is thought unnecessary to specify their number.

MUNTIN (Fr.), any upright piece in a framing.

MYNCHERY, Saxon name for nunnery.

NAOS, the cella or interior part of a temple.

NARTHEX, in Early Christian churches an enclosed space near the entrance for catechumens.

NERVES, a term sometimes applied to the ribs of a vault.

conventual churches the nave was generally, if not always in this country, separated from the choir by a screen, which in most instances still remains; on the western side of this, next the nave, one or more altars were occasionally placed; one is recorded, for instance, to have stood thus at Canterbury Cathedral, previous to the fire in 1174; the same arrangement appears also to have been formerly common in France, though, with but very few exceptions, the old screens have been removed to make way for light open partitions. Previous to the Reformation the pulpit was always placed in the nave, as it still is at Ely and Chichester, and always in Roman Catholic churches on the Continent; the font also stood there, usually near the west end, sometimes in the middle, and sometimes in an aisle, or adjoining one of the pillars. [See *Cathedral, Church, Choir,* &c.]

Neck. The plain part at the bottom of a Roman Doric or other capital, between the mouldings and the top of the shaft. In Gothic architecture the mouldings at the bottom of the capital are frequently called *Neck-mouldings.*

Newel (Old Eng. forms, Noel, Nowel, and Nuel), the central column round which the steps of a circular staircase wind; in the northern parts of the kingdom it is sometimes continued above the steps up to the vaulting of the roof, and supports a series of ribs which radiate from it, as at Belsay. The term is also used for the principal post at the angles and foot of a staircase. The newel staircase occurs in all turrets, as no other staircase could be designed to occupy so small a space. It is essentially Gothic in its construction, and though it constantly occurs in Norman work it is not found in the Classical styles. See also *Vise.*

Belsay Castle.

Niche (Fr.), a recess in a wall for a statue, vase, or other erect ornament. Among the ancients they were sometimes square, but oftener semicircular at the back, and terminated in a half-dome at the top; occasionally small pediments were formed over them, which were supported on consoles, or small columns or pilasters placed at the sides of the niches, but they were frequently left plain, or ornamented only with a few mouldings. In middle-age architecture niches (often called *Tabernacles*), were extensively used, especially in ecclesiastical buildings, for statues.

Gateway of the Bishop's Palace,
Peterborough, c. 1220.

The figures in the *Early English* style were sometimes set on small pedestals, and *canopies* were not unfrequently used over the heads; they were often placed in suites or arranged in pairs, under a larger arch; when in suites they were very commonly separated by single shafts, in other cases the sides were usually moulded in a similar way to windows: the arches of the heads were either cinquefoiled, tretoiled, or plain, and when canopies were used they were generally made to project: good examples of the thirteenth century are to be seen on the west front of the cathedral at Wells.

In the *Decorated* style they

Coombe Church, Oxon, c. 1350.

very frequently had ogee canopies over them, which were
sometimes placed flat against the wall and sometimes
bowed out in the form of an ogee; triangular canopies were
also common: several kinds of projecting canopies were
likewise used, especially when the niches were placed separately. In the tops of buttresses niches were sometimes
made to occupy the whole breadth of the buttress, so as to
be entirely open on three sides, with small piers at the front
angles; pedestals were very common, particularly in niches
with projecting canopies, and in such cases were either
carried on corbels or rose from other projecting supports
below; sometimes corbels were used instead of pedestals.

In the *Perpendicular* style the panelling, which was so
profusely introduced, was sufficiently recessed to receive

Magdalen Church, Oxford, c. 1500.   Kidlington, Oxfordshire, c. 1450.

figures, and these varied considerably in form, but of the

more legitimate niches the general character did not differ very materially from those of the preceding style. In plan the canopies were usually half an octagon or hexagon, with small pendants and pinnacles at the angles; and crockets, finials, and other enrichments were often introduced in great profusion: buttresses, surmounted with pinnacles, were also very frequently placed at the sides of niches in this style. [See illustrations under *Buttress*, *Canopy*, *Image*, *Pinnacle*, and *Tabernacle*.]

Norman Architecture, or the Anglo-Norman style. This variety of the Romanesque style was first used in this country about the time of the Conquest, the little which we have of the time of Edward the Confessor or earlier is very rude. In the early stages it was plain and massive, with but few mouldings, and those principally confined to small features, such as the string, impost, *abacus*, and base, the archways being either perfectly plain or formed with a succession of square angles, and the capitals of the pillars, &c., were for the most part entirely devoid of ornament. Sculpture was very sparingly used before the twelfth century, and was frequently added to the earlier buildings at some later period.

Early Norman Arch, Westminster Hall, A.D. 1090.

As the style advanced, greater lightness and enrichment were introduced, and some of the later specimens exhibit a profusion of ornaments. The mouldings were but little varied, and consisted principally of rounds and hollows,

NIGGED ASHLAR, stone hewn with a pick or pointed hammer instead of a chisel; called also *Hammer-dressed*.

with small fillets and sometimes splays intermixed. A very common mode of decorating buildings in this style was with rows of small shallow niches or panels, which were often formed of intersecting arches, and some of them were also frequently pierced to form windows. The doorways were often very deeply recessed, and had several small shafts in the jambs, which, when first introduced, were cut on the same stones with the other parts of the work and built up in courses, but at the latter end of the style they were frequently set separately like the Early English, and occasionally were also banded; in many doorways, especially small ones, the open-

Late Norman Doorway, Middleton Stoney, Oxon, c. 1160.

ing reached no higher than the level of the springing of the arch, and was terminated flat, the tympanum or space above it being usually filled with sculpture, or other ornament. The windows were not usually of large size, and in general appearance resembled small doors; they had no mullions, but sometimes they were arranged in pairs (not unfrequently under a larger arch), with a single shaft between them; towards the end of the style they were occasionally grouped together in threes, like the Early English. The pillars at first were very massive, but subsequently became much lighter; they were sometimes channelled, or moulded in zigzag or spiral lines, as at Durham Cathedral; in plan they differed considerably, though not so much as in some of the later styles; the commonest forms were plain circles, or polygons, sometimes with small shafts attached, and a cluster of four large semicircles with smaller shafts in rectangular recesses between them. The buttresses were most commonly broad, and of small projection, either uniting with the face of the parapet, or terminating just below the cornice; sometimes they had small shafts worked on the angles, and occasionally half-shafts were used instead of buttresses. Spires and pinnacles were not used in this style, but there are some turrets, of rather late date, which have conical tops, as at the west end of Rochester Cathedral, and in Normandy several small church towers have steep pyramidal stone roofs. It was not till

Norman Window, St. John's, Devizes, c. 1160.

towards the end of the Norman style that groining on a large scale was practised ; at an early period the aisles of churches were vaulted with plain groining without bosses or diagonal ribs, but the main parts had flat ceilings, or were covered with cylindrical vaults, as at the chapel in the White Tower of London. The Norman arch was round, either semicircular or horse-shoe, and sometimes the impost moulding or capital was considerably below the level of the springing, and the mouldings of the arch were prolonged vertically down to it; this arrangement was common in the arches round the semicircular apses of churches, as at St. Bartholomew's, in West Smithfield, London; it was not till the latter part of the twelfth century, when the Norman style was in a state of transition into Early English, that the pointed arch was commonly introduced, but some buildings erected at this period retained the Norman characteristics in considerable purity. The best example in the kingdom of an early ecclesiastical structure in this style is the chapel in the White Tower of London; later specimens are to be found in very many of our cathedrals and parish churches; the churches of Iffley, Oxon., and Barfreston, Kent, are striking examples of late date; the latter of these shews considerable signs of the near approach of the Early English style.

The earliest dated example of this style in England is probably the portion of the refectory and the substructure of the dormitory of Westminster Abbey usually attributed to the time of Edward the Confessor. The following are other dated examples, arranged in chronological order:—

WILLIAM THE CONQUEROR, 1066—1087.

Canterbury Cathedral—Part of the Dormitory.

St. Alban's Abbey—Central tower and transepts, begun 1077.

Rochester Cathedral—Tower on north side.

Malling Abbey—West front.
     ,,   St. Leonard's Tower, (Gundulph).

London, Tower of—Keep.

WILLIAM II., 1087—1100.

Canterbury Cathedral—Part of the crypt, and walls of the choir aisles.

Ely Cathedral—Transepts.

Lincoln Cathedral—Part of West Front.

Lastringham, Yorkshire—Crypt.

Thorney Abbey, Cambridgeshire—Walls of the nave.

Hurley Priory Church—Berkshire.

Chichester Cath.—Some parts.

Worcester Cathedral—Ditto.

Gloucester Cathedral—Ditto.

Carlisle Cathedral—South transept and a fragment of the nave.

Durham Cathedral—Nave and transepts.

Lindisfarne Priory Ch., Durham.

Christ Church, Hampshire—Part of nave.

Norwich Cathedral—Choir and transept, and the lower part of central tower.

Colchester Castle.

Bury St. Edmund's — Abbey Church.

Winchester Cathedral—Transepts.

[The above were all building during the reign of William Rufus, but some had been commenced in the previous reign, and many were carried on into the reign following.]

HENRY I., 1100—1135.

Canterbury Cathedral—Part of the crypt, and walls of the choir aisles.

Tewkesbury—Abbey Church.

Colchester—St. Botolph's Priory.

Durham Cathedral—Nave.

Sherborne Castle, Dorsetshire.

Croyland—Abbey Church.

Peterborough Cathedral—Choir.

Boxgrove Priory, Sussex.

Kirkham Priory, Yorkshire.

Bury St. Edmund's—St. James's Tower.

Norwich Cathedral—Nave.

Castor Church, Northants.

London, St. Bartholomew's Priory Church, Smithfield—Choir and aisles.
Leominster Priory, Herefordshire—The old choir.
St. Margaret's-at-Cliffe, Kent.
Rochester Cathedral—Nave.
Porchester Church, Hampshire—The west front.

STEPHEN, 1135—1154.

St. Cross, Hampshire—Choir.
Buildwas Abbey, Shropshire.
Shobden Church, Herefordshire.
Roche Abbey Church, Yorkshire.
Hereford Cathedral—Nave.
Bristol—St. Augustine's Priory Gateway.
    ,,   —Chapter-house.
Birkenhead Priory Ch., Cheshire.
Northampton, St. Peter's.
Kenilworth Priory Church—Doorway.

HENRY II., 1154—1189.
Generally late and Transitional.
Iffley Church, Oxfordshire.
Stewkley Church, Bucks.
Jervaulx Abbey, Yorkshire.
Peterborough Cathedral—Nave and transepts.
Oakham Castle, Rutlandshire.
Lanercost Priory, Cumberland.
Ely Cathedral—Nave.
Canterbury Cathedral—Rebuilding of choir under William of Sens, 1175—1184.
Byland Abbey, Yorkshire.
Oxford, Christ Church Cath.
Durham Cathedral—Galilee.
Romsey Abbey Church, Hants.
Witham Priory Ch., Somerset.
London, Temple Church.
Glastonbury—St. Joseph's Chap.
Oxford, St. Peter's—Choir and crypt.

Ogee, or Ogyve (Old Fr.), a moulding formed by the combination of a round and hollow, part being concave and part convex. In Classical architecture ogees are extensively used, and are always placed with the convex part upwards, [see *Cyma Reversa*]: among the Greeks they were

Quirked Ogee, Arch of Constantine, Rome.

formed with quirks at the top, but by the Romans these were very frequently omitted.

In Gothic architecture also ogees are very abundantly employed, but they are, quite as often as not, used with the hollow part upwards, and in such cases might in strictness be called cyma recta; they are almost invariably quirked: in Norman work they are very rarely found, and are less common in the Early English than in either of the

NOSING, the prominent edge of a moulding or drip. A term often applied to the projecting moulding on the edge of a step.

OCTOSTYLE, a portico having eight columns in front.
OCULUS, a round window.
OFF-SET. See *Set-off*.

later styles. This moulding assumed different forms at different periods, and the variations, although not sufficiently constant to afford conclusive evidence of the date of a building, often impart very great assistance towards ascertaining its age : fig. 1 is Early English ; fig. 2 is used at all periods, but less frequently in the Early English than in the other styles ; fig. 3 is Decorated ; fig. 4 is late Perpendicular.

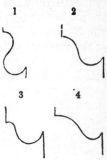

The term *Ogee* is also applied to a pointed arch, the sides of which are each formed of two contrasted curves. [See *Arch*, and, under *Decorated*, Higham Ferrars.]

Order, in Classical architecture, a column entire, consisting of base, shaft, and capital, with an entablature. There are usually said to be five orders, the Tuscan, Doric, Ionic, Corinthian, and Composite ; but the first and last, sometimes called the two Roman orders, are little more than varieties of the Doric and Corinthian, and were not used by the Greeks.

The *Tuscan Order*, the simplest of the five orders of Classical architecture : it was unknown to the Greeks, and by many is considered only as a Roman variety of the Doric order. The column is usually made six times the diameter of the lower part of the shaft in height ; the entablature is varied both in character and proportion by different authors, but it is always simple and without any enrichment ; the capital has a square abacus, with a small projecting fillet on the upper edge ; under the abacus is an ovolo and a fillet, with a neck below ; the base consists of a square plinth and a large torus ; the shaft of the column is never fluted.

OGIVAL, French equivalent for Gothic, i.e. from *Ogive* = a pointed arch. Whence also the terms adopted by some ecclesiologists, First Pointed, Second or Middle Pointed, and Third Pointed, meaning Early English, Decorated, and Perpendicular.

OILLETS. See *Loop-holes*.

OPISTHODOMUS, the enclosed space in the rear of a cell in a Greek Temple.

ORATORY, a small private chapel. See *Oriel*.

ORB, a blank window or panel.

The *Doric Order*, the oldest and simplest of the three orders used by the Greeks, but it is ranked as the second of the five orders adopted by the Romans. The shaft of the column has twenty flutings, which are separated by a sharp edge, and not by a fillet, as in the other orders, and they are less than a semicircle in depth: the moulding below the abacus of the capital is an ovolo: the *architrave* of the entablature is surmounted with a plain fillet, called the tenia: the frieze is ornamented by flat projections, with three channels cut in each, which are called triglyphs; the spaces between these are called metopes: under the triglyphs and below the tenia of the architrave are placed small drops, or guttæ; along the top of the frieze runs a broad fillet, called the capital of the triglyphs: the soffit of the cornice has broad and shallow blocks worked on it, called mutules, one of which is placed over each metope and each triglyph: on the under surface are several rows of guttæ or

Grecian Doric.

Roman Doric.

drops. In these respects the order, as worked both by the Greeks and Romans, is identical, but in other points there is considerable difference. In the pure Grecian examples the column has no base, and its height rises from about four to six and a-half diameters; the capital has a perfectly plain square abacus, and the ovolo is but little if at all curved in section, except at the top, where it is quirked under the abacus; under the ovolo are a few plain fillets and small channels, and a short distance below them a deep narrow channel is cut in the shaft; the flutes of the shaft are continued up to the fillets under the ovolo. In the Roman Doric the shaft is usually seven diameters high, and generally has a base, sometimes the Attic and sometimes that which is peculiar to the order, consisting of a plinth and torus with an astragal above it; the capital has a small moulding round the top of the abacus, and the ovolo is in section a quarter-circle, and is not quirked; under the ovolo are two or three small fillets, and below them a collarino or neck. According to the Roman method of working this order, the triglyphs at the angles of buildings must be placed over the centre of the column, and the metopes must be exact squares. Sometimes the mutules are omitted, and a row of dentels is worked under the cornice.

The *Ionic Order.* The most distinguished feature of this order is the capital, which is ornamented with four spiral projections called volutes; these are arranged in the Greek examples, and the best of the Roman, so as to exhibit a flat face on the two opposite sides of the capital, but in later works they have been made to spring out of the mouldings under the angles of the abacus, so as to render the four faces of the capital uniform, the sides of the abacus being

Erectheum.

worked hollow like the Corinthian: the principal moulding is an ovolo, or echinus, which is overhung by the volutes, and is almost invariably carved; sometimes also other enrichments are introduced upon the capital: in some of the Greek examples there is a collarino, or necking, below the echinus, ornamented with leaves and flowers. The shaft varies from eight and a quarter to about nine and a half diameters in height; it is sometimes plain, and sometimes fluted with twenty-four flutes, which are separated from each other by small fillets. The bases used with this order are principally varieties of the Attic base, but another of a peculiar character is found in some of the Asiatic examples, the lower mouldings of which consist of two scotiæ, separated by small fillets and beads, above which is a large and prominent torus. The members of the entablature in good ancient examples, are sometimes perfectly plain, and sometimes enriched, especially the bed-mouldings of the cornice, which are frequently cut with a row of dentels. In modern or Italian architecture, the simplicity of the ancient entablature has

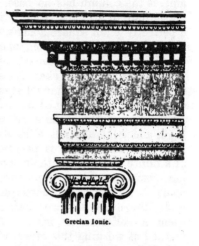

Grecian Ionic.

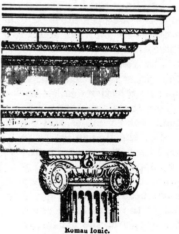

Roman Ionic.

been considerably departed from, and the cornice is not unfrequently worked with modillions in addition to dentels.

The *Corinthian Order* is the lightest and most ornamental of the three orders used by the Greeks. "The capital," says Rickman, "is the great distinction of this order; its height is more than a diameter, and consists of an astragal, fillet, and apophyges, all of which are measured with the shaft, then a bell and horned abacus. The bell is set round with two rows of leaves, eight in each row, and a third row of leaves supports eight small open volutes, four of which are under the four horns of the abacus, and the other four, which are sometimes interwoven, are under the central recessed part of the abacus, and have over them a flower or other ornament. These

volutes spring out of small twisted husks, placed between the leaves of the second row, and which are called cauli-coles. The abacus consists of an ovolo, fillet, and cavetto, like the modern Ionic. There are various modes of indent-ing the leaves, which are called from these variations, acanthus, olive, &c. The column, including the base of half a diameter, and the capital, is about ten diameters high."

The base, which is considered to belong to this order, resembles the Attic, with two scotiæ between the tori, which are separated by two astragals: the Attic base is also frequently used, and other varieties sometimes occur.

The entablature of this order is frequently very highly enriched, the flat surfaces, as well as the mouldings, being sculptured with a great variety of delicate ornaments. The architrave is generally formed into two or three faces or faciæ; the frieze in the best examples is flat, and is sometimes united to the upper fillet of the architrave by an apophyges: the cornice has both modillions and dentels.

The *Composite Order*, called also Roman, being invented by that people, and composed of the Ionic grafted upon

the Corinthian; it is of the same proportion as the Corinthian, and retains the
same general character,
with the exception of the
capital, in which the Ionic
volutes and echinus are
substituted for the Co-
rinthian caulicoli and the
scrolls. It is one of the
five orders of Classic architecture, when five are ad-
mitted, but modern archi-
tects allow of only three,
considering the Tuscan and
the Composite as merely
varieties of the Doric and
the Corinthian. [See also
Column.]

In Gothic architecture the term *Order* is applied to the
divisions or recesses of an arch. [See p. 16.]

Organ: originally this term appears to have been applied to almost every kind of musical instrument use l in
churches, but at an early period it began to be confined to
wind instruments formed of a col-
lection of pipes; these, however,
were very different from the large
structure now in use, and of very
much smaller size; they were supplied with wind by means of bel-
lows at the back, which were
worked by an attendant, and not
by the player. Besides these large
instruments there was also a small
portable organ, sometimes called
a "pair of *Regals*," formerly in
use, and this was occasionally of

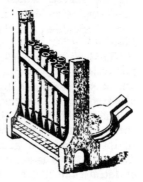

such a size as to admit of its being carried in the hand
and inflated by the player; one of these is represented
among the sculptures in the cornice of St. John's, Ciren-
ester, and another on the crozier of William of Wykeham,
at Oxford.

Oriel, or Oriole (Lat. *Oratoriolum,* or little place for prayer, its original meaning). It was a portion of an apartment set aside for prayer. In mediæval houses it was not an uncommon practice to arrange the domestic *oratory* so that the sacrarium was the whole height of the building, while there was an upper floor looking into it for the lord and his guests to attend to the service. This upper part more especially received the name of Oriole. Thus any projecting portion of a room, or even of a building, was called an Oriole, such as a penthouse, or such as a closet, bower, or private chamber, an upper story, or a gallery, whether it was used for prayer or not; and the term became more especially applied to a project-

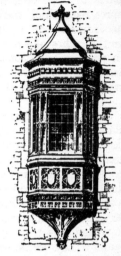

Vicars' Close, Wells.

ing window, (in which there was sometimes an altar, as in Linlithgow Palace, Scotland). This name is even given to the Bay-window of a hall for the sideboard.

Ovolo (Ital.), a convex moulding much used in Classical architecture; in the Roman examples it is usually an exact quarter of a circle, but in the Grecian it is flatter, and is most commonly *quirked* at the top: in middleage architecture it is not extensively employed; it is seldom found in any but the

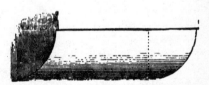

Roman Ovolo, Theatre of Marcellus, Rome.

Grecian Ovolo, quirked, Temple at Corinth.

Decorated style, and is not very frequent in that. [See also *Column.*]

OVERSTORY, the clearstory or upper story.

Pane, an old term formerly used in reference to various parts of buildings, such as the sides of a tower, turret, spire, &c., which were said to be of four, eight, &c., panes, according to the number of their sides; it was also applied to the lights of windows, the spaces between the timbers in wooden partitions, and other similar subdivisions, and was sometimes synonymous with the term panel: occasionally it was applied to a bay of a building.

Panel: this term is probably only a diminutive of Pane; it was formerly often used for the lights of windows, but is now almost exclusively confined to the sunken compartments of wainscoting, ceilings, &c., and the corresponding features in stone-work, which are so abundantly employed in Gothic architecture as ornaments on walls, ceilings, screens, tombs, &c. Of the *Norman* style no wooden panels remain; in stone-work, shallow recesses, to which this term may be applied, are frequently to be found; they are sometimes single, but oftener in ranges, and are commonly arched, and not unusually serve as niches to hold statues, &c.

In the *Early English* style, the panellings in stone-work are more varied; circles, trefoils, quatrefoils, cinquefoils, &c., and the pointed oval called the vesica piscis, are common forms; they are also frequently used in ranges, like shallow arcades, divided by small shafts or mullions, the heads being either plain arches, trefoils, or cinque-

Lincoln Cathedral.

foils, and panels similar to these are often used singly; the backs are sometimes enriched with foliage, diaperwork, or other carvings.

In the *Decorated* style wood panelling is frequently enriched with tracery, and sometimes with foliage also, or with shields and heraldic devices: stone panelling varies considerably; it is very commonly arched, and filled with tracery like windows, or arranged in squares, circles, &c., and feathered, or filled with tracery and other ornaments in different ways; shields are often introduced, and the backs of the panels are sometimes diapered.

Monument of Aymer de Valence, Westminster.

In the *Perpendicular* style the walls and vaulted ceilings of buildings are sometimes almost entirely covered with panelling, formed by mullions and tracery resembling the windows; and a variety of other panels of different forms, such as circles, squares, quatrefoils, &c., are profusely used in the subordinate parts, which are enriched with tracery, featherings, foliage, shields, &c., in different ways: in

Monument of John Langston, Esq., Caversfield, Bucks.

wood panelling the tracery and ornaments are more minute than was usual at an earlier period: and towards the end of the style these enrichments, instead of being fixed on to the panel, are usually carved upon it, and are sometimes very small and delicate. There is one kind of ornament which was introduced towards the end of the Perpendicular style, and prevailed for a considerable time, which deserves to be particularly mentioned; it consists of a series of straight mouldings worked upon the panel, so arranged, and with the ends so formed, as to represent the folds of linen: it is usually called the *linen pattern.* Many churches have wooden ceilings of the Perpendicular style, and some perhaps of earlier date, which are divided into panels, either by the timbers of the roof, or by ribs fixed on the boarding: some of these are highly ornamented, and probably most have been enriched with painting. After the expiration of Gothic architecture, panelling in great measure ceased to be used in stone-work, but was extensively employed in wainscoting and plaster-work; it was sometimes formed in complicated geometrical patterns, and was often very highly enriched with a variety of ornaments.

Paradise, the eastern term for a large garden (and applied to the garden of Eden), was chosen for the open court, or area, in front of the old church of St. Peter's at Rome, which was surrounded by a colonnade (*quadriporticus*). Hence it came to be applied to the cloisters of monasteries generally, and more especially to the burial-place within the precincts, wherever it was. Probably a corruption of this is the word *Parvise,* which is still in use in France for the open space round cathedrals and churches. With us this latter word seems to have been applied by antiquaries of two centuries ago, not only to the western porch, but to any porch, and more especially to the room over it.

PACE, a broad step, or raised space about a tomb or altar.

PALÆSTRA, a gymnasium.

PALLADIAN, a name applied to the revived Classical styles.

PANTRY (Fr. *Panneterie*), one of the offices in a monastic building, or castle, or manor-house, in which the bread (Fr. *Pain*) was kept, and with it much of the garniture of the table. It is especially distinguished from the *Botellerie* or buttery, where the wine and beer, &c. were decanted, and the flagons, cups, &c., kept. This office is still kept up in our colleges, and in large houses the *butler* is still retained as the officer, but the pantry has lost its original signification.

PARAMENT (Fr.) the furniture, ornaments, and hangings of an apartment, especially of a state-room.

Parapet, a breastwork or low wall used to protect the ramparts of military structures, and the gutters, roofs, &c., of churches, houses, and other buildings. On military works the parapets are either plain walls or battlemented, and they are frequently pierced with loopholes and oillets, through which arrows and other missiles might be discharged against assailants. (See *Allure, Battlement, Coping,* &c.) On ecclesiastical buildings parapets are of a different kind: in the Norman style they are perfectly plain, or occasionally have narrow embrasures in them at considerable intervals apart.

Early English Parapet, Salisbury Cathedral.

In the Early English style a few examples are probably to be found of embattled parapets, but they are generally straight at the top, and are usually perfectly plain. though in rich buildings they are sometimes panelled on the front, and in some instances are pierced with trefoils, quatrefoils, &c. Decorated parapets on plain buildings frequently consist of simple battlements, but on rich structures are ornamented in various ways; they are frequently straight at the top and panelled, or, more

Decorated Parapet, Beverley Minster, c. 1350.

commonly, pierced with a series of trefoils, quatrefoils, and other geometrical forms, or with running patterns of tracery, especially one peculiar to this style, in which the leading line of the stone-work forms a continuous undulation; embattled parapets are also panelled and pierced in a similar manner; the coping also of the battle-ments began to be car-ried up the sides of the merlons so as to form a continuous line round them. In the Perpendi-cular style a plain bat-tlemented parapet was very common, but this was also very frequent-ly panelled or pierced. There are many exam-ples which are straight at the top, and these are almost all either panelled or pierced.

Tower, Merton College, Oxford, A.D. 1440.

Parclose, or Perclose, an enclosure, screen, or railing, such as may be used to protect a tomb, to separate a chapel from the main body of a church. [See *Screen.*] Also to form the front of a gallery, or for other similar purposes; it is either of open-work or close. A distinct chapel is often formed in this manner, e.g. a chantry chapel. [See *Chapel.*]

Pargeting, or Pergeting, called also Parge-work: the term appears formerly to have been used in several senses, sometimes for plain plastering on walls, but usually for such as was made ornamental; this was effected by mouldings, fo-liage, figures, and other en-richments, applied in relief, and by various patterns and ornaments sunk in the surface

Banbury, Oxfordshire.

of the work or formed on it in a smoother material than the rest. Timber houses of the time of Queen Elizabeth

PARGE-BOARD = Barge-board.	(2.) A set of dressings or orna-ments for a fireplace.
PARRELL (1.) A chimney-piece;	

are often to be found with the exterior ornamented with pargeting; in the market-place at Newark is a wooden house with small figures and canopies over them in plaster-work, between some of the timbers, of earlier date. This term is now seldom used, except for the coarse plastering applied to the insides of chimney-flues.

Parlour (Fr. *Parloir*), a private apartment to which persons can withdraw for conference or retirement: the room in a convent in which the inmates were allowed to speak with their friends, sometimes called the "speke-house."

Paten, a small plate or salver for the *Bread*, used in the celebration of the Eucharist: it was so formed in ancient times as to fit the Chalice, or cup, as a cover; and was most commonly made of gold or silver, often silver-gilt, and with some sacred device or inscription. The word is still retained in our Prayer-book.

Paten, Chichester Cathedral.

Patera (Lat. = a bowl), a circular ornament resembling a dish, often worked in relief on friezes, &c. in Classical architecture; the term has also come to be applied to a great variety of flat ornaments used in all styles of architecture, to many of which it is extremely inappropriate.

Pax (Lat.), a small tablet, having on it a representation of the Crucifixion, or some other Christian symbol, which was offered to the congregation to be kissed during the celebration of the Mass: it was introduced when the *osculum pacis,* or kiss of peace, was abrogated on account of the confusion which it entailed   It was usually of silver or other metal, with a handle at the back, but was occasionally of other materials; sometimes it was enamelled and set with precious stones.

PARVISE. See *Paradise.*

PASCHAL, a stand or candlestick supporting a candle of very large size used in the early churches at Rome. See illustration under *Ambo.*

PASTORAL STAFF. See *Crozier.*

PATAND, the bottom plate or sill of a partition or screen.

PAVEMENT (Lat. *Pavio* = to beat, the Roman floor being often of earth beaten hard). The word signifies flooring, whether of Roman tesseræ, tiles, or stone.

Pedestal (Gr. *Pous* = a foot, and *stulos* = a column), a substructure frequently placed under columns in Classical architecture. It consists of three divisions: the *Base* or foot, next the ground; the *Dado* or die, forming the main body; and the *Cornice*, or surbase mouldings, at the top.

Pediment (Lat.), the triangular termination used in Classical architecture at the ends of buildings, over porticoes, &c., corresponding to a gable in middle-age architecture: it is much less acute at the top than a gable. Most of the porticoes on the fronts of Greek and Roman buildings support pediments; in Roman work the dressings over doors and windows are sometimes arranged in a similar form, and called by the same name; in debased Roman work pediments of this last-mentioned kind are occasionally circular instead of angular on the top, a form which is also common in Italian architecture. The term is sometimes applied by modern writers to the small gables and triangular decorations over niches, doors, windows, &c., in Gothic architecture.

Pelican, the representation of this bird vulning herself, as expressed heraldically, occurs not unfrequently as a sacred emblem among the ornaments of churches. A beautiful specimen is preserved at Ufford, Suffolk, at the summit of the elaborately carved spire of wood which forms the cover of the font; and another occurs over the font at North Walsham, Norfolk. The lectern of brass was occasionally made in the form of a pelican, instead of that of an eagle, a specimen of which is to be seen in Norwich Cathedral. It was also used as an heraldic device; e.g. in the arms of the founder of Corpus Christi College, Oxford.

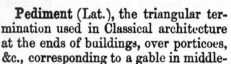

PELE-TOWER. See *Pile-tower*.

PENDANT-POST, is a short post in a mediæval roof-truss, placed against the wall, the lower end resting on a corbel, the upper end fixed to the tie-beam.

PENTASTYLE, a portico of five columns.

Pendant (Lat. *Pendens* = hanging). (1.) A hanging ornament much used in Gothic architecture, particularly in late Perpendicular work, on ceilings, roofs, &c.: on stone vaulting they are frequently made very large, and are generally highly enriched with mouldings and carving; good specimens are to be seen in Henry the Seventh's Chapel, West-

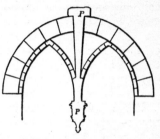

Section of a roof shewing a Pendant.

minster; the Divinity School, Oxford; St. Lawrence, Evesham, &c. In open timber roofs pendants are frequently placed under the ends of the hammer-beams, and in other parts where the construction will allow of them. About the period of the expiration of Gothic architecture, and for some time afterwards, pendants were often used on plaster ceilings, occasionally of considerable size, though usually small. (2.) This name was also formerly used for the *spandrels* very frequently found in Gothic roofs under the ends of the tie-beams, which are sustained at the bottom by corbels projecting from the walls.

Henry the Seventh's Chapel, Westminster, A.D. 1510.

Peristyle (Gr.), a court, square, or cloister, in Greek and Roman buildings, with a colonnade round it; also the colonnade itself surrounding such a space. In mediæval Latin it is called the *Quadriporticus*, and was the usual arrangement in Italy in front of the churches as well as in front of houses. We have no examples remaining in England. The nearest approach is our *Cloister*. [See *Atrium* and *Paradise*.]

Pendentive, the portion of a groined ceiling supported by one pillar or impost, and bounded by the apex of the longitudinal and transverse vaults; in Gothic ceilings of this kind the ribs of the vaults descend from the apex to the impost of each pendentive where they

Pendentive (Gothic).

Pendentive (Byzantine).

become united. Also the portion of a domical vault which descends into the corner of an angular building when a ceiling of this description is placed over a straight-sided area. Pendentives of this kind are common in Byzantine architecture, but not in Gothic.

Penthouse (old form Pentee), an open shed or projection over a door, window, flight of steps, &c., to form a protection against the weather. A double penthouse forms a convenient design for a *Lich-gate.*

Perpendicular Style (Rickman). The last of the styles of Gothic architecture which flourished in this country; it arose gradually from the Decorated during the latter part of the fourteenth century, and continued till the middle of the sixteenth: the name is derived from the arrangement of the tracery, which consists of perpendicular lines, and forms one of its most striking features. At its first appearance the general effect was usually bold, and the mouldings, though not

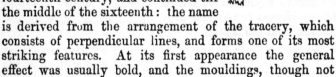

PERCH, (1.) An old name given to a bracket or corbel; (2.) The long wax candles used in churches were also sometimes so called.

PERGENYNG. See *Pargeting.*

PERIBOLUS, a wall built round ancient temples enclosing the whole of the sacred ground.

PERIPTERAL, a form of *Temple,* entirely surrounded with columns.

PERPENDER == Perpent-stone.

equal to the best of the Decorated style, were well defined; the enrichments were effective and ample without
exuberance; and the details delicate without extravagant
minuteness. Subsequently it underwent a gradual debasement; the arches became depressed; the mouldings
impoverished; the ornaments shallow and crowded, and
often coarsely executed;
and the subordinate fea-
tures confused, from
the smallness and com-
plexity of their parts.
A leading character-
istic of the style, and
one which prevails
throughout its con-
tinuance, is the square
arrangement of the
mouldings over the
heads of *doorways,*
creating a spandrel
on each side above
the arch, which is
usually ornamented
with tracery, foliage,
or a shield; the jambs
of doorways have some-

St. Michael's, Oxford, c. 1460.

times niches in them, but are generally moulded, frequently with one or more small shafts, and sometimes
the round mouldings have bases but no capitals. The
perpendicular arrangement of the *window tracery* has been
already alluded to; the same principle is also followed
in panellings. Another peculiarity of this style is the
frequent use of *transoms* crossing the mullions at right
angles, and in large windows these are occasionally repeated several times; bands of quatrefoils and other
similar ornaments are also more frequently employed than
in the earlier styles, and are often carried across the
panellings and vertical lines, creating a rectilinear arrangement, which also pervades most of the subordinate
parts, that gives an air of stiffness which is peculiar.
Panelling is used most abundantly on walls, both inter-

nally and externally, and also on vaulting; some buildings are al-
most entirely
covered with
it, as Henry
the Seventh's
Chapel at
Westminster.
Vaulting of
fan - tracery,
which is gene-
rally charac-
teristic of this
style, is al-
most invari-
ably covered
with panel-
ling.

The arch-
es are either
two - centred
or four - cen-
tred; at the
commence-
ment of the
style of good
elevation, but
subsequently
much flatten-

Yelvertoft, c. 1500.

ed: in small openings ogee arches are very often used;
and a few rare examples of elliptical arches are to be
found. The timber *Roofs* of this style are often made ornamental, having the whole of the framing exposed to view;
many of them are of high pitch, and have a very magnificent effect, the spaces between the timbers being filled with
tracery, and the beams arched, moulded, and ornamented in various ways; and sometimes pendants, figures of
angels, and other carvings, are introduced: the largest
roof of this kind is that of Westminster Hall, erected in
the reign of Richard II. The flatter roofs are sometimes
lined with boards and divided into panels by ribs, or have

the timbers open, and both are frequently enriched with mouldings, carvings, and other ornaments. [Illustrations of this style will be found under the parts of buildings referred to, e.g. *Gateway, Lantern, Niche, Pillar.*]

The Perpendicular style may be said to commence about the middle of the fourteenth century in some parts of England, as at Gloucester and Windsor; but the Decorated and Perpendicular styles overlapped each other for a long period, some districts retaining the older style much longer than others. The following are some of the chief dated examples of the fourteenth century:—

Gloucester Cathedral—Choir and transept, 1350—1370(?).
York Cath.—Choir, 1372—1403.
Warwick—St. Mary's—Choir, 1370—1391.
Lynn, Norfolk—Chapel of St. Nicolas, 1371—1379.
Selby Abbey, Yorkshire, 1375.
Winchester Cathedral—West front, 1360—1366.
Canterbury Cath.—Nave and western transepts, 1378—1411.
Oxford—New Coll., 1380—1386.

Howden, Yorkshire—Chapter-house and tower, 1389—1407.
Saltwood Castle, Kent—Gate-house, 1381—1396.
Gloucester Cathedral—Cloisters, 1381—1412.
Winchester College, 1387—1393.
„ Cathedral—Nave, 1394—1410.
Westminster Hall—Roof, 1397—1399.
Maidstone—College and Church, 1395.

In the fifteenth century the Perpendicular is the general style of England for churches, houses, castles, barns, cottages, and buildings of every kind. It would be tedious to attempt to enumerate the various buildings which we know from records to have been built during that and in the early part of the sixteenth century. The Universities of Oxford and Cambridge owe many of their colleges to this period, and there we find vestiges of the style still lingering when in other places it had been lost. There are many good examples as late as the time of James I., and even Charles I. to A.D. 1640.

Perpent-stone (Fr. *Perpeigne*), a large stone reaching through a wall so as to appear on both sides of it; the same as what is now usually called a *bonder*, bond-stone, or through, except that these are often used in rough-walling, while the term perpent-stone appears to have been applied to squared stones, or ashlar; bonders also do not always reach through a wall. The term is still used in some districts; in Gloucestershire, ashlar thick enough to reach entirely through a wall, and shew a fair face on both sides, is called *Parping ashlar.* This name may perhaps also have been some-times given to a corbel. The term *Perpent-wall* would signify a wall built of perpent ashlar.

Also a pier, buttress, or other support projecting from a wall to sustain a beam, roof, &c. In Lincoln Cathedral the dwarf walls separating the chapels in the transepts are also called perpeyn-walls, although they do not sustain a roof.

Perpeyn-wall, Lincoln Cathedral.

Pew, or Pue (probably from the Dutch). It is un-necessary in a work of this kind to say anything of the modern style of pews, with which most of our churches had been filled; till within the last few years the ugly pues were intro-duced subse-quently to the Reformation, and the use of

Headington, Oxfordshire.

them was considerably promoted by the Puritans. Up to

PERRON, external steps with landings on the first floor.

PIAZZA (Ital.), an open area or square, usually with arcades.

a period some time after the Reformation the naves of
churches, which were occupied by the congregation, were
usually fitted with fixed seats, as they had been from the
fourteenth century or earlier downwards; these seats
varied in height from about two feet and a-half to three
feet, and were partially enclosed at the ends next the passages, sometimes with what are called Bench-ends; sometimes these rose considerably above the wainscoting, and
were terminated with carved finials, or *poppies*, but they
are more frequently ranged with the rest of the work, and
were often straight at the top and finished with the same
capping-moulding; these end enclosures occupied about
the width of the seat, and the remainder of the space was
left entirely open. The partitions sometimes reached down
to the floor, and some-
times only to a little
below the seats; they
were usually perfectly
plain, but the wains-
coting next the cross
passages was generally
ornamented with pan-
elling, tracery, small
buttresses, &c.: op-
posite to the seat at
the back of each divi-
sion, or pew, a board
was frequently fixed,
considerably narrower,
intended to support
the arms upon when
kneeling. This mode
of fitting the naves of
churches was certainly
very general, but it is
difficult to ascertain
when it was first in-

Steeple Aston, c. 1500.

troduced, the great majority of specimens that exist being
of the Perpendicular style. A large proportion of these
are of the time of Henry VII. and VIII., many of them
after the Reformation.　[See also *Standard*.]

Pier (Sax.): (1.) The solid mass between doors, windows, and other openings in buildings; (2.) The support of a bridge, on which the arches rest. (3.) This name is constantly given to the *Pillar* in Norman, and sometimes in Gothic architecture, but not so correctly. Although perhaps the same in their absolute meaning, the word 'pier' is more properly applied to large masses in the construction of a building. The pillar is the support of an arch, and generally partakes of an ornamental character as well as *structural*.

Pilaster (Ital.), a square column or pillar, used in Classical architecture, sometimes disengaged, but generally attached to a wall, from which it projects a third, fourth, fifth, or sixth of its breadth. The Greeks formed their pilasters of the same breadth at the top and bottom, and gave them capitals and bases different from those of the orders with which they were associated; the Romans usually gave them the same capitals and bases as the columns, and often made them diminish upwards in the same manner. [See *Antæ*.]

Pillar (Fr.): the column supporting the arch. In the *Norman* style the pillars are generally massive, and are frequently circular, with capitals either of the same form, or square; they are sometimes ornamented with channels, or *flutes*, in various forms, spiral, zigzag, reticulated, &c. In plain buildings a square or rectangular pillar, or pier, is occasionally found; a polygonal, usually octagonal, pillar is also used, especially towards the end of the style, and is generally of lighter proportions than most of the other kinds. But, besides these, clustered or compound pillars are extremely numerous and much varied; the simplest of them consists of a square with one or more rectangular recesses at each corner, but a more common form is one resembling these, with

St. Peter's, Northampton,
c. 1160.

a small circular shaft in each of the recesses, and a larger one, semicircular, on two (or on each) of the faces: most

of the compound pillars partake of this arrangement, though other varieties are by no means rare.

In the *Early English* style, plain circular or octagonal shafts are frequently used, especially in plain buildings, but many other, and more complicated kinds of pillars are employed; the commonest of these consists of a large central shaft, which is generally circular, with smaller shafts (usually four) round it; these are frequently made of a finer material than the rest, and polished, but they are often worked in courses with the central part of the pillar, and are sometimes filleted; in this style the pillars are very constantly banded.

In the *Decorated* style the general form of clus-

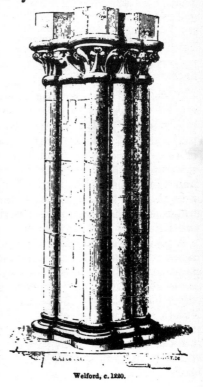

Welford, c. 1220.

tered pillars changes from a circular to a lozenge-shaped
arrangement, or to a square placed diagonally, but many

other varieties
are at times to
be met with;
they some-
times consist
of small shafts
surrounding a
larger one, and
are sometimes

moulded; the small shafts and
some of the mouldings are often
filleted; plain octagonal pillars
are also very frequently employed
in our vill-
age churches:
towards the
end of this
style a pillar
consisting of
four small
shafts sepa-
rated by a
deep hollow
and two fil-
lets is com-

mon, as it is also in the Perpendicular
style, but in that style the hollows
are usually shallower, and the disposition of the fillets is different.

A plain octagonal pillar continues
in use throughout the *Perpendicular*
style, though it is not so frequent as
at earlier periods, and its sides are
occasionally slightly hollowed. In
Decorated work a few of the mouldings of the piers occasionally run up
into the arches and form part of the
archivolt, as at Bristol Cathedral, but
in Perpendicular buildings this ar-

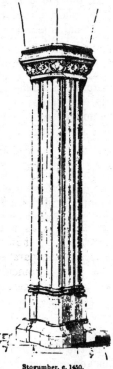

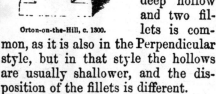

Stogumber, c. 1450.

rangement is much more common, and in some cases the whole of the mouldings of the pillars are continued in the arches without any capital or impost between them : the forms are various, but in general arrangement they usually partake of a square placed diagonally ; sometimes however they are contracted in breadth so as to become narrower between the archways (from east to west) than in the opposite direction : the small shafts attached to the pillars in this style are usually plain circles, but are occasionally filleted, and in some instances are hollow-sided polygons.

Pile-tower, or Pele-tower, or more correctly *Pele* only : this term is almost peculiar to the northern parts of the kingdom ; it seems to have signified a small *Donjon,* or fortified dwelling, or tower, capable of being defended against any sudden marauding expedition. Church towers appear to have been sometimes used for the same purpose. Some of these towers, which were used for habitations, have had additions made to them subsequent to their erection : Heifer-haw tower, near Alnwick, and a tower in Corbridge churchyard, were probably pele-towers only. Pile, a fortress, occurs only in names of places in the Isle of Man, Lancashire, and the neighbouring parts, but it is an archaic term not exclusively northern.

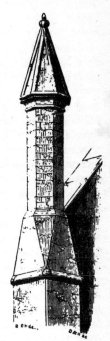

Battle Church, c. 1250.

Pinnacle (Low Lat.), a small turret or tall ornament, usually tapering towards the top, much used in Gothic architecture as a termination to buttresses, &c. ; it is also very frequently employed in parapets, especially at the angles, and sometimes on the tops of gables and other elevated situations : it consists of a shaft and top ; this last is generally in the form of a small spire, surmounted with a finial, and often crocketed at the angles, and is then sometimes called a finial.

Pinnacles are not used in the *Norman* style, though
there exist a few small turrets, of late
date, with pointed terminations, which appear to be their prototypes, as at the west
end of Rochester Cathedral, and the north
transept of St. Etienne at Caen.

In the *Early English* style they are not
very abundant; they are found circular,
octagonal, or square; some are perfectly
plain, as at the east end of Battle Church,
Sussex; others are surrounded with small
shafts, as at Peterborough and Wells; and
in some instances the tops are crocketed.
Towards the latter part of this style the
system of surmounting each face of the
shaft with a small pediment was introduced, and about the same period the shafts
began to be occasionally made of open-
work, so as to form niches for statues.

Decorated pinnacles are very numerous;
they have the shafts sometimes formed into
niches, and sometimes panelled or quite
plain, and each of the sides almost invariably terminates in a pediment; the
tops are generally crocketed, and always

Peterborough Cathedral,
A.D. 1238.

have finials on the points: in form they are most usually
square, but are sometimes octagonal, and in
a few instances hexagonal and pentagonal;
occasionally, in this style, square pinnacles
are placed diagonally. [See the illustration
from Caythorpe, under *Spire*.]

In the *Perpendicular* style they do not in
general differ much from those of the Decorated; polygonal forms are not very frequently found, and square pinnacles are very
much oftener placed diagonally on buttresses,
&c.; they are also in rich buildings, abundantly used on the offsets of buttresses, as well
as at the tops: instead of the small pediments
over the sides of the shaft, it is sometimes
finished with a complete moulded cornice, or

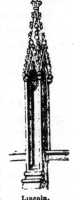

Lincoln.

capping, out of which the top of the pinnacle rises, and
sometimes in the place of a top of this kind the figure
of an animal holding a vane, or some other device, is
used: there are a few examples of pinnacles in this style
with ogee-shaped tops. In the fine Perpendicular towers
the pinnacles are often the most striking feature. Examples are seen on Merton and Magdalen towers in Oxford,
and many of the towers in Somersetshire.

This term is sometimes applied to turrets, and William
of Worcester uses it for a spire.

Piscina (Lat. = a reservoir of water), originally the
reservoir and filter connected with the aqueducts of
Rome, but long applied to a water-drain formerly placed
near to an altar in a church; this consists of a shallow
stone basin, or sink, with a hole in the bottom, to carry

Crowmarsh, c. 1150.   Warmington, c. 1220.

off whatever is poured into it; it is fixed at a convenient
height above the floor, and was used to receive the water
in which the priest washed his hands, as well as that with
which the chalice was rinsed at the time of the celebration
of the mass; it is placed within a niche, though the basin
very frequently projects before the face of the wall, and is

sometimes supported on a shaft rising from the floor; in many instances, particularly in those of Early English and early Decorated date, there are two basins, and drains, and occasionally three; within the niche there is also often found a wooden or stone shelf, which served the purpose of a *credence-table*, to receive certain of the sacred vessels that were used in the service of the mass, previous to their being required at the altar; sometimes there is room at the bottom of the niche for these to stand at the side of the basin: in this country the piscina is almost invariably on the south side of the altar, and usually in the south wall (though sometimes in the eastern), but in Normandy it is not uncommon to find it on the north side, when the situation of the altar is such as to render that more convenient than the south. No piscinas are known to exist in this country of earlier date than the middle of the twelfth century, and of that age they are extremely rare: of the thirteenth and succeeding cen-

Cumnor, c. 1350.   Tackley, c. 1450.

turies, down to the period of the Reformation, they are

very abundant, and are to be found (or at least traces of them) in the chancel of most churches that have not been rebuilt, and very frequently at the eastern ends of the aisles of the nave also : their forms and decorations are very various, but the character of the architectural features will always decide their date.

Pix, Pyx (Lat. *Pyxis*), the ornamented box, or casket, in which the consecrated Host is preserved in the Roman Catholic Church for the use of the sick, or the wafers previously to consecration ; it was made of the most costly materials, and was placed upon the altar under a tabernacle, or canopy, within which it was sometimes suspended, and sometimes raised upon a stand or foot. In form it was frequently circular, and closed with a cover ; occasionally, when suspended, it was in the form of a dove.

Ashmolean Museum, Oxford.

Plate, Platt, a general term applied to almost all horizontal timbers which are laid upon walls, &c., to receive other timber-work : that at the top of a building immediately under the roof, is a *wall-plate;* those also which receive the ends of the joists of the floors above the ground-floor are called by the same name. *Plate tracery* is the term applied to that kind of solid tracery which appears as if formed by piercing a flat surface with ornamental patterns. It is used in contradistinction to *Bar* tracery. [See *Tracery.*]

Plinth (Gr.), a square member forming the lower division of the base of a column, &c.: also the plain projecting face at the bottom of a wall immediately above

PITCH of a roof, the slope of a roof. See *Gable.*

PLANCEER, the soffit or underside of the corona of a cornice in Gothic architecture.

PLAT-BAND, (1.) a flat fascia, band, or string whose projection is less than its breadth ; (2.) the lintel of a door is sometimes so called.

the ground. In Classical buildings the plinth is sometimes divided into two or more gradations, which project slightly before each other in succession towards the ground, the tops being either perfectly flat or only sloped sufficiently to prevent the lodgment of wet; in Gothic buildings the plinth is occasionally divided into two stages, the tops of which are either splayed or finished with a hollow moulding, or covered by the base-mouldings.

Polychrome, the name applied to the colouring of walls and architectural ornaments. There is no doubt that all mediæval buildings were intended to be coloured, and the colour formed part of the original design, which in most cases has been lost from the practice of whitewashing them over, which prevailed in the seventeenth and eighteenth centuries. Whenever this whitewash is carefully removed the original colouring appears; but unfortunately, in getting off the whitewash the original thin coat of fine plaster which formed the *gesso* or ground to paint upon is removed along with it. In some instances the stone itself seems to have been painted upon, and the colour mixed with wax varnish, which is impervious to moisture; and though these have been whitewashed over again and again, the colouring still re-appears. In some cases also the colouring was executed while the plaster was wet. in what is called fresco painting, and thus becomes part of the plaster itself, and can only be destroyed by destroying the plaster. There is the same change of style in the colouring as in the carved ornament, and a treatise on the succession of styles in mediæval colouring is still a desideratum. [See *Wall-painting.*]

Pomel (Lat. *Pomellum*, from *Pomum*=an apple), a knob, knot, or boss; the term is used in reference to the finial, or ornament on the top of a conical or dome-shaped roof of a turret, the summit of a pavilion, &c., and is especially applied to articles of plate and jewellery. It also denotes generally any ornament of globular form.

PODIUM, (1.) a continuous basement, or *Pedestal*, q.v.; (2.) a dwarf wall used as a substructure for the columns of a temple.

POLE-PLATE, a small kind of wall-plate used in modern *Roofs* to receive the feet of the rafters.

Poppie, Poppy, Poppy-head, (from Fr. *Poupé* = a doll, or Lat. *Puppis* = the "poop" of a ship,) an elevated ornament often used on the tops of the upright ends, or elbows, which terminate seats, &c., in churches: they are sometimes merely cut into plain fleurs-de-lis or other simple forms, with the edges chamfered or slightly hollowed, but are frequently carved with leaves, like finials, and in rich work are sculptured into animals and figures, and are often extremely elaborate. No examples are known to exist of earlier date than the Decorated style, and but few so early; of Perpendicular date specimens are to be found in very many churches, especially in the cathedrals and old abbey churches. [See *Stall* and *Standard.*]

Kidlington, c. 1450.

Porch (Lat. *Porticus*), an external erection protecting the doorway of a large building. (Compare with the Portico of the Palladian style, which was carried round the whole of the exterior of the building.) In some instances the lower story of the tower of a church forms the porch, as at Cranbrook, Kent, and in several instances in Somerset. Porches appear originally not to have had close doors, but there are some wooden ones of Decorated date which have marks about the entrances seeming to indicate that they have been fitted with moveable barricades, sufficient to keep out cattle. Porches were used at an early period, and many fine examples of Norman date exist, as at Southwell, Nottinghamshire; Sherborne, Dorsetshire; Malmesbury, Wiltshire; Castle Ashby, Northamptonshire, &c.: these are of stone and rectangular, with a large open doorway in front, and the sides either entirely closed or pierced only with a small window: that at Southwell has a small room over it, a feature which is not very common in this style. Early English porches also remain in considerable numbers, as at the cathedrals of Wells, Salisbury, and Lincoln; St. Alban's Abbey; and the churches of Great Tew and Middleton Stoney, Oxfordshire; Barnack,

Norman Porch, Great Addington, c. 1180.

Northamptonshire, &c.   At Chevington, Suffolk, is a wooden porch of Early English date, but much impaired by modern work. In the Decorated style wooden porches are not unfrequently found; they are of one story only in height, sometimes entirely enclosed at the sides, and sometimes with about the upper half of their height formed of open screen-work; the gables have barge-boards, which are almost always feathered, and more or less ornamented: good specimens remain at Warbling-ton, Hampshire; Horsemonden and Brookland, Kent; Aldham, Essex; Hascombe, Surrey; Northfield, Worces-tershire, &c. Stone porches of this date have, not un-usually, a room over them, as they have also in the

Early English Porch, Skelton, Yorkshire, c. 1250.

Decorated Porch, Aldham, Essex, c. 1350.

Perpendicular style. [See next Article.] Of this last-mentioned style there are many wooden porches, which differ but little from those of the preceding, except that the upper half of the sides is almost always formed of open screen-work; examples remain at Halden, Kent; Albury, Surrey, &c.

It is common to find porches of all ages considerably

West Porch, Woodstock, Oxfordshire.

ornamented; those of the Norman style, and perhaps also the Early English, have the decorations principally on the inside and about the doorway; those of later date are often as much enriched externally as internally, and sometimes more so. Some porches have the roofs entirely formed of stone, both externally and internally, as at Barnack, Northamptonshire; St. Mary's, Nottingham; Strelly, Nottinghamshire; All Saints, Stamford; Arundel, Sussex, &c.

The foregoing observations apply to church porches, but some domestic buildings are also provided with them, of which a fine example, of Decorated date, exists attached to the hall of the Archbishop of Canterbury's palace at Mayfield, Sussex: they have sometimes rooms over them, and are carried up as many stories in height as the rest

of the building, and this projection is called the porch-
tower; in houses of the time of Elizabeth the porch is
almost always carried up to the main roof of the building.
Small chapels attached to churches are sometimes called
porches. [See *Galilee*.]

Porch, Rooms over the. Over very many porches, dating
from the twelfth up to the fifteenth century, a chamber
has been made, and in some few instances even two chambers, one above the other.

Very many theories have been held as to the original
purposes of these chambers, but the truth is, that not
only were there often different reasons for their erection,
but that many have been at subsequent times applied
to different uses. One to which they were more frequently applied than others, was for the preservation of
the books and documents of the church, and of the parish
also, providing as they did, a place of safe-keeping, safer
from fire or from destruction, than in domestic buildings.
Many churches also, and parishes, had libraries of books
left for their use, just as all cathedrals have now libraries;
and when books were scarce, such a gift was very valuable.

From the account-books of the parish, long kept there,
it was sometimes called the Treasury, as at Hawkhurst,
Kent; at Wimborne, the muniment-room. At Bodmin,
where there are two chambers, one above the other, the
upper was used as the record-room, and the lower for
the meetings of the Corporation. And at Great Malvern
it was long a depository for wills. In very many, *chests*
are still found, and in some an aumbry, or cupboard, for
keeping, no doubt, especially valuable property. At
Chelmsford, it was always used as the library for the
books granted to the church; while at Plympton, Devon,
it has been only recently fitted up as a parish library,
and books placed there: at Loddewell, it is used as the
Vicar's study.

The presence in a large number of them of a fireplace,
has led many to suppose them to be sleeping or dwelling-
rooms, but this does not necessarily follow, since where
books and documents were kept, it would be found that
ta times a fire was necessary to prevent decay from damp.
That many also have one of the windows opening into

the church, has also led to the theory of the room being for the use of recluses; and to another, that they were used for watching chambers.

In some few cases there are evidences of there having been an altar, with the piscina, &c., as at Fotheringhay. This would imply that some chantry was founded here, and it was chosen by the founder as a convenient place for the altar.

Access to the room over the porch is as often from the church, as from the porch itself, and sometimes from outside.

Portcullis (Fr. *Porte-coulisse*), a door sliding up and down in *coulisses* or gutters, consisting of a massive frame, or grating, of iron or wooden bars, used by the ancient Romans, as at Pompeii and in the walls of Rome, and continued in the Middle Ages to defend gateways. It was made to slide up and down in a groove formed for the purpose in each

Portcullis.

jamb, and was usually kept suspended above the gateway, but was let down whenever an attack was apprehended: the principal entrances of almost all fortresses were provided with several portcullises in succession, at some little distance apart: the old grooves for them are found in buildings of the Norman style. [See *Killesse.*]

The portcullis will be found constantly carved as an ornament upon buildings of the time of Henry VII. and Henry VIII., it being one of the Tudor badges.

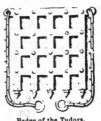

Badge of the Tudors.

PORTICUS, in Classical architecture = Peristyle. Used by Bede and other early writers in the sense probably of what we should best term apsidal chapels. Gervase of Canterbury uses the word evidently for such (see Willis, p. 39), though in some instances the word may be translated the *Aisle.*

POST, an upright timber in a building; e.g. *kingposts* or *queen posts*, [see *Roof*]: the vertical timbers in the walls of wooden houses, with the intervals filled with plastering, were sometimes

Portico, a range of columns in the front of a building: when of four columns it is called *tetrastyle;* when of six, *hexastyle;* of eight, *octostyle;* of ten, *decastyle*. The Latin *porticus,* however, from which the Italian *portico* and the French *portique,* as well as the English porch is derived, (e.g. Solomon's Porch, Acts iii. 11), has a more extended signification in all these languages; comprehending, in fact, every kind of covered ambulatory of which one or more sides are opened to the air, by rows of columns or of arches, whether it be attached to the front of a building or to its sides, or to the inner sides of an area, so as to form a cloister. [See *Temple.*]

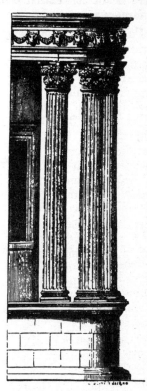

Temple of Vesta, Tivoli.

Presbytery (Gr., the place of the elders or priests), the part of a church in which the high altar is placed; it forms the eastern termination of the choir, above which it is raised by several steps, and is occupied exclusively by those who minister in the services of the altar. The name is not unfrequently used for the space behind the high altar, as at Lincoln, and in a more extended sense to include the whole of the choir. [See *Choir,* and plan under *Basilica.*]

---

called *post and pane.* [See *Pane.*]

POSTERN, a private or concealed entrance behind or outside of a castle, town, or monastery.

POYNTELL, paving formed into small lozenges or squares laid diagonally.

PRECEPTORY, a subordinate establishment of the Knights Templars, governed by a preceptor.

Priory, a monastery governed by a prior. Alien priories were small conventual establishments, or cells, belonging to foreign monasteries.

Pulpit (Lat.), an elevated stage or desk from which sermons are delivered. They were formerly placed not only in churches but also in the Refectories of monasteries, as at Beverley, Shrewsbury, Chester, Beaulieu, &c.; in the Cloisters, as at St. Dié, in France; and occasionally in public thoroughfares, as on the north side of the church of Notre Dame, at St. Lô in Normandy, and in the outer court of Magdalen College, Oxford. In churches the pulpits were formerly always placed in the nave, attached to a wall, pillar, or screen, and the ecclesiastics and others who occupied the choir during the mass removed into the nave to hear the sermon: this custom

Beaulieu, Hants.

was long continued at Ely, and has of late been revived at Lincoln, and in some other cathedrals. Many ancient

PRICK-POSTS, an obsolete term for the queen-posts in a roof.

PRINT, a plaster cast of a flat ornament.

PRISMATORIES occurs in one contract = Sedilia, but probably an error of copyist.

PROCESSION-PATH, or Procession, the passage or way round and behind the presbytery in a large church.

PRONAOS, the vestibule or portico in front of the cell of a temple.

PROPYLEUM, a portico, court, or vestibule before the gates of a building.

PROTHESIS, a credence-table.

pulpits exist in our churches, particularly in Somerset-shire, and the adjoining counties: some are of wood, others of stone. The wooden ones are usually polygonal, with the panels enriched with featherings, tracery, and other architectural ornaments, and raised upon a single stem; few, if any, of these are earlier than the Perpendicular style: an example exists in the church of Kenton, Devonshire, which retains some of its original painting. Stone pulpits are sometimes met with of Decorated date, as at Beaulieu, Hampshire, already noticed, but by far the greater number are of Perpendicular work. In design they are very various, but their plan is usually polygonal, and in many cases they are formed like niches in the wall, with projecting fronts, and are approached by concealed stairs (especially in the case of those in Refectories), in others the steps are exposed to view; some of them are very highly enriched with architectural ornaments and sculpture, and some are nearly plain. It is not unusual to find ancient pulpits, both of wood and

Fotheringhay, Northamptonshire.

PROPYLON (Gr.), a gateway before an Egyptian temple.

PROSTYLE, a portico in which the columns stand out quite free from the wall to which it is attached.

PSEUDO-DIPTERAL, a temple whose general plan is dipteral, but the inner range of columns omitted. See *Temple.*

PTEROMA, a space between the walls of the cell of a temple and the column of the peristyle.

PTEROMATA (Gr.),= Side-walls.

stone, surmounted with ornamental canopies. Numerous wooden pulpits were erected in this country soon after the Reformation in the churches not previously provided with them, in accordance with the injunctions of Edward VI. and subsequent orders; a number of these still remain: some are considerably ornamented, and have a rich effect, although the majority are poor. Most of these, especially those of Jacobean work, have flat testoons over them, but some have elevated canopies; a remarkably fine specimen of this kind of pulpit remains at Castle Ashby, Northamptonshire. Another example occurs at Eddlesborough, an engraving of which is given under *Tabernacle*. The pulpits in the large churches on the Continent are often of very considerable size, capable of holding more than one person, and most elaborately enriched with a profusion of architectural and sculptured ornaments; a fine specimen, of Flamboyant date, exists in the cathedral at Strasburg.

Purlins, Perlings, the horizontal pieces of timber which rest on the principals, or main rafters, of a roof, and support the common rafters. In some districts purlins are called *ribs*, and rafters *spars*. [See *Roof.*]

Putlog-holes, small holes left in walls for the use of the workmen in erecting their scaffolding: the cross pieces of the scaffold, on which the planks forming the floor are laid, are called "putlogs." These holes are found in walls of almost every age: they are common in Roman work; Vitruvius calls them "columbaria," from their resemblance to pigeon-holes. [See also *Hourds.*]

Quadrangle (Lat. *quatuor* = four, *angulus* = a corner), a square or court surrounded by buildings: the buildings of monasteries were generally arranged in quadrangles, as, for instance, the cloisters; colleges and large houses are also often disposed in the same way.

PUNCHEONS, small upright timbers in wooden partitions, now called studs or quarters.

PURFLED-WORK (Fr. *Pour-filer* = to embroider), signifies any delicately sculptured tracery, &c.

PYCNOSTYLE, an arrangement of columns in Greek and Roman architecture in which the intercolumniations are equal to one diameter and a half of the lower part of the shaft.

PYNUN - TABLE, probably the coping-stones of a gable, from the French *Pignon*.

PYX. See *Pix.*

QUADRIPORTICUS. See *Peristyle.*

QUATREFOIL. See *Foil.*

Quarrel (Fr. *Carré* = square): (1.) A stone quarry; (2.) A diamond-shaped pane of glass, or a square one placed diagonally; (3.) A small piercing in the tracery of a window; also, (4.) A small square, or diamond-shaped paving-brick or stone.

Quarter (Cater), a square panel, or a piercing in tracery, divided by cusps or featherings into four leaves (= *Quatrefoil*). Bands of small quatrefoils are much used as ornaments in the Perpendicular style, and sometimes in the Decorated; when placed diagonally they appear formerly to have been called "cross-quarters." [See for illustrations *Foil*, also under *Band, Font, Panel, Parapet.*] (2.) The pieces of timber used in the construction of wooden partitions are called quarters.

Quirk, a small acute channel or recess, much used between mouldings. In Grecian architecture ovolos and ogees are usually quirked at the top, and sometimes in Roman; in Gothic architecture quirks are abundantly used between mouldings. [See examples under *Ogee* and *Ovolo;* also see *Column.*]

Quoin (Fr. *Coin*), the external angle of a building. In middle-age architecture, when the walls are of rough stonework, or of flints, the quoins are most commonly of ashlar: brick buildings also frequently have the quoins formed in the same manner; and occasionally they are plastered in imitation of stonework, as at Eastbury House, Essex. The name is sometimes used for ashlar-stones with which the quoins are built; and it appears formerly to have also signified vertical angular projections formed on the face of a wall for ornament.

Rafters (Saxon), the inclined timbers forming the sides of a roof, which meet in an angle at the top, and on which the laths or boards are fixed to carry the external covering. [See *Roof.*]

QUEEN-POST. See *Roof.*

QUIRE, Quier, = *Choir.*

RABBIT, corruption of *Rebate.*

RAILS, horizontal pieces of timber between the panels of wainscoting, doors, &c. The upright pieces of such frames are termed *Styles.* Rails are also those pieces which lie over and under balusters in balconies, or extend from post to post in fences.

RAMPARTS. See *Step.* This name is also given to a parapet, the passage behind the parapet, and to the walls of a town.

Rag-stone, or Rag-work, buildings of rough stone in thin layers resembling

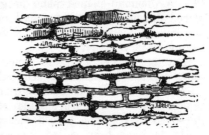

tiles. It is found only in certain districts, depending entirely on the nature of the materials. Some kinds of stone split up naturally or easily into thin layers, which are readily broken to the size required. These thin stones are usually laid flat, with a considerable thickness of mortar between them sometimes, in herring-bone fashion. [See *Herring-bone* and *Rubble.*] This kind of masonry is frequently plastered and rough-cast: but in some counties neatly pointed with large joints, and looking very well: in rubble-work the stones are more irregular both in size and shape, and are sometimes larger.

Rear-vault, the small vault which is interposed between the tracery or glass of a window, and the inner face of the

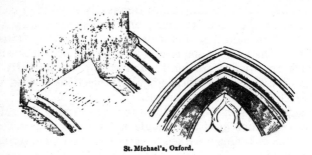

St. Michael's, Oxford.

wall. It is only employed when the wall is thick, and the glass placed nearer to the outer face of the wall than to the inner; and it is usually bounded on the inside by a rib, which either abuts against the splay of the jambs, or else rests upon corbels or shafts fixed against the inner edges of the jambs.

Rebate (Fr. *Rebattre*), a rectangular recess or groove cut longitudinally in a piece of timber, to receive the edge of a plank, or other work required to fit into it. The notch or recess  in a door-post, into which the door fits, is a rebate; boarding is rebated together when the edges are worked in this manner. Stones fitted together in the same way are said to be *joggled*.

Refectory (Lat.), the dining-hall, or fratery, of a convent, college, &c.: the internal arrangements and fittings were very similar to those of the ordinary domestic halls, except that it was usually provided with a raised desk or pulpit, from which, on some occasions, one of the inmates of the establishment read to the others during meal-time.

Reliquary (Lat.), a small chest, box, or casket, to contain reliques. Depositories of this kind were very common in our churches previous to the Reformation; they were made of wood, iron, or other metals, and occasionally of stone; they were always more or less ornamented, frequently with arcades and other architectural ornaments, and sometimes were covered with the most costly embellishments. [See *Shrine*.]

Renaissance (Fr.), the name employed to describe the revival of Classical details in the French Gothic styles. It corresponds, in point of date, to the Elizabethan and Jacobean styles in England, though it commenced rather earlier abroad than in this country.

RATCHEMENTS of a herse, a kind of flying buttresses which spring from the corner principals and meet against the central or chief principal.

RECESSED ARCH means an arch divided into two or more portions or orders, receding one behind the other.

REGALS. See *Organ*.

REGLET (Lat. *Regula*=a rule), a flat narrow moulding employed to separate panels or other members.

REGRATING or skinning, among masons, is taking off the outer surface of an old hewn stone with the hammer and ripe in order to whiten and make it look fresh again.

RELIEVING ARCH. See *Discharging Arch*.

RELIEVO, RELIEF, the projection given to carved work. See *Bas-relief*.

Reredos (written also Lardos, from Fr. *L'Arrière-dos*), the wall or screen at the back of an altar, seat, &c.; it was usually ornamented with panelling, &c., especially behind an altar, and sometimes was enriched with a profusion of niches, buttresses, pinnacles, statues, and other decorations, which were often painted with brilliant colours; reredosses of this kind not unfrequently extended across the whole breadth of the church, and were sometimes carried up nearly to the ceiling, as at St. Alban's Abbey, Durham Cathedral, Gloucester Cathedral, St. Saviour's Church, Southwark; Christ Church, Hampshire, &c. In village churches they were generally simple, and appear very frequently to have had no ornaments formed in the wall, though sometimes corbels or niches were provided to carry images, and sometimes that part of the wall immediately over the altar was

Reredos of Altar, Enstone, c. 1420.

panelled; remains of these, more or less injured, are to be found in many churches, particularly at the east ends of aisles, where chantry-altars have stood, as at St. Michael's, Oxford, &c.; and against the east wall of transepts, as in St. Cuthbert's, Wells. It was not unusual to decorate the wall at the back of an altar with panellings, &c., in wood, or with embroidered hangings of tapestry-work, to which the name of reredos was given; it was also applied to the screen between the nave and choir of a church.

Ressaunt (probably Fr. *Ressentir*), an old English term for an ogee-moulding. It was also applied to other architectural members that had the inflected outline of this moulding. It is a purely technical word, and seldom used.

Ressaunt, Redcliffe Church, Bristol.

Respond, a half-pillar or pier, in middle-age architecture, attached to a wall to support an arch, &c. They are very frequently used by themselves, as at the sides of the entrances of chancels, &c., and are also generally employed at the terminations of ranges of pillars, such as those between the body and aisles of churches. In these last-mentioned situations they usually correspond in general form with the pillars, when of the same date; but it often happens they belong to work of another period. The name occurs frequently in mediæval contracts, and may have its origin in the notion of the two pilasters responding to each other: thus the breadth of the nave of Eton College Chapel "between the *responders*" was directed by the will of King Henry VI. to be thirty-two feet; or else that the shaft 'responds to,' i.e., 'meets' the arch.

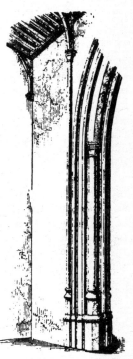

Respond, Fotheringay, Northants.

Reticulated Work (Lat. *Opus reticulatum* = net-work), masonry constructed with small diamond-shaped stones, or square stones placed diagonally. In the city of Rome this mode of decorating the surface of a wall is generally characteristic of the period of the Early Empire; it was frequently imitated in Romanesque work, especially in the tympanum of a doorway in Norman work.

Return, the terminations of the dripstone or hood-mould of a window or door. Several examples will be found under *Dripstone*. The term is also sometimes applied to the seats and desks which are set against the screen at the west end of a choir.

Rib, a projecting band on a ceiling, &c. In middle-age architecture ribs are very extensively employed to ornament ceilings, both flat and vaulted; more especially the latter, when groined. In the earliest *Norman* vaulting the ribs generally consist of mere flat bands crossing the vault at right

Oxford Cathedral, c. 1180.

angles, the groins as well as the apex being left perfectly plain. As the style advances the ribs become moulded, and are also applied to the groins, as in Oxford Cathedral, and are sometimes enriched with zigzags and other ornaments peculiar to the style, with carved bosses at the intersections, as in the churches of Iffley, Oxfordshire, and Elkstone, Gloucestershire.

In *Early English* vaulting, and that of all subsequent periods, the groins are invariably covered by ribs, and the intersections are generally ornamented with bosses or other decorations, as is the case in the chapter-house at Oxford. [See illustration under *Boss*.] In the Early English style it is

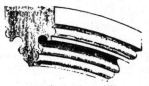

Westminster Abbey, c. 1220.

REREDOS. Sometimes used for the open fireplace in halls, &c.

RETABLE. See *Table*.

REVEAL (Lat. *Revello*), the side of an opening for a window, doorway, &c., between the framework and the outer surface of the wall.

REVESTRY = vestry.

RISER, or RAISER. See *Step*.

ROMAN ORDER, a name given sometimes to the Composite order.

ROUNDEL, (1) in Classical architecture same as *Astragal;* (2) in armour. See illustrations to *Brass*.

seldom that more ribs are used than those which cross the
vault at right angles (cross-springers) and the (diagonal)
ribs upon the groins, with sometimes one at the apex.
[See illustration from Westminster Abbey, under *Vault*.]

In the *Decorated* style additional ribs are introduced
between the diagonal and cross-springers, following the
curve of the vault, and frequently also in other parts,
running in different direc-
tions, and uniting the whole
into a kind of net-work, as
at Tewkesbury Abbey, Gloucestershire : the apex of the
vault is almost invariably
occupied by a rib, which is
often slightly curved up-
wards between the bosses.
When they are numerous

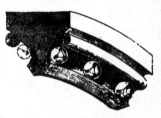

Gloucester Cathedral, c. 1320.

it is not unusual to find that the more important ribs
are of larger size than the
others. In this style the
ribs are sometimes orna-
mented with the characteristic ornament, the *Ball-
flower*, as in Gloucester Cathedral.

In ordinary *Perpendicu-
lar* vaulting, ribs are applied much in the same
way as in the preceding
style, but they are some-
times employed in greater
profusion and in more complicated arrangements, by
which the effect is by no
means always improved, as
at St. Mary Redcliffe Church,
Bristol. Occasionally the
mouldings are made to in-
tersect each other. In *fan-
tracery* vaulting the ribs
radiate from the springing

Thornton Abbey, Lincolnshire, c. 1420.

of each pendentive, and generally become multiplied as they rise upwards, so that the whole surface is covered with tracery, which is usually enriched with featherings and other decorations.

Divinity School, Oxford, A. D. 1480.

Many churches, and some other ancient buildings, have raised ceilings, of wood or plaster, formed on the undersides of the timbers of the roof; a few of these, which are as old as the Decorated and Early English styles, are sparingly ornamented with small ribs; there is generally one along the top and others crossing it at considerable intervals: in some instances the ribs are more numerous in both directions, so as to divide the surface into rectangular compartments or panels.

In the Perpendicular style ceilings of this kind are divided into squares by small ribs with bosses, shields, or flowers, at the intersections; flat ceilings also, which are common in this style, are frequently divided into squares, and sometimes into other patterns, by moulded ribs. In

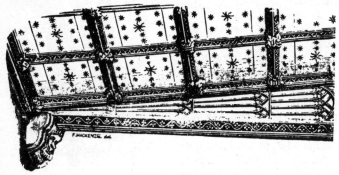

Wymington, Bedfordshire.

the time of Queen Elizabeth and James I., ribs were even used on plaster ceilings, and were often arranged with considerable intricacy.

Ridge, the upper angle of a roof. It has usually though by no means always, a piece of timber running along it, called the *ridge - piece*, upon which the upper ends of the rafters rest: the tiles with which it is covered are called *ridge-tiles;* these are

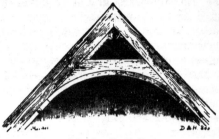

Ridge-piece, Llan Tysilio.

sometimes made ornamental, good instances of which are found at Great Malvern and Lincoln. [See *Crest-tiles*.] Not unfrequently the ridge along the roof, when covered with lead, was made ornamental.

Roll-moulding. This term has been popularly, but somewhat vaguely, given to a moulding much used in Decorated and late Early English work, especially in strings and dripstones. The varieties of such mouldings are numerous, some of them bearing resemblance to a roll of parchment, others are very different. Where the square fillet is more decidedly marked, it has been called "The Roll and Fillet Moulding." It appears to have become confused with the *Scroll-moulding,* so called from resemblance to a scroll of parchment with the edge overlapping. The name of

Roll and Fillet.

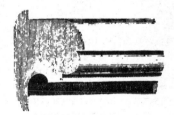

String, Dorchester, Oxfordshire.

Roll-moulding also is often applied to the common *Round* or *Bowtell.*

Roman Architecture. Before the conquest of Greece the Romans were gradually developing an architecture of their own, quite distinct from what is now usually called by that name, which is a variation of the Greek style, adopted after the conquest of Greece, when the superior civilization of the conquered race had great influence on the conquerors. In the time of the kings of Rome, the style of architecture was of the same rude and massive character as that of other nations at the same period, not only in the cities of the Latins, such as Tusculum, or the Sabines as at Varia, or the Etrurians as at Fiesole, Volterra, Perugia, and many others; but also in distant countries, as in Palestine at Jerusalem, and in Africa at Tunis, where we see the same construction of large quadrangular blocks with wide joints, similar to what we have in Rome in the walls of Roma Quadrata, and on the other hills; and of the time of the later kings in the Capitolium, containing the Ærarium, Tabularium, &c., of which we have considerable remains. In this venerable building we have also a very early example of the use of the *Arch* in a porticus, or arcade, on the western side. The only other building of any importance of the time of the Republic is the Emporium of Commerce near the Port. Here we have arcades as a leading feature, and the face of the wall is of the kind called by Vitruvius "Opus incertum," which preceded the "Opus reticulatum" of Sylla and the early emperors; but there are no columns here. The rude Tuscan or Etruscan columns in front of the Tabularium are, however, quite as early as the Emporium, the exact date of which is not recorded, but it is mentioned about two centuries before the Christian era. This example of the use of the Arch at so early a period has not been observed elsewhere. The vaults of the early Etruscan tombs are cut out of the rock, not built; but they may have given the idea of the arch, though they are sometimes cut in the form of timbers, as at Orvieto and Veii.

The style usually called Roman architecture differs considerably from Grecian, both in general aspect and in the details; it also embraces two additional orders, the

Tuscan and Composite, which were unknown to the Greeks. The mouldings are rounder and often more prominent; the enrichments both in design and execution are bolder, and are frequently used in greater profusion, while figures are comparatively seldom introduced; the Entablatures in many cases are broken over the columns; the pediments are steeper, and the shafts of the columns, instead of diminishing in a straight line from the base to the capital, are very often slightly curved. The arch also, which appears to have been unknown to the Greeks, was brought into general use by the Romans, and greatly affected the character of their architecture; at its first introduction it was made subordinate to the columns and entablature, but it soon came to be regarded as a more important principle, and was adopted as one of the leading features. In general appearance Roman architecture is less chaste and simple than the Grecian, but it is bolder, richer, and in many respects more imposing.

The construction of nearly all the great Roman buildings in Rome itself is concrete faced with brick, or with small ashlar masonry in diamond-shaped patterns, called reticulated masonry; the latter is more usual in the two first centuries of the Christian era, the best period of art in Rome, and the brickwork of that period is also superior to that of any other. In the third century there is scarcely a perceptible change, but in the fourth there is a very decided falling off and deterioration of all kinds, and old materials were extensively used again, as in the Arch of Constantine. The vaults are usually one mass of concrete, with the walls plastered and painted on the inside, and faced with brick or stone on the outside. The walls are of enormous thickness: those of the Pantheon are thirty feet thick, and as the interior is lighted by a large circular opening in the centre of the vault, no windows were required. The brick casing is full of arches, called arches of construction, and the use of them is to bind the brick casing on to the concrete mass securely. The concrete or rubble walls frequently have layers of the flat bricks or tiles at intervals to bind them together. but this fashion seems to have been introduced at rather a later time, or at least it is not left outside in the earlier work as it is in later times. The construction gets gradually worse, until in the tenth century it is as bad as it well could be to stand at all, and the only dated building of the eleventh century in Rome is of herring-bone work. The revival of the art of building began later in Rome than in the distant provinces of the empire. France and England took the lead in this real Renaissance. Germany followed next, and Italy, especially Rome, was the latest. Throughout the Middle Ages the building art at Rome may be said to be a century behind the rest of Europe.

Of the buildings constructed by the Romans in this country during their occupation, we have none remaining at all perfect. We can judge of their extent by the traces of foundations, and sometimes of their plan by the finding of hypocausts, baths, &c. The walls of fortification are also in part remaining round several places known to have been important Roman towns; but beyond these we have very little to guide us as to the style and character of the ornamental work of their buildings. It is probable that in many of the Roman villas the lower part of the wall only was of stone, and the superstructure of wood, and there is no reason to suppose that in any of the remains of villas, &c., which have hitherto been discovered in this country, there were upper storeys. The best remains of Roman houses have been excavated at Silchester.

Romanesque Style, a general term for all the debased styles of architecture which sprang from attempts to imitate the Roman, and which flourished in Europe from the period of the destruction of the Roman power till the introduction of Gothic architecture. It is thus described by Dr. Whewell: "Its characters are a more or less close imitation of the features of Roman architecture. The arches are round; are supported on pillars retaining traces of the Classical proportions; the pilasters, cornices, and entablatures, have a correspondence and similarity with those of Classical architecture; there is a prevalence of rectangular faces and square-edged projections; the openings in walls are small, and subordinate to the surfaces in which they occur;

the members of the architecture are massive and heavy, very limited in kind and repetition, the enrichments being introduced rather by sculpturing surfaces, than by multiplying and extending the component parts.   There is in this style a predominance of *horizontal* lines, or at least no predominance and prolongation of vertical ones.   For instance, the pillars are not prolonged in corresponding mouldings along the arches; the walls have no prominent buttresses, and are generally terminated by a strong horizontal tablet or cornice."   "This same kind of architecture, or perhaps particular modifications of it, have been by various persons termed Saxon, Norman, Lombard, Byzantine, &c.   All these names imply suppositions, with regard to the history of this architecture, which it might be difficult to substantiate; and would, moreover, in most cases, not be understood to describe the style in that generality which we learn to attribute to it, by finding it, with some variations according to time and place, diffused over the whole face of Europe."   The Pisan style has a very disdinct character of its own, the chief feature of which is the number of small arcades with detached shafts or *colonettes* along the upper part of the walls, and especially round the apse; the arches are round, but the work is very light and elegant.   It is contemporary with the Early Gothic of England and France.   In Italy small *antique* columns are often used again, as in the apse of the cathedral at Pisa.   This style is adopted in the Rhine churches in the first half of the thirteenth century.

Rood-beam, Rood-loft, and **Rood-screen.** The custom of separating the choir and presbytery from the nave by a high screen appears to have begun in the large monastic churches, and afterwards to have set the fashion for the smaller, and parish churches; for this reason there are no remains of Rood-screens earlier than the thirteenth century, or any account of such.   In the earlier churches of Rome, the choir was always separated by a low screen or railing (see *Chancel*), and never by a high one, nor was the presbytery even shut in by any lofty structure.   But apart from the Rood-*screen*, the Rood-*beam* had its origin, probably, in the ancient *trabes* or beam, frequently referred to in the earlier writers, e.g., Anastasius. In the Middle Ages the rood-beam became part and parcel of the screen, and with it a rood-loft, which was found convenient for lighting candles, decorating, and other offices required in connection with the images which essentially belonged to it. These Rood-lofts do not appear to have been common in this country before, if so soon as the fourteenth century; they were approached from the inside of the church, generally by a small stone staircase in the wall, which is often to be found in churches which have lost all traces of the screens themselves. The front was often richly panelled, and the under side formed into a large coved cornice, or ornamented with small ribs and other decorations, connecting it with the screen below. Although most of the rood-lofts in

Rood-screen, Charlton-on-Otmoor, Oxfordshire, c. 1500.

this country have been destroyed, a considerable number of examples (more or less perfect) remain, as at Long Sutton, Kingsbury Episcopi, Barnwell, Dunster, Timberscombe, Minehead, and Winsham, Somersetshire; Newark, Nottinghamshire; Charlton-on-Otmoor, and Handborough, Oxfordshire; Merevale, Knowle, and Worm-Leighton, Warwickshire; Flamsted, Hertfordshire; Uffendon, Bradninch, Collumpton, Dartmouth, Kenton, Plymptree, and Hartland, Devon, &c. The rood-loft was occasionally placed above the chancel-arch, as at Northleach, Gloucestershire. It sometimes extended across the first arch of the nave, as in Castle Hedingham Church, Essex. There are very fine and rich rood-lofts in Wales, in churches which are in other respects plain and poor.

The rood-lofts were ordered to be taken down as superstitious, but strict injunctions were given by the Commissioners of Queen Elizabeth, Oct. 10, 1561, to the effect that only the loft was to be removed down to the beam, that the screen itself was to be left standing, and if removed to be replaced.

Rood (Saxon), a cross or crucifix; the term was more particularly applied to the large cross erected in all our churches over the entrance of the chancel or choir; this was often of very large size, and when complete was, like other crucifixes, accompanied by the figures of St. John and the Blessed Virgin, placed one on each side of the foot of the cross: in front of these roods lights were frequently placed, especially on certain festivals of the Church. Of course, all such were destroyed, some probably as early as Henry the Eighth's reign, most in that of Edward the Sixth. What remained, or were restored during

Rood, Sherborne, Dorset.

Mary's reign, were taken down in the early years of that of Elizabeth. Only a few examples of the Crucifix remain, and those in stone.

ROOD-TOWER, Rood-steeple: this name is sometimes applied to the tower built over the intersection of a cruciform church.

Rood-arch is sometimes applied to the arch between the nave and chancel, from its being immediately over the rood-loft.

Roof, the external covering on the top of a building; sometimes of stone, but usually of wood overlaid with slates, tiles, lead, &c. The form and construction of the timber-work of roofs differ materially according to the nature of the building on which it is to be placed, and any attempt to notice all the varieties would far exceed the limits of this work. The main portions of the framing, which in most cases are placed at regular intervals, are each called *a truss, principal,* or *pair of principals;* these, in ornamental open roofs, are the leading features, and in some ancient roofs are contrived with an especial view to appearance. The accompanying diagrams of two of the simplest kinds of modern roofs will serve to explain the names of the most important timbers: a *king-post* roof has one vertical post in each truss, a *queen-post* roof has two.

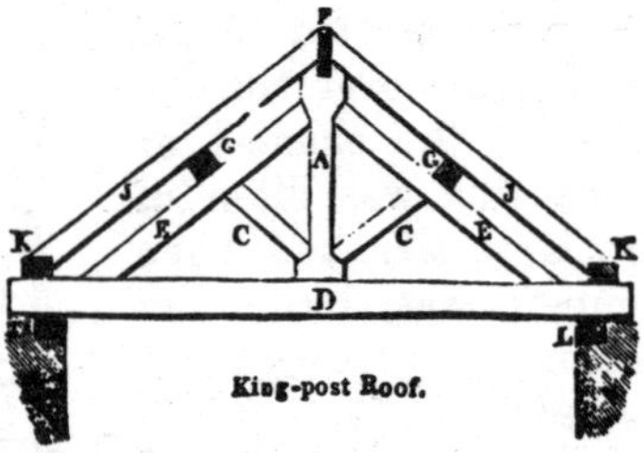

Mediæval roofs vary so much in their structure, on account of the ornamental disposition of the pieces, that it is not easy to establish a universal nomenclature for them. Many names of beams and timbers occur in old contracts of which the original application is often uncertain.

King-post Roof.

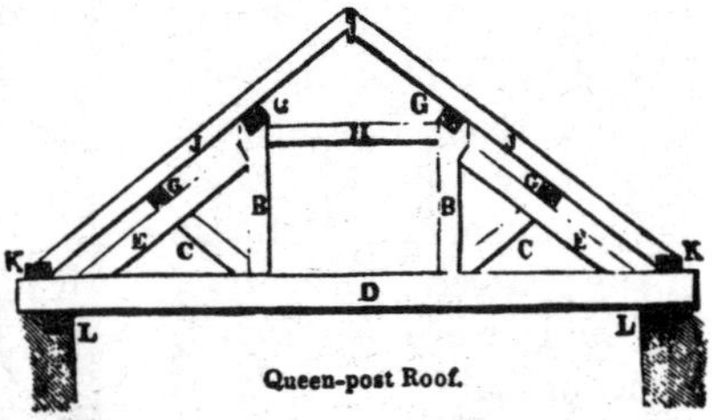

Queen-post Roof.

A. King-post.
BB. Queen-posts.
CCCC. Braces, or struts.
DD. Tie-beams.
EEEE. Principal rafters, blades, or backs.

FF. Ridge-pieces.
GGGGGG. Purlins.
H. Collar.
JJJJ. Common rafters.
KKKK. Pole-plates.
LLLL. Wall-plates.

The *Hammer-beam* roofs contain most of the peculiarities of structure that distinguish the mediæval roofs from the modern roofs, and the following nomenclature may be adopted in describing them:—

Sometimes one hammer beam is repeated over another, forming, as it were, two storeys. It is then called a *double hammer-beam* roof, and the nomenclature runs,—*Lower hammer-beam, upper hammer-beam, lower hammer-brace, upper hammer-brace, lower side-post, upper side-post, &c.*

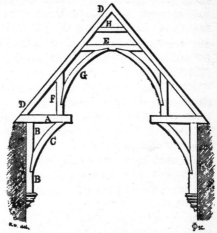

A. Hammer-beam.

BB. Pendant-post.

C. Hammer-brace.

DD. Rafter.

E. Collar.

F. Side-post.

G. Collar-brace.

H. Upper collar.

Hammer-beam Roof.

It must be remembered that all upright pieces may be called *posts*, with an epithet, if necessary, e.g. Pendant-post. Inclined pieces, if not *rafters*, are *braces*, and commonly derive their epithet from the piece under which they are placed, or which they principally stiffen, as *Collar-brace*. *Ashlar pieces* are fixed to every one of the rafters in most mediæval roofs, but they are sometimes concealed by cornice-mouldings and frieze-boards. The example from Dorchester shews the hammer-beam construction with *collar-brace, side-post*, &c.

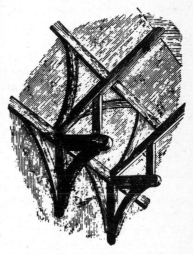

Hammer-beam Roof, North Aisle, Dorchester, Oxon.

Of the construction of the wooden roofs of the *Ancients* very little is known, but it was probably of the most inartificial kind, and judging from the form of their pediments, the pitch of them was low: some small buildings still retain their original roofs of marble, as the Tower of the Winds, and the Choragic Monument of Lysicrates at Athens. The Mausoleum of Theodoric at Ravenna has a domed roof, formed of a single block of stone, nearly thirty-six feet in diameter.

Saxon roofs were elevated, but to what degree we have no certain account, neither is there satisfactory evidence of their internal appearance; the illuminations in manuscripts seem to represent them as often covered with slates, tiles, or shingles.

Norman roofs were also raised, in some cases to a very steep pitch, but in others the elevation was more moderate, the ridge being formed at about a right angle. It does not appear that at this period the construction was made ornamental, although, doubtless, in many cases the framing was open to view. The covering was certainly sometimes of lead, but was probably oftener of a less costly material.

Early English roofs were generally, if not always, made with a steep slope, though not universally of the same pitch; sometimes the section of the roof represented an equilateral triangle, and sometimes the proportions were flatter. A few roofs of this date still exist, as on the nave of Hales Owen Church, Shropshire; this originally had tie-beams across it, and under every rafter additional pieces of timber are fixed, which are cut circular, so that the general appearance is that of a series of parallel ribs forming a barrel-vault. This seems to have been a common mode of improving the appearance of roofs in this style before any important ornaments were applied to them. The additional pieces under the rafters were usually either quite plain or only chamfered on the edges; a moulded rib sometimes ran along the top, and a cornice next the wall-plate, both of which were generally small; the tie-beams also were frequently moulded.

When first the approach of the *Decorated* style began to exercise an influence, the roofs, though still of the same construction, became somewhat more ornamental. There are also roofs existing of this date, and some probably earlier, in country churches, the insides of which are formed into a series of flat spaces, or cants; they are usually quite plain, with the exception of the tie-beam and cornice, which are frequently moulded, and the king-post, which is commonly octagonal with a moulded capital or base. Of a later period roofs of this kind are extremely common in some districts, but they are generally to be distinguished from the earlier specimens by being arranged in seven cants instead of six; of the older description good examples remain at Chartham Church, Kent, and on the south aisle of Merrow Church, Surrey. Most of these roofs are now ceiled, but probably many of them were originally open.

As the Decorated style advanced, the leading timbers of the principals were often formed into an arch by the addition of circular braces under the tie-beams, the beams themselves being also frequently curved; the spandrels formed by these braces were very usually filled with pierced tracery, and the timbers generally were more moulded and enriched than in the earlier styles. Where the lines of mouldings were interrupted they very

South Aisle, Kidlington, Oxon.

commonly terminated in carved leaves or other ornaments: sometimes the tie-beams were omitted in roofs of high pitch, but the principals were generally arched. The roofs of domestic halls, in the Decorated style, appear to have been more enriched than those of churches; that of Malvern Priory had a variety of cross-braces above the tie-beams cut into ornamental featherings; that of the Archbishop of Canterbury's palace at Mayfield, Sussex, was supported on stone arches spanning the whole breadth of the room (about forty feet): this construction is also partially used in the hall at the Mote, Ightham, Kent. This kind of construction, a wooden roof supported on stone arches instead of the large timbers necessary for the principals, seems to have been more common than is generally supposed, and at all periods [d].

In the *Perpendicular* style *hammer-beam* roofs were introduced, (one of the finest specimens of which is that on Westminster Hall,) and, together with them, most numerous varieties of construction for the sake of orna-

St. Mary's, Devizes, Wilts, c. 1450.

ment. These are far too manifold to be enumerated; many specimens exist in churches and halls, some of which are extremely magnificent, and are enriched with tracery, featherings, pendants, and carvings of various kinds, in the greatest profusion. Many roofs in this style were nearly or quite flat; these, when plain, had the timbers often exposed to view, and moulded; in other cases they

[d] Besides those mentioned in the text, there is one over the hall and chapel of Conway Castle, and there is reason to believe t at the old roof of the Guild-hall in London had stone principals, some portions of them having been found during the repairs in 1864. Such roofs are common in some parts of France, especially over the aisles of churches, as at Montmartre in Paris, and many churches in the Isle de France, and remains of them have been found in Normandy in work of the eleventh and twelfth centuries.

were ceiled with oak and formed into panels, and were usually enriched with bosses and other ornaments of similar description to those of the higher roofs; good examples remain at Cirencester Church, Gloucestershire. On halls hammer-beam roofs were principally used, but on churches other kinds of construction were more prevalent. There are some mediæval buildings, principally vestries, apses, and portions of churches, which are entirely roofed with stone. They are generally of high elevation, and often have ribs answering to the rafters in a wooden roof. They occur at all periods, and in some cases may have been erected for protection against fire; in other cases, when the material was suitable, perhaps from economy.

The name of roof is often applied to what are in fact ceilings having an external covering, or outer roof, distinct from that which is seen. Vaulted roofs are also frequently spoken of, but a vault usually has an outer roof over it, and is more properly a vaulted ceiling.

Rose. A kind of rose was sometimes used as an ornament on the face of the abacus on Corinthian capitals. It also occurs in ornamental mouldings during the Norman style; but the full rose, as in the accompanying illustration, was a badge of the Tudors, and during their reigns it is often found carved on buildings in conjunction with the *Portcullis*.

Badge of the Tudors.

Rubble, Rubble-work, Rough-walling: coarse walling constructed of rough stones, not large but of great irregularity both in size and shape, and not so flat-bedded as in rag-work: in some districts it is often formed of

ROSE WINDOW, a name sometimes given to a circular window. See *Window*.

ROUGH-CAST, coarse plaster-work, used on the outsides of buildings.

ROUGH-SETTER, Rough-mason: an old term for a mason who only built coarse walling, as distinguished from a free-mason, who worked with mallet and chisel.

ROUND, a name for the *Torus*.

ROUNDEL, a bead or *astragal* moulding.

flints : in large buildings, in neighbourhoods where better materials can be obtained for the outer face of the walls.

it is in general only used for the insides, or backing, but in other districts the whole substance of the walls is not unfrequently of this construction; it is often found to have been plastered on both sides, but sometimes it was only pointed externally.

Rustic-work, ashlar masonry, the joints of which are worked with grooves, or channels, to render them conspicuous; sometimes the whole of the joints are worked in this way, and sometimes only the horizontal ones; the grooves are either moulded or plain, and are formed in several different ways; the surface

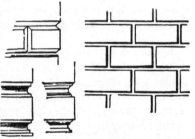

of the work is sometimes left, or purposely made rough, but at the present day it is usually made even. Rustic-work was never employed in mediæval buildings, but it is said to have had its origin in the buildings of Augustus and Claudius at Rome.

Sacristy (Fr., from Lat. *Sacer*, but written also *Secretarium*), a room attached to a church, in which the *sacred* vessels, vestments, and other valuables connected with the religious services of the building, were preserved, and in which the priest put on his robes; sometimes included within the main walls of the fabric, and sometimes an adjunct. In England this name does not appear to have been so common as Vestry, but on the Continent it still prevails. [See *Vestry*.]

Sancte-bell, Sanctus-bell, Saints'-bell, Mass-bell, (old English forms, Sacring-bell, Saunce-bell,) a small bell used in the Roman Catholic Church to call attention to the more solemn parts of the service of the Mass, as at the conclusion of the ordinary, when the words "Sanctus, Sanctus, Sanctus, Deus Sabaoth," are pronounced by the priest, and on the elevation of the Host and chalice after consecration; it is now usually, if not always, a small hand-bell carried by an attendant, and was generally of this kind in England previous to the Reformation, made sometimes of silver; but in some instances a larger bell was used, and was suspended on the outside of the church in a small turret, made to receive it, over the archway leading from the nave into the chancel, and rung by a rope from within;

Long Compton, Warwickshire.

many of these turrets still exist, as at Isham, Rothwell, and Desborough, Northamptonshire; Boston, Lincolnshire: Bloxham, Brize-norton, Swalcliffe, and Coombe, Oxfordshire, &c.; a few still retain the bell, as at Long

SACRAMENT-HOUSE. See *Tabernacle.*

SACRYNGE - BELL, or Saunce-bell = *Sancte-bell.*

SADDLE-BARS, in casement or quarry glazing the small iron bars to which the lead panels are tied.

SADDLE-ROOF of a tower, so called where the roof has two gables, sometimes termed a *Pack-saddle Roof* and a *Saddle-back Roof.*

SALLY-PORT, a postern gate or passage underground from the inner to the outer works of a fortification, intended as a passage for the garrison to *sally* from, or pass through.

SARCOPHAGUS. See *Tomb.*

SARRAIME = a portcullis.

Compton, Warwickshire. Occasionally also a number of "little bells were hung in the middle of the church, which the pulling of one wheel made all to ring, which was done at the elevation of the hoste."

Sanctuary (Lat.), the presbytery, or eastern part of the choir of a church, in which the altar is placed. [See *Choir* and *Presbytery*.]

Saxon Architecture. This name was given to the style of building supposed to be erected by the English in this country before the Norman Conquest. But the word was at first wrongly applied, and arches of twelfth-century date were frequently called Saxon. In later years it was applied in a more restricted sense to the architecture of buildings which were either before the Conquest or of the eleventh century: certain towers which were known to have been built after the Conquest being of a style which was earlier than Norman.

The buildings of the English, after their arrival here, were perhaps, at first, usually of wood; but the writings of historians, such as Bede, as well as incidental mention in the early Chronicles, shew that as early as the seventh and eighth century stone buildings, especially those for ecclesiastical purposes, were as frequent as those in wood.

The scant and uncertain references to special buildings, leaves it very difficult to apply definite dates to the few existing remains which we have of buildings before the Conquest. Even in the cases of Jarrow and Monks' Wearmouth, where we have more historical data than usual, there is some difficulty in saying what part of the work should be assigned to Benedic Biscop. At both the churches there are considerable remains of moulded balusters, which probably fulfils the description by Bede, that the churches were built "more Romano." How far, and how much of the walls were restored after the fire, and desertion on account of the ravages of the Danes, leaves it difficult to lay down any laws as to the character of the masonry itself of this period. But for the most part, all that can possibly belong to this date is of very coarse and irregular rubble-work, with rather irregular ashlar stones used for the coins, and in the case in point, the stone of the neighbourhood, and the circumstances attending their history, have to be taken into account before referring to them as a type of the usual building of that time. Of nearly the same age, that is before the close of the seventh century, are probably the crypts of Hexham and Ripon, all that remain of the churches founded there, at that time.

But while the rough masonry may be characteristic of those buildings in the north, we have, in the south, adjoining the fine stone quarries of Bradford-on-Avon, the remains of a church of very good masonry; it is close to the large twelfth-century church, and as William of Malmesbury implies that the smaller church is of Aldhelm's foundation, we may fairly attribute it to the early part of the eighth century. It is very complete, with its continuous arcade and external pilasters, and may be said to possess certain characteristics, especially the use of pilasters, which are found in other churches which there is reason for assigning to a period before the Conquest. A characteristic example of the style occurs at Deerhurst, when, from the inscription of Duke Odda being preserved, we know that it was built either in, or soon after 1053, and here there is richer ornament than in early Norman work.

Doorway in Vaults under the Dormitory, Westminster, A.D. 1066.

Again, some of the work of Edward the Confessor, at Westminster, is very rude, while the masonry in places is of ashlar work, which might be thought to be of Henry the First's reign, or even later. But here, again, we have no very certain data for differentiating the building actually completed before the Conquest, and that completed afterwards.

After the Conquest, we have the two towers at Oxford, namely, that of St. Michael's Church, and that in the Castle. Both these there is good reason to assign to Robert D'Oili, and the date of about 1070-80; though, as far as masonry is concerned, they belong to a class ruder than Deerhurst. The Castle tower lays no claim to any special feature, but the tower of St. Michael's, besides the quoins forming long-and-short work, has also central baluster or mid-wall shafts, as they may be also called, to the three windows. These have only of late years been opened out.

Tower, St. Michael's, Oxford.

From such examples— and as regards ascertained dates, it is not easy to add many more—it might be thought that there was not sufficient evidence on which to base any theories as to the style.

Still, there is a distinct character belonging to portions of very many churches, and especially to a large number of towers which may well be called Saxon, in the sense in which the word has been accustomed to be used, namely, the English style before the arrival of the Normans, since that is ruder and earlier than Norman, while the germs of Norman are plainly visible. But in the classification of these towers, we have equally to include the Lincoln towers, which were erected by the inhabitants *after* the Norman Bishop, Remigius, had driven them down from their habitations on the hill to the plain below, and the towers which they built after the Conqueror had arrived.

The following may be said to be the marked features belonging to this class :—

The execution is rude and coarse: the walls are built either of rag or rubble, sometimes partly of herring-bone work, without buttresses, and in many cases, if not always, have been plastered on the outside; the quoins are usually of hewn stones placed alternately flat and on end, a kind of construction to which the name "*long and short*" has been given: an example of this is shewn very clearly in the tower of St. Michael's Church, Oxford. But perhaps one of the most singular and marked features in the ornamentation of towers of this style, and so presumably of this date, is, that the walls are often ornamented externally with flat vertical strips of stone projecting slightly from the surface, resembling wooden framing, generally of the same "long and short" construction as the

Barton-on-the-Humber, Lincolnshire.

quoins: on towers there are sometimes several tiers of these, divided from each other by plain strings, or bands: semicircular arches and triangles, formed of similar strips of stone, are also sometimes used as ornaments; and plain projecting blocks are frequently associated with these, either as imposts, or as bases for the vertical strips which often stand above them. Barnack, Northants, is a remarkable example of this kind of work, which covers all the lower part of the tower, and on the inside of this a recess for a seat, apparently for a schoolmaster, of distinctly Norman character, has been made, not going through the wall, but only part of the way, and the pilaster strips continue to the ground on the exterior. *Within* the tower also, the original level of the floor is two feet below the present one, so that the seat looks like a doorway now; the tower-arch opposite to this doorway is also a fine example of the Saxon style.

The jambs of doorways and other openings are very commonly of "long and short" work, and when imposts are used, as they generally are, they are usually rude, and often extremely massive, sometimes consisting of plain blocks and sometimes moulded. Round the arch there is very often a projecting course, occupying the situation of a hood-moulding, which sometimes stops upon the imposts, but more frequently runs down the jambs to the ground, forming a kind of pilaster on each side of the opening;

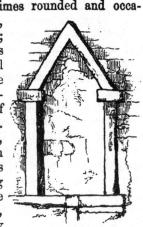

Earl's Barton, Northamptonshire.

it is usually flat, but is sometimes rounded and occasionally notched on the edges, as at Dunham Magna, Norfolk; in some instances the impost is arranged so as to form a capital to each of these projections on the jambs, and they are sometimes provided with bases either formed of plain blocks or rudely moulded. The arches are generally plain, but are occasionally worked with rude and massive mouldings, as the chancel-arch at Wittering Church, Northamptonshire; some arches are constructed with brick, as at Brixworth, where probably all of them were taken from some

Barnack, Northamptonshire.

Roman building, as at St. Michael's Church, Colchester, or thin stones, and these usually have a course of stones or bricks laid upon the top of the arch, as at Britford

Church, Wiltshire: the arches are always semicircular, but some small openings, such as doors and windows, have pointed or triangular heads formed of two straight stones placed on end upon the imposts, and resting against each other at the top, as at Barnack. The windows are not large, and, when splayed, have often nearly or quite as much splay externally as internally; in belfries and other situations where they do not require to be glazed, they are frequently of two or more lights, divided by small shafts or pillars, which are very usually made like balusters, and encircled with bands of rude mouldings. Balusters of the time of Benedict Biscop, c. 680, remain in large numbers at Jarrow and Monks' Wearmouth; and in the old portion of St. Alban's Abbey, erected in the latter half of the eleventh century, specimens are seen, one of which is engraved under *Baluster*. These generally have capitals, or imposts, formed of long stones reaching entirely through the wall; in some instances the balusters are oblong in plan, and in others two are placed together, one behind the other, in order to give better support to these long capitals.

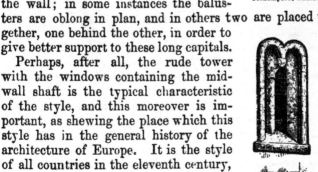

Corhampton, Hants.

Belfry window, with section. Tower, Sompting, Sussex.

Perhaps, after all, the rude tower with the windows containing the midwall shaft is the typical characteristic of the style, and this moreover is important, as shewing the place which this style has in the general history of the architecture of Europe. It is the style of all countries in the eleventh century, but it lingered on in Germany, and still lingers in Italy, and became a style of its own fully developed; while in England and in Normandy also it gave way before the special characteristics which make up the Norman style.

The whole of these peculiarities are not to be met with in any one building, and in some churches, in which several of them are to be found, they are associated with other features, evidently original, which so clearly belong to the Norman style as to prove that these buildings are not of præ-Conquest date, as at the churches of Daglingworth, Gloucestershire, and Syston, Lincolnshire. In other instances the lower parts of buildings consist exclusively of this peculiar kind of construction, and are surmounted by pure Norman work, which has been raised upon it subsequently to the first erection, as at the tower of Clapham Church, Bedfordshire, and Woodstone, near Peterborough. Such instances afford strong evidence of the buildings with such characteristics as have been described, being anterior to the Conquest, certainly anterior to the time of Henry I.; for some of the churches in which the peculiarities under consideration are found, are clearly Norman (and not early in the style), but it may reasonably be supposed that in many parts of the country the Saxon style would have lingered for a considerable time after the Norman invasion, and would have continued to be employed (with an increasing admixture of Norman features) in buildings erected by native workmen. Brixworth, Northants, is a very remarkable example, the arches being all built of Roman bricks, but these may have been brought from a Roman villa near at hand. An excavation by the side of the choir shews that the original level of the floor was several feet below the present one, and yet the Norman doorways are at the more recent level; the original parts of the church were built not later than the eighth century.

The following is a tolerably complete list of examples of this so-called Anglo-Saxon style:—

Bedfordshire—Knotting; Clapham, tower.

Berkshire — Wickham, tower; Cholsey, tower.

Buckinghamshire—Caversfield, tower; Iver; Lavendon, tower, nave, and chancel.

Cambridgeshire—St. Benet's and St. Giles's, Cambridge.

Cornwall—Tintagel.

Derbyshire—Repton, east end, and crypt.

Durham—Monks' Wearmouth, tower; Jarrow, walls of church and chancel.

Essex—Boreham, church; Colchester, Trinity Church, part of the tower, &c.; Felstead, church; Great Maplestead, north door.

Gloucestershire—Daglingworth church, except the tower; Deerhurst, tower; Miserden, church; Stretton, north doorway; Upleaden, chancel-arch.

Hampshire — Boarhunt; Corhampton; Headbourne Worthy; Hinton Ampner; Little Sombourn; Kilmeston; Tichborne.

Hertfordshire—St. Michael's, at St. Alban's, and part of the Abbey church.

Kent—Dover, part of the ruined church in the Castle; Swanscombe, tower.

Leicestershire—Barrow on Soar.

Lincolnshire — Aukborough; Barton on the Humber, St. Peter's, tower; Branston; Caburn; Clee, tower; Holtonle-Clay, tower and chancelarch; Heapham; Lincoln, St. Peter's at Gowt's; St. Maryle-Wigford; Nettleton; Ropsley, part of the west end; Rothwell; Scartho; Skellingthorpe; Skillington, part of the church; Springthorpe; Stow, transepts; Swallow; Syston, tower; Waith, tower and chancel-arch; Winterton.

Middlesex—Kingsbury, part of church (now hid by plastering).

Norfolk—Norwich, St. Julien's; Beeston St. Lawrence; Dunham Magna, church; Elmham, ruins of bishop's palace; Howe; Newton, tower.

Northamptonshire — Barnack, tower; Brigstock, church; Brixworth, church; Earl's Barton, tower; Green's Norton, west end; Pattishall;

Stow-nine-churches; Wittering, chancel.

Northumberland--Bolam, tower; Bywell, St. Andrew; Bywell, St. Peter; Corbridge; Hexham, crypt; Ovingham; Whittingham.

Oxfordshire—St. Michael's, Oxford, tower; Oxford Castle, tower; Northleigh, tower.

Shropshire—Barrow, chancelarch; Church Stretton; Clee; Stanton Lacey, nave and transept; Stottesdon.

Somersetshire—Cranmore, doorhead; Milbourne Port.

Suffolk—Barham, part of ch.; Debenham; Claydon, part of church; Flixton; Gosbeck; part of church; Hemingstone; Ilketshall; Leiston.

Surrey—Albury; Stoke d'Abernon, some portions.

Sussex — Bishopstone, church; Bosham, tower; St. Botolph, chancel - arch; Burwash; Sompting, tower; Worth; Yapton.

Warwickshire–Wootten Wawen, substructure of tower.

Wiltshire—Bradford-on-Avon; North Burcombe, east end; Brytford, north and south doors; Bremhill, west end; Somerford Keynes.

Worcestershire — Wyre Piddle, chancel-arch.

Yorkshire—Bardsey; Kirkdale, west end and chancel-arch; Kirk Hamerton; Laughtonen-le-Morthen, north doorway; Maltby; Ripon minster, crypt, called Wilfred's Needle; York Cathedral. portion of crypt (Bloxham); York, church of St. Mary, Bishophill Junior.

Scamilli, plain blocks or sub plinths, placed under columns, statues, &c., to elevate them: they differ from ordinary pedestals in having no mouldings about them, and in being usually of smaller size.

Scotia (Gr.), or *Trochilus,* a hollow moulding constantly used in the bases of columns, &c., in Classical architecture: the old English name for a corresponding mould-ing very frequently em-ployed in Gothic archi-tecture is *Casement.* [See *Column.*]

Scotia, Trochilus, or Casement; Baths of Diocletian, Rome.

Screen, a partition, enclosure, or *parclose* separating a portion of a room, or of a church, from the rest. In the domestic halls of the Middle Ages a screen was almost invariably fixed across the lower end, so as to part off a small space, which became a lobby (with a gallery above it) within the main entrance doors, the approach to the body of the hall being by one or more doorways through the screen; these were of wood, with

SCAFFOLD, a temporary erection of poles, planks, &c., for the use of the workmen in building walls, or executing any work which they cannot otherwise reach. A gallery in a church is sometimes called a scaffold.

SCALLAGE, Scallenge, a provincial word used in Herefordshire for the detached covered porch at the entrance of the churchyard, commonly called a Lich-gate.

SCANTLING, in carpentry the dimensions of a piece of timber in breadth and thickness, but not including length. In masonry, on the other hand, it is the size of a stone in length, breadth, and thickness. *Scantling* is also the name of any piece of timber under five inches square.

SCAPPLE. To scapple a stone is to reduce it to a straight surface without working it smooth; usually done by chopping imme-

diately it is dug in the quarry: the term is now used exclusively (or nearly so) in reference to stone, but was formerly applied to timber also, and must have signified the barking of a tree, or, more probably, squaring it with the axe.

SCAPUS, Scape, the shaft of a column; also the apophyges of the shaft.

SCARCEMENT, a plain flat set-off in a wall; the term is but little used at the present day.

SCHEME, the crown of an arch.

SCHEME-ARCH (Ital. *Arco scemo*), a segmental arch.

SCOINSON. See *Escoinson.*

SCONCE = *Squinch.* Also used for a candlestick.

SCOUCHON, SKOUCHON, in some instances *Scutcheon,* in others *Squinch.*

SCRINIUM (Lat.): (1.) a small circular box in which documents were deposited; (2.) a *Shrine* or chest containing relics.

the lower part, to the height of a few feet, formed of close panelling, and the upper part of open-work. The passage behind the screen for the use of the servants was called "the Screens."

In churches, screens were used in various situations, to enclose the choir, to separate subordinate chapels, to protect tombs, &c. The chief was at the west end of the choir, or chancel, and was called the *Rood-screen*, from the Rood having been placed over it; these were formed either of wood or stone, and were enriched not only with mouldings and carvings, but also with most brilliant colouring and gilding. The screens at the west end and sides of the choir in cathedrals and large churches were usually close throughout their whole height, as they also occasionally were in other situations; but in general the lower part only, to the height of about four feet from the ground, was close, and the remainder was of open-work. The oldest piece of wooden screen-work that has been noticed is at Compton Church, Surrey; it is of transition character from Norman to Early English, consisting of a series of small octagonal shafts with carved capitals supporting plain semicircular arches, and forms the front of an upper chapel over the eastern part of the chancel.

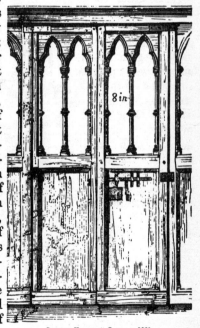

Stanton Harcourt, Oxon., c. 1260.

Of the *Early English* style the existing examples are almost invariably of stone; some are close walls, more or less ornamented with panelling, arcades, and other decorations, and some are close only at the bottom, and have the upper part formed of a series of open arches. That at Stanton Harcourt is of wood, but is late in the style. Specimens of wooden screens of *Decorated* date remain at Sparsholt, Berks., and in the north aisle of the choir of Chester Cathedral; these have the lower part of plain boarding, and the upper of small feathered arches supported on circular banded shafts. Stone screens of this date are variously, and often very highly, enriched; some have the upper part of open-work, similar to those of wood, and others are entirely close, and are enriched with arcades, panels, niches, pinnacles, diapering, and other decorations characteristic of the style: specimens remain at Lincoln and several other cathedrals and large churches. *Perpendicular* screens exist in great variety in very many churches, both of wood and stone; some of them are profusely ornamented with panellings, niches, statues, pinnacles, tabernacle - work, carvings, and other enrichments : the lower part usually consists of close panels, and the upper part of openwork divided by mullions supporting tracery, but sometimes the whole is close, with

Parclose Screen, Fyfield, Berks., c. 1480.

the same general arrangement of panelling. The illustration given from Fyfield Church Berkshire. is an example of a *Parclose*.

Scroll. A name given to a numerous class of ornaments, which in
general character
resemble a band
arranged in un-
dulations or con-
volutions

Scroll-moulding, a term applied to a particular kind
of moulding, used much for string-
courses in work of Edward I. and Edward II.'s reign. It is called the scroll
or *Roll - moulding*, from the resemblance to a roll of parchment, the
last fold overlapping.

Chacombe, Northants.

Scutcheon (old form Scouchon; Lat. *Scutum* = a shield):
the explanation of this term when signifying an *Escutcheon* has been already given. It is also an old name
for the angles of buildings or parts of buildings, such as
window-jambs, &c., but apparently for those only which
are more obtuse than right angles.

Section, the representation of a
building cut asunder vertically so
as to shew the interior; also of a
moulding or other member in architecture cut asunder so as to shew
its profile.

Sedile, or **Sedilia,** the Latin name for a seat, which
in modern times has come to be pretty generally applied
by way of distinction to the seats on the south side
of the choir near the altar in churches, used in the
ancient service by the Priest and his attendants, the
deacon and subdeacon, during certain parts of the Mass:
they were sometimes moveable, but more usually in this
country were formed of masonry and recessed in the wall

Scullery = Scutellerie (Lat.
Scutellum = a dish), the office
in a mediæval mansion or monastery where the plates and
dishes were kept.

Scutable, a term occurring
in the Westminster accounts,
probably = escutcheon.

See, a seat: the term is sometimes applied particularly to the
seat of dignity, or dais, in a domestic hall, &c.

like niches. Very numerous examples remain in our churches, a few of which are of as early date as the latter part of the twelfth century, but the majority are later,

Chesterton, Oxon.

extending to the end of the Perpendicular style. In general they contain three separate seats, but occasionally two, or only one, and in a few rare instances four, as at Rothwell Church, Northamptonshire, and Furness Abbey; or five, as at Southwell Minster; sometimes a single seat under one arch, or formed on the back of a window, is found, long enough for two or three persons. They are very commonly placed at different levels, the eastern seat being a step the highest and the western the lowest; but sometimes, when three are used, the two western seats are on the same level, a step below the other, and sometimes the two eastern are level and the western a step below them. The decorations used about them are various, and in enriched buildings they are occasionally highly ornamented, and sometimes surmounted

with tabernacle-work, pinnacles, &c. Some ancient sedilia
consist of plain benches
formed of masses of ma-
sonry projecting from the
wall, and it is not improbable that such may have
once existed in some of the
churches in which no traces
of these seats are now to be
found. At Lenham Church,
Kent, is a single seat projecting considerably from
the wall (though the back
is slightly recessed) with
stone elbows resembling an
arm-chair: this is popularly
called the confessional; at
Beckley Church, Oxford-
shire, is also a single stone
seat with one elbow.

Sedile, Lenham. Kent.

Sepulchre, The Easter, a representation of the entomb-
ment of our
Saviour, set
up in our
churches at
Easter, on
the north
side of the
chancel, near
the altar: in
this country
previous to
the Refor-
mation, it
was most
commonly
a wooden
erection, and
placed with-
in a recess

Easter Sepulchre, Stanton St. John's, Oxon.

in the wall or upon a tomb, but several churches still

contain permanent stone structures that were built for
the purpose, some of which are very elaborate, and are
ornamented with a variety of decorations, as at Navenby
and Heckington, Lincolnshire, and Hawton, Nottinghamshire, all of which are beautiful specimens of the Decorated style: sepulchres of this kind also remain in the
churches at Northwold, Norfolk; Holcombe Burnell,
Devonshire, and several others. The Host consecrated
on Maundy Thursday was placed in the sepulchre with
great solemnity on Good Friday, and continually watched
from that time till Easter-day, when it was taken out
and replaced upon the altar with especial ceremony.
Altar-tombs in this position are often mistaken for Easter
sepulchres.

Set-off, or Off-set: the part of a wall,
&c., which is exposed horizontally when
the portion above it is reduced in thickness. Set-offs are not unfrequently covered,
and in great measure concealed, by cornices or projecting mouldings, but are more
usually plain; in the latter case, in Classical architecture, they are generally nearly
or quite flat on the top, but in Gothic
architecture are sloped, and in most instances have a projecting drip on the lower
edge to prevent the wet from running
down the walls; this is especially ob-
servable in the set-offs of buttresses.

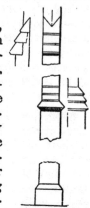

Cockington, Devon.

Shaft, the body of a column or pillar; the part between
the capital and base. It is particularly applied to the
small columns which are clustered round pillars, or used
in the jambs of doors, in arcades and various other situa-

SEELING=Ceiling and *Wainscot.*

SEGMENTAL. See *Arch.*

SELER. See *Tester.*

SELL. See *Cell.* It is also applied to a small retired habitation for an anchorite or other
religious recluse, and to a subordinate establishment of monks
dependent on one of the larger
monasteries.

SEPT (Lat. *Septum*), a railing.

SERGES, the great wax candles
burnt before the altars in Roman
Catholic churches.

SEVERANS, an old term not
now in use; it seems to have
signified a kind of cornice, or
string-course.

tions; they are sometimes cut on the same stones as the main body of the work to which they are attached, and sometimes of separate pieces: in the latter case they are very commonly of a different material from the rest of the work, and are not unfrequently polished: this mode of construction appears to have been first introduced towards the end of the Norman style. In early *Norman* work they are circular, but later in the style they are occasionally octagonal, and are sometimes ornamented with zig-zags, spiral mouldings, &c. In the *Early English* style they are almost always circular, generally in separate stones from the other work to which they are attached, and very often banded, in some instances they have a narrow fillet running up them. In the *Decorated* style they are commonly not set separate, and are frequently so small as to be no more than vertical mouldings with capitals and bases; they are usually round, and filleted, but are sometimes of other forms. In the *Perpendicular* style they are cut on the

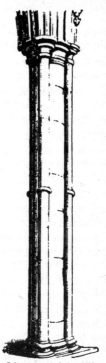

Salisbury Cathedral, c. 1250.

same stones with the rest of the work; they are most generally round, and are sometimes filleted; in some cases they are polygonal, with each side slightly hollowed. The part of a chimney-stack between the base and cornice is called the shaft.

Shingle, a wooden tile for covering roofs, spires, &c., made of cleft oak. Shingles were formerly very extensively employed in some districts, but their use has, for

SEVEREY, a bay, division, or compartment, of a vaulted ceiling.

SEXTRY = Sacristy.

SHANKS, Legs: a name sometimes applied to the plain spaces between the channels of the triglyphs in the Doric frieze.

the most part, been superseded by more durable kinds of covering; they are, however, still to be found on some church roofs, and on many timber spires, especially in the counties of Kent, Sussex, Surrey, and Essex.

Shrine (Lat. *Scrinium*), a *feretory* or repository for relics, whether fixed, such as a tomb, or moveable; the term is also sometimes applied to the tomb of a person not canonized. Shrines were often made of the most splendid and costly materials, and enriched with jewellery in profusion, as that of St. Taurin, at Evreux, in Normandy; those which were moveable were on certain occasions carried in religious processions;

Ely Cathedral.

others were substantial erections, generally the tombs of saints, as that of Edward the Confessor, in Westminster Abbey, and that of St. Cuthbert, formerly in Durham Cathedral, &c.; these were not unfrequently rebuilt (with additional splendour) subsequently to their first erection.

Sill, Cill, or Sole (Fr. *Seuil*, from Lat. *Solum*). (1.) The horizontal piece of timber or stone forming the bottom of a window, doorway, or other similar opening. (2.) Also the horizontal piece of timber, or plate, at the bottom of a wooden partition. (3.) Also the horizontal piece of timber near the base of houses which are

Window-sole, Fotheringhay.

built partly of timber and partly of brick. [See illustration under *Timber-built house*.]

Skew, A skew-table: the term skew is still used in the north for a stone built into the bottom of a gable or other similar situations to support the coping above (A); it appears formerly to have been applied to the stones forming the slopes of the set-offs of buttresses and other projections. Skew-table was probably the course of stone weathered, or sloped, on the top, placed over a continuous set-off in a wall.

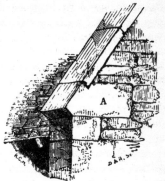

A. Skew.

Soffit, a ceiling: the word is seldom used except in reference to the subordinate parts and members of buildings, such as staircases, entablatures, archways, cornices, &c., the under sides of which are called the soffit.

SS. Soffit.

Solar, Soller (Lat. *Solarium*), a loft, garret, or upper chamber. In a mediæval house it was *usually* situated behind the dais, separated from it by the end of the hall, and

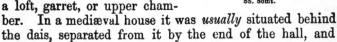

SCREW STAIRS. See *Newel, Vise,* and *Step.*

SHOAR, a sloping piece of timber acting as a temporary buttress to support a structure that threatens ruin, or that needs such help during repairs.

SHOULDERING · PIECE, in carpentry called also *Bragger,* is an obsolete term, probably the same as *Bracket:* "pieces of timber in building called *Braggers,* or shouldering-pieces (*mutuli*), in mason's work they be called *corbells.*"

SHROUDS, the crypt of a church.

SIDE-POSTS in a roof-truss are posts placed in pairs at an equal distance from the middle. See *Roof.*

SIMA = Cyma.

SLEEPER, a piece of timber, or plate, laid under the ground-floor of a building, on which the joists rest. The walls which support these timbers are called sleeper-walls.

SOCLE, Zocle: a plain block or plinth forming a low pedestal to a statue, column, &c.; also a plain face, or plinth, at the lower part of a wall; the term is used only in reference to Classical architecture.

SOLE = Sill.

SOUDLETS, Sowdels = Saddle-bars.

had a cellar under it; these two storeys together were frequently not so high as the hall, leaving the gable of the lofty roof with the window in it free above them.   It was usually the lord's chamber, and there was sometimes a small opening from the solar into the hall, from which the lord could overlook the proceedings, and hear all that passed.   The term is also occasionally applied to the rood-loft in a church, as in an inscription to the memory of John Spicer in Burford Church, Oxfordshire, bearing the date of A.D. 1437: and in some mediæval writers it is applied to the triforium.

Sommer, Summer, Sommer-beam: a main beam, or girder, in a floor, &c.; the name is now seldom used except in the compound term *Breast-summer*.

Spandrel, the triangular spaces included between the arch of a doorway, &c., and a rectangle formed by the outer mouldings over it: the term is also applied to other similar spaces included between arches, &c., and straight-sided figures surrounding them;

St. Alban's Abbey Church, c. 1400.

they are usually ornamented with tracery, foliage, shields or other enrichments.   In the Perpendicular style the doorways most commonly have the outer mouldings arranged in a square over the head so as to form spandrels above the arch.   In the earlier styles, this arrange-

SOUND-HOLE, the small ornamental openings often seen in towers: probably intended for giving passage to the sound of the bells.

SOUNDING, or SOUND-BOARD, the wooden projection often seen over pulpits, and supposed to diffuse the sound of the preacher's voice over the church.

SOWDELS, or SOUDLETS = saddle bars.

SPAN of an arch, the breadth of the opening between the imposts.

SPAN-PIECE, the name given to the *Collar-beam* of a roof in some districts.

SPAN-ROOF, a roof consisting of two inclined sides, in contradistinction to a shed-roof or penthouse, which consists of one only. Thus the body of a church is span-roofed, and its aisles shed-roofed.

SPARVER. See *Tester*.

ment is very seldom found in the doorways, but spandrels
are sometimes used in other parts of buildings, especially in
Decorated work, in which they are frequent, as at Ely. In

the west door of the
chapel of Magdalen
College, Oxford, the
spandrels of the
outer arch (which
stands considerably
in front of the ac-
tual doorway, so as
to form a shallow
porch) are cut quite
through and left
open. The spandrels
of a door were some-
times termed the *hanse* or *haunch* of a door.

Ely Cathedral.

Sper, Spur, Spar, a name applied by old writers to pieces
of timber of various kinds, such as quarters, rafters, wooden

bars for securing doors, &c.;
the term is still used in some
districts for rafters: sper-batten
is not an unusual name with
middle-age authors for a rafter;
they also frequently speak of
spering a door, meaning the
securing it with a wooden bar,
or fastening it with a bolt.
Another sense of the word *spur*
is for the ornamented wooden
brackets which support the
sommer-beam by the sides of
doorways at York, this usage
is believed to be quite local.
[See *Bracket* and *Haunch.*]

Walmgate, York.

Spire (Lat.), an acutely pointed termination given to
towers and turrets, forming the roof, and usually carried

SPEKE-HOUSE; i.q. *Parlour.*

SPERE, the screen across the
lower end of the hall in domestic buildings.

SPERVER, the wooden frame
at the top of a bed or canopy;
the term sometimes includes
the tester, or head-piece.

SPITAL, a hospital. The term
usually denotes one for lepers.

up to a great height. It is doubtful whether any very decided approach towards a spire was made till a considerable time after the introduction of the *Norman* style: at this period spires were sometimes adopted both on turrets and towers, and were generally made to correspond with them in their plan. Thus the circular turrets at the east end of the church of St. Peter, at Oxford, terminate in small circular spires; an octagonal turret at the west end of Rochester Cathedral has an octagonal spire; and the square towers of several churches in Normandy are surmounted with pyramids or square

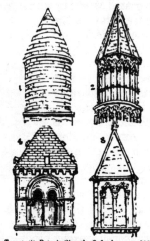

1. Turret. St. Peter's Church, Oxford, c. A.D. 1160.
2. Turret. Rochester Cathedral, c. A.D. 1160.
3. Pinnacle, Bishop's Cleeve Church, Gloucestershire, c. A.D. 1180.
4. Than Church, near Caen, Normandy, c. A.D. 1080.

spires: they were at first of very low proportions compared with later structures, and in truth were little more than pyramidal roofs. The whole of the existing specimens of this date are of stone, and rise from the outer surface of the walls, so as to have no parapet or gutter round the base. These pyramids become gradually more elongated as they are later in date, and clearly led the way to the spire

As the *Early English* style arose, considerably greater elevation was given to spires, although they were still very frequently less acute than they afterwards became, as at Ry-

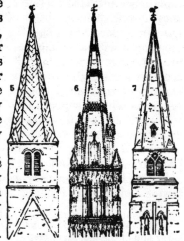

5. Almondsbury Church, Gloucestershire, c. A.D. 1250.
6. Salisbury Cathedral, c. A.D. 1350.
7. St. Mary's Church, Cheltenham, c. A.D. 1300.

hall, Rutland; Barnack and Ringstead, Northamptonshire; and Christ Church Cathedral, Oxford. With the
exception of a few rare examples, spires at this period
were always octagonal, and
when placed on square
towers, the angles of the
tower not covered by the
base of the spire were occupied by pinnacles or by
masses of masonry made to
slope back against the spire.
At the bottom of each of the
four cardinal sides was usually a large opening with
the jambs built perpendicularly, so that the head stood
out from the spire and was
usually finished with a steep
pediment. Above these, at
some considerable distance,
smaller openings of a similar
kind were generally introduced on the alternate sides;
these openings are called
spire-lights: the top of the
spire terminated with a finial
and a cross or *vane.* Spires
were still usually made to
rise from the exterior of the
tower walls without a parapet, a mode of construction

Ringstead, c. 1300.

which is distinguished in some districts by the term
Broach, the name of *Spire* being confined to such structures as have gutters and parapets round their bases.
Fine examples of spires of this date exist in Normandy,
and at Bampton and Witney, Oxfordshire, and various
other places.

During the prevalence of the *Decorated* style spires
were almost always very acute; they generally had parapets and gutters round them, though the *Broach* spires
are by no means uncommon at this date, as at Stamford

and Crick, Northamptonshire. Decorated spires did not differ materially from Early English spires, except in the character of the details and the amount of enrichments, which now began to be introduced in profusion : crockets were often carved on the angles, as at Caythorpe, and small bands of panelling or other ornaments formed round them at different heights ; the openings also were more enriched, and the pinnacles on the angles of the tower were enlarged, and were not unfrequently connected with the spire by small flying buttresses. Fine examples of this style are the spires of Salisbury Cathedral and of St. Mary's, Oxford.

Spire, Caythorpe, c. 1320.

In the *Perpendicular* style the same general arrangement was continued, although the character of the details and enrichments was altered in common with those of the other features of Gothic architecture : at this period broach spires appear to have been abandoned—at least no example of one of this date can be referred to. The foregoing observations refer to spires of stone, but they were often also made of timber and covered either with lead or shingles ; the greater part of these were broaches, but they were sometimes surrounded by a parapet at the base : many specimens of timber spires, covered with shingles, are to be met with in the counties of Surrey, Sussex, Kent, and Essex, and in some other places.

Splay, (old Fr. *Disployer*), the expansion given to doorways, windows, and other openings in walls, &c., by slanting the sides. This mode of construction prevails in Gothic architecture, especially on the insides of windows, but is very rarely, if ever, used in Classical architecture. The term is also applied to other slanted or sloped surfaces, such as *cants, bevels,* &c.

Spout. The usual contrivance for throwing off the water from the roofs of mediæval buildings was by means of a carved stone spout called a *gargoyle,* or *gurgoyle.* It is quite possible some were of lead, but none are found remaining till the sixteenth century.

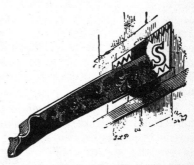

Leaden Spout, Woodford Church, Northamptonshire.

Springing, Springer, the impost or point at which an arch unites with its support. The bottom stone of an arch, which lies immediately upon the impost, is sometimes called a springer or springing-stone. Also the bottom stone of the coping of a gable. [See *Voussoir* and *Skew.*]

Squinch, or Sconce, small arches or projecting courses of stone formed across the angles of towers, &c., in Gothic architecture, to support the alternate sides of octagonal spires, lanterns, &c., above. Sometimes the overhanging side of the spire or octagon, when rising from a square tower, is supported by a series of projecting courses of stone (as at Tong), which

Squinch, Canon's Ashby, Northamptonshire.

answer the same purpose as the arches, but are more substantial because they have no tendency to expand the walls, which is always to be feared when the arched squinch is used. The straight squinch is often employed externally, as at St. Cross, where it is used to carry the *alure*, or parapet walk, across the angle at the junction of the choir and transept with the tower. The construction of the arched squinch or *tromp* was a favourite exercise with the French professors of the art of stone-cutting.

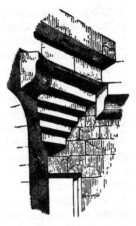

Tong Church, Salop.

Squint: an opening through the wall of a church in an oblique direction, for the purpose of enabling persons in the transepts or aisle to see the elevation of the Host at the high altar. The usual situation of these openings is on one or both sides of the chancel-arch, and there is frequently a projection, like a low buttress, on the outside across the angle to cover this opening: these projections are more common in some districts than in others; they are particularly abundant in the neighbourhood of Tenby, in South Wales; but the openings themselves are to be found everywhere, though they have commonly been plastered over, or sometimes boarded at the two ends, in other cases filled up with bricks. In some

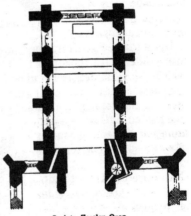

Squints, Haseley, Oxon.

SPLANDREL = Spandrel.
SQUILLERIE = Scullery.

SPUR. See *Sper*.

instances they are small narrow arches by the side
of the chancel-arch,
extending from the
ground to the height
of ten or twelve feet,
as at Minster Lovell,
Oxon: usually they
are not above a yard
high and about two
feet wide, often wider
at the west end than
at the east. They are
commonly plain, but
sometimes ornament-
ed like niches, and
sometimes have light
open panelling across
them; this is par-
ticularly the case in
Somersetshire and
Devonshire. There
are many instances
of these openings in
other situations be-
sides the usual one,
but always in the

Crawley, Hampshire.

direction of the high altar, or at
least of an altar: sometimes the
opening is from a chapel by the
side of the chancel, as at Chipping-
Norton, Oxon. In Bridgewater
Church, Somerset, there is a series
of these openings through three
successive walls, following the
same oblique line, to enable a person standing in the porch to see
the high altar: in this and some
other instances, as at Burford, it
seems to have been for the use
of the attendant who had to ring
the sanctus-bell at the time of

Squint, Mayor's Chapel, Bristol.

the elevation of the Host. While there seems to be no good or ancient authority for the name of Squint applied to these openings, it has been long in use, and has a priority to the name of *Hagioscope*, which has of late been applied to them. It is true that they, as a rule, are directed towards the altar, and the name is, therefore, more fortunate than that given to the Low-side window, by those who prefer Greek names to English; still it is a question whether there is any reason for the disuse of the older and more simple word.

Stage, a step, floor, or storey; the term is particularly applied to the spaces or divisions between the set-offs of buttresses in Gothic architecture, and to the horizontal divisions of windows which are intersected by transoms.

Stained-glass, or Painted-glass windows were in use at all periods, or as early as white glass, both in houses and in churches : those of houses were in moveable casements, which were articles of furniture for a long period, and were carried from one manor-house to another. In churches the windows were fixtures, and often very richly coloured, the style changing along with that of the architecture, and requiring a separate treatise, which has been admirably supplied by the late Mr. Winston in his "Hints on Glass-Painting, by an Amateur."

The earliest examples known in this country are of the end of the twelfth century, as in the clear-story of Canterbury. In France there is a small portion of painted glass believed to be of the eleventh century, at Le Mans. The greater part of our glass belongs to the fifteenth century, though small portions of earlier date may generally be found in our country churches, especially in the smaller openings of the tracery, where it has escaped notice, and so destruction, by the Puritans. As in Gothic architecture generally, so especially in glass, has the revival of taste and knowledge shewn itself during the last few years, so that now no restoration of a church is considered complete without stained-glass windows, if not in the body of the church at least in the chancel.

Stall (Lat.), a fixed seat enclosed, either wholly or partially, at the back and sides. All large churches and most small ones previous to the Reformation had a range of wooden stalls on each side and at the west end of the choir, which were separated from each other by large projecting elbows, with desks fixed before them. In cathedrals and other large buildings they were enclosed at the back with panelling, and were surmounted by overhanging canopies of open tabernacle-work, which were often carried up to a great height, and enriched with numerous pinnacles, crockets, pierced tracery, and other ornaments: examples of stalls of this kind remain in most of our cathedrals and in many other churches. In some cases two rows were used, the outer one only being surmounted by canopies; it was also raised a step or two higher than the other, as in Henry the Seventh's Chapel, Westminster. In ordinary parish churches the stalls were without canopies, and frequently had no panelling at the back above the level of the elbows, but in many instances the walls over them were lined with wooden panels, with a cornice above, corresponding with the screen under the rood-loft, of which a very good speci-

Oxford Cathedral, c. 1450.

STAY-BAR, the horizontal iron bar which extends in one piece along the top of the mullions of a traceried window; the smaller bars, or *transoms*, extend only from mullion to mullion, and serve to support the vertical bars or stanchions.

men remains at Etchingham, Sussex: when the chancel
had aisles behind the stalls, the backs were formed by the
side screens, which were sometimes close and sometimes
of open-work.   The chief seat on the dais in a domestic
hall was sometimes a stall, as in (the ruins of) the palace
of the Archbishop of Canterbury at Mayfield, Sussex,
where it is of stone.

Standard. (1.) This name seems to have been applied
formerly to various arti-
cles of furniture which
were too ponderous to
be easily removed, as to
large *chests*, or the massive candlesticks placed
before altars in churches,
&c. (2.) Also the vertical
poles of a scaffold; and
the vertical iron bars in
a window, or *Stanchions*.
(3.) It was also applied
to the ends of the oak
benches in churches, and
that is the common use
of the term now.   They
were often very hand-
somely carved, some-
times having poppy-
heads and sometimes
without.   A good illus-
tration is taken from
Dorchester, but others
will be found under *Pew*
and *Stall*.

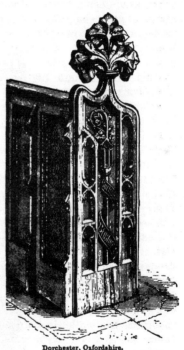

Dorchester, Oxfordshire.

Steeple, Stepull, the tower of a church, &c., including
any superstructure, such as a spire or lantern, standing upon it.   In some districts small churches have
the steeples formed of massive wooden framing, standing
on the floor, and carried up some little distance above the
roof; these are usually at the west end, parted off from
the nave by a wooden partition, as at Ipsden and Tets-
worth, Oxfordshire.

Stanchion (old Fr. *Estançon*), the upright iron bar between the mullions of a window, screen, &c.; they were frequently ornamented at the top with fleurs-de-lis, leaves, &c. The upright bars or railings round tombs may be called stanchions, and these were often very elaborately ornamented at the top. [See illustrations under *Ironwork*.] The name is also sometimes applied to the quarters or studs of wooden partitions, and is used in the north of England for the stone mullions also.

Warborough, Oxon.

Step or **Stair.** It may be convenient in this place to give the nomenclature of the different parts of a stair. The vertical surface is called the *riser* (or *raiser*), the horizontal surface the *tread*. If the edge have a moulding, it is called the *nosing :* this never appears in mediæval steps. When the *tread* is wider at one end than the other, it is called a *winder*, but if of equal breadth a *flyer*. When the *tread* is so broad as to require more than one step of the passenger, it is called a *landing* or *landing-place*, sometimes a *resting-place* or *foot-pace*. A number of successive steps uninterrupted by landings is a *flight*, or simply *stairs ;* the part of the building which contains them is the *staircase*. A flight of *winders* of which the narrow ends of the steps terminate in one solid column was called a *vyse, screw stairs*, sometimes a *turngresse*, now often termed *corkscrew stairs ;* the central column is the *newel*, whence the term newel staircase is often used. Sometimes the newel is omitted, and in its place we have a *well-hole*. Stairs that have the lowermost step supported by the floor, and every succeeding step supported jointly by the step below it and the wall of the staircase at one end only, are termed *geometrical stairs*. Stairs constructed in the form nearly of an inclined plane, of which the treads are inclined and broad, and the risers small, so that horses may ascend and descend them, are called *marches rampantes*, or *girons rampantes* (as at the Mausoleum of Hadrian at Rome, St. Mark's at Venice, and in Italy commonly). Large external stairs are called *perrons*.

Stilted-arch, a name proposed by Professor Willis for an arch which has the capital, or impost mouldings, of the jambs below the level of the springing of the curve, the mouldings of the archivolt being continued, vertically, down to the impost mouldings. This mode of construction was frequently employed at the latter end of the Norman style, especially as a means of maintaining an uniform height, when arches of different widths were used in the same range. [See *Arch*, fig. 5.]

Story, Storey: one of the divisions of a building, in the vertical direction; the space between two contiguous floors, or between two contiguous entablatures, or other architectural dividing lines that indicate floors or separations of the building. In English mediæval documents it is often Latinized into *historia*. In domestic and palatial architecture the storeys are thus enumerated, from the lowest upwards: basement or underground storey; ground-storey or ground-floor, at about the level of the ground; first-storey, usually the principal floor or storey. Then follow second, third, and so on, the upper being the garrets. Entresols or mezzanini are considered as intermediate storeys not interfering with the enumeration of the principal ones. The word is applied also to a window where the lights appear one above the other, as a "storied window."

Strut, or Strutting-piece. In carpentry, any piece that keeps two others from approaching, and is therefore itself in a state of compression; in contradistinction to a tie, which keeps the two points of the frame to which its extremities are attached from receding, and is therefore in a state of tension. [See *Roof*.]

Stoup, Stope, a vessel to contain consecrated water, such as is placed near the entrance of a Roman Catholic church, into which all who enter dip their fingers and cross themselves. In this country a small niche with a stone basin was formed in the wall, either in the porch or within the church, close to the door, or in one of the

STAYKFALD-HOLE=Putlog-hole.   STEREOBATE (Gr.), base of a wall.
STOA (Gr.) = Latin *Porticus*.

pillars nearest to the door, as a receptacle for holy-water, but sometimes a vessel placed on a stand or pedestal was used; the niches resemble piscinas, except that they differ

Pylle Church, Somerset.

Romsey, Hants.

in situation, are smaller and plainer, and very rarely have any hole in the bottom: examples in a mutilated condition remain in various churches, as in the south porch of Coton Church, Cambridgeshire; in the north porch of Thornham Church, Kent, is one in a perfect state. It is also called *Holy-water Stone*, and answers to the French *Benitier*.

String or **Stringcourse**, a projecting horizontal band or line of mould-ings in a build-ing. Round the exterior of a building the string is car-ried across the buttresses, and sometimes over

Lincoln Cathedral, c. 1220.

the windows, forming the dripstone.

STUDS, the intermediate posts in partitions of wood-work. They are also termed *Uprights* and *Quarters*.

STYLES, in joining, are the upright pieces of a frame, as of a door, shutter, screen, or other panel-work, of which the horizontal pieces are termed *rails*.

Tabernacle. The Latin *tabernaculum* signifies a booth or small *taberna* of boards capable of being put together or taken asunder, as a tent is pitched. In the Vulgate it is thus employed for the portable temple of the Jews, the "Tabernacle of the Wilderness." Hence the word came to signify any small cell or other place in which some holy or precious thing was deposited, and thus was applied to the ornamental receptacle for the pix over the altar. It was similarly extended to the niches for images, at first of saints, and next for any images. Lastly, sepulchral monuments, and the stalls of a choir, and the sedilia, being surmounted by rich canopy-work of the same kind as that which was employed over the heads of niches, such work was called *tabernacle-work*, and the seat with its canopy, *a tabernacle;* and not only over the seats of the choir, but over the pulpit also, the same design was employed. Tabernacles were also called *Maisons, Habitacles, Hovels,* and *Housings* in old contracts, all reverting to the original derivation of the word. It is worth remarking that Inigo Jones applies it to the niches of Roman architecture. The tabernacle was sometimes in the form of a tower. The *Sacrament-Hauslein,* in the church of St. Laurence, Nuremberg, constructed by Adam Kraft, 1496—1500, is sixty-four feet high, and tapers upwards in the form of a spire until it reaches the roof. In the early ages of Christianity the name of tabernacle was sometimes applied to a church, as well as to the ciborium or canopy of the altar.

Canopy of Pulpit, Edlesborough, Bucks.

The forms and arrangements of tabernacles for images have been varied at different times, but at first they consist of little else than an ornamental arch of the period, recessed so as to form a niche of sufficient depth for the reception of the statue. Various kinds of hoods or canopies over the head of the figure are soon introduced, and projecting corbels or other pedestals for its support beneath.

In the *Norman* style the tabernacles are generally shallow square recesses, often plain, and in many cases the figures in them carved on the backs in alto-relievo, and built into the wall. They were not unfrequently placed in ranges, sometimes under a series of intersecting arches, but were also used singly, especially over doorways, as at Hadiscoe.

In the *Early English* style tabernacles became more enriched and their niches more deeply recessed; the figures were sometimes set on small pedestals, and canopies were not unfrequently used over the heads. They were often placed in suites, or arranged in pairs, under a larger arch; when in suites they were very commonly separated by single shafts, in other cases the sides were usually moulded in a similar way to windows. The arches of the heads were either cinquefoiled, trefoiled, or plain, and when hoodmoulds were used they were generally made to project. Good examples are to be seen on the west front of the cathedral at Wells.

Decorated tabernacles were more varied than those of

STYLOBATE, Stereobate, the basement or substructure of a temple below the columns, resembling a continuous pedestal. See *Podium*.

SUBSELLUM = *Miserere*.

SUMMER, a horizontal beam or girder, usually called *Breastsummer*.

SUPER ALTARE. (1.) A small portable stone altar, (see an example engraved in Archæological Journal, vol. iv. p. 245). (2.) Commonly but erroneously applied to the shelf or raised portion at the back of the altar, on which the candlesticks, &c., are placed.

SURBASE, the upper mouldings of a cornice of a *Pedestal*.

SURBASED ARCH, an arch which rises less than half the breadth of the opening above the level of the springing.

SYLE, or Sule. See *Sill*.

SYSTYLE, one of the five species of intercolumniation defined by Vitruvius. In this the columns are set at a distance equal to twice the diameter of the shaft measured at its lower part just above the apophyge, or (which is the same thing according to the Vitruvian proportions) the distance between the plinths is exactly equal to the diameter of the plinths.

the earlier styles. Their niches were usually of considerable depth, in the form either of a semi-octagon or semi-hexagon, with the top cut into a regular vault with ribs and bosses, but sometimes they were made shallower and plainer; they were placed either singly or in ranges, and they very frequently had ogee crocketed hoodmoulds over them, which were sometimes placed flat against the wall, and sometimes bowed out in the form of an ogee; triangular hoodmoulds were also common. Several kinds of projecting canopies were likewise used, especially when the niches were placed separately; some of these were conical, like spires, with a series of flat triangular, or ogee, subordinate canopies round the base; others resembled these without the central spire, and some were flat at the top, partaking some-what of the form of turrets; in the tops of buttresses taber-nacles were sometimes made to occupy the whole breadth of the buttress, so as to be entirely open on three sides, with small piers at the front angles. The arches of tabernacles in this style were either plain or feathered; the sides, in addition to the mouldings, were very frequently ornamented with small buttresses and pinnacles; crockets, finials, and pinnacles, were also abun-dantly used on the canopies; pedestals were very common, par-ticularly in niches with project-ing canopies, and in such cases were either carried on corbels or rose from other projecting sup-ports below; sometimes corbels were used instead of pedestals. Queen Eleanor's crosses furnish excellent examples of enriched Decorated tabernacles.

Walpole St. Andrew's, Norfolk.

In the *Perpendicular* style the numerous kinds of

panelling, which were so profusely introduced, were sometimes deeply recessed and made to receive figures, and these varied considerably in form, but of the more legitimate tabernacles the general character did not differ very materially, although there was often considerable variety in the details; they were usually recessed in the form of a semi-hexagon or semi-octagon, with a vaulted top carved with ribs and bosses; the canopies projected, and were sometimes flat on the top, sometimes conical like spires, and occasionally were carried up a considerable height with a variety of light open-work, with buttresses and pinnacles; in plan the canopies were usually half an octagon, or hexagon, with small pendants and pinnacles at the angles; and crockets, finials, and other enrichments were often introduced with great profusion. Buttresses, surmounted with pinnacles, were also very frequently placed at the sides of the niches in this style; the arches were sometimes plain and sometimes feathered.

St. Michael's, Oxford.

In early French work tabernacles are frequently formed at the tops and at the set-offs of buttresses, &c., with three sides open, the front of the canopy being supported on small shafts; the canopies are sometimes triangular, and sometimes in the form of small spires. [See *Canopy* and *Niche*.]

TABERNACLE-WORK, ornamented open-work, such as is used over niches, stalls, &c.

TABLE, Holy Table, the Lord's Table. See *Altar*.

Table, Tablet, a mediæval term applied generally to all horizontal *bands* of mouldings, such as base-mouldings, strings, cornices, &c. The word table, when used separately without any adjunctive term to point out its position, appears to have signified the cornice, but it is very usually associated with other epithets which define its situation, as *base-table, earth-*

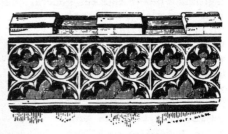

Great Addington, c. 1350.

table, or *ground-table*, *bench-table*, *corbel-table*, &c.

The word TABLE also, according to its ancient signification, denoted a level expanded surface, as a flat piece of board : a picture was termed a table as late as the seventeenth century : the folding boards used for the game of chess were called tables. In like manner any construction adapted for superficial decoration was termed *tabula*, or *tablementum*, such as the decorative front of an altar, when formed of solid workmanship, enriched with ornaments of gold or silver, with gems, ivory, or other costly substances. Occasionally the term *tabula* denotes the decorative work which more correctly should be called *posttabula*, or *retro-tabula*, in French *retable*, which in common parlance would be termed the altar-piece, being affixed over the altar to the wall or screen against which the altar is placed. A remarkable example of the *tabula*, destined for the front of the altar, is preserved in Westminster Abbey; it is formed of wood, elaborately carved, painted, and enriched with a kind of mosaic work of coloured glass superficially inlaid—a species of decoration which appears to have been of Italian origin. Amongst the benefactions of the abbots to the church of St. Alban's, as recorded by Matthew Paris, several instances may be found, which shew the extraordinary richness of such decorations, as used in England ; William of Malmesbury, in the " Antiquities of the Church of Glastonbury," describes the rich *tabula* given by Abbot Brithwy, 1017, formed of gold, silver, and ivory.

Temple, (1.) a building set apart for the services of religious worship, and generally dedicated to some heathen deity; (2.) a building erected by the Jews for worship. The temples of the ancients were generally oblong in their plan, and consisted of a body, or cell, with a portico at one or both of the ends supporting a pediment, and were often entirely surrounded by a colonnade, but occasionally they were circular: of this latter form there were but two kinds, the *monopteral*, which was merely an open circle of columns supporting a roof or entablature, and the *peripteral*, which had a circular cell surrounded by a colonnade. Of the oblong temples there were several varieties, the simplest of which was called *in antis;* this consisted of a plain cell, the side walls of which projected at one end, or front of the building, and were terminated with antæ, between which were two columns. The *prostylos* temple differed from the preceding in having a portico of four columns standing in front of the antæ, the columns between the antæ being omitted. The *amphiprostylos* had a portico of this last-mentioned kind at each end, or front, of the cell. The *peripteral* temple had a portico of six columns on each front, and a detached colonnade of eleven at each side of the cell, the columns at the angles being included in both computations. The *pseudo-peripteral* was like the peripteral, with the breadth of the cell increased, so that the side walls became united with the columns of the lateral colonnades. The *dipteral* had porticoes of eight columns on the fronts and a double colonnade at the sides, the outer one consisting of fifteen columns. The *pseudo-dipteral* was precisely the same as the dipteral, with the inner range of columns omitted throughout. Some large temples had the cells left open at the top, without any roof, and when so constructed were called *hypæthral.* Temples were also classified according to the number of columns in the front porticoes; *tetrastyle* had four columns; *hexastyle*, six; *octastyle*, eight; *decastyle*, ten. The width of the spaces between the columns varied considerably, and the porticoes were designated accordingly *aræostyle, diastyle, eustyle, systyle,* and *pycnostyle.*

Tænia, or Tenia, the fillet or band on the top of a Doric frieze.

Templet, Template: a pattern or mould used by workmen, especially by masons and bricklayers, as a guide for the shape of their work; it is usually formed of a thin board, or sheet of metal. Also a short piece of timber sometimes laid in a wall under the end of a girder or other beam.

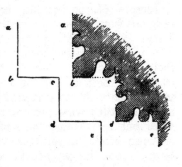

Tenon, Tenant: a common term in carpentry, used to signify the projection left at the end of a piece of timber to be inserted into a socket, or *mortise*, made to receive it.

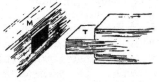

M. Mortise.　　　　　T. Tenon.

Terrace, a raised space or platform adjoining to a building, frequently encompassed with a balustrade or steps, as at Versailles, where there are a succession of terraces one above the other. A level area on the side of a sloping bank or other situation overlooking lower scenery in a garden, pleasure-ground, &c. Terraces were very extensively employed about houses in the time of Queen Elizabeth and King James I.

Tessellated Pavement, pavement formed of small pieces of brick, stone, marble, &c., which are called *tessellæ* or *tesseræ*, much used by the Romans; the rudest description was formed of small cubes of brick about an inch square, but the better kinds were of finer materials and in smaller pieces, and were generally very ornamental, representing architectural patterns, or animals and figures. [See *Mosaic.*]

Tester (old French, *Teste* or *Téte*), a flat canopy over a pulpit, tomb, bed, &c. According to Ducange, (voc. *Testerium,*) the Italian *testiera* is that side of the bed which is next the bolster, or as we now call it, the *head* of the bed; and not the *tester* in its modern sense. It may be, however, that the *tester* was drapery drawn upwards into the form of a kind of dome or canopy which crowned the *sparver*, while the *celura* or *seler* was the horizontal lining below it, and therefore immediately over the bed. The canopy over Queen Eleanor's tomb at Westminster is called a *tester* in old documents.

Thatch, a covering for roofs, formed of reeds, flags, straw, heath, or other similar materials. Thatch was formerly used more generally and on more important buildings than is usual in the present day, though in some districts it is still employed to a considerable extent; the best kind is made of reeds, a material which was employed at an early period. The old word *to thack, theak,* or thatch, frequently signifies no more than to cover, and is used in reference to tiles, lead, or other materials, e.g. *thack-tiles* are tiles or slates for covering a roof.

Through Carved-work. carved work in which the spaces between the ornamental parts are pierced entirely through the substance of the material on which it is cut and left open: this is the way in which wooden tabernacle-work is usually formed, and also the foliage of Decorated capitals.

Through, a stone in a wall which reaches entirely through it, and shews itself on both sides; called also a *Bonder, Bond - stone,* and *Perpent - stone.* The name Through or Through - stone, sometimes spelt Trough, is also applied to a flat gravestone, and is still common in some of the northern parts of the kingdom.

TELAMONES, statues of men employed as columns or pilasters in Classical architecture; sometimes called also Atlantes or Caryatides.

TEPIDARIUM, or tepid bath, also the vessel used for heating the water for the bath; and the room in which the warm-bath was placed.

TETRASTOON (Gr.), a court-yard having porticoes on each of its four sides.

TETRASTYLE (Gr.), a portico having four columns in front.

TEWEL, a term which seems to imply the louvre, or flue for smoke. It is derived from the old French word *Tuiel,* 'a pipe or conduit.'

THERMÆ, public institutions of the ancient Romans, of which the Baths were an important part.

THOLOBATE, the substructure on which a dome or cupola rest.

THROATING, the undercutting of a projecting moulding beneath, so as to prevent rainwater from dripping down the surface of the wall.

Thurible (Lat.), a vessel in which to burn incense, which was used in some of the services of the Church. It was made of metal commonly, and in the form of a vase, with a cover perforated to allow the scented fumes of the burning incense to escape; it is carried by three chains, which are attached to three points around the lower portion of the censer, whilst a fourth, connected with them above, being united to the ring or handle, which serves for carrying the censer, is used to raise at intervals the upper portion or covering of the censer,

Thurible, Sixteenth century.

and allows the smoke of the incense to escape.

Tiles. (1.) Thin plates of baked clay used to cover roofs. In this country there are but two kinds of tiles in ordinary use, plain tiles and pan-tiles: the former of these, which are by far the commonest, are perfectly flat, the latter are curved, so that when laid upon a roof each tile overlaps the

Pan Tiles.

edge of the next to it, and protects the joint from the wet. The Romans used flat tiles turned up at the edges, with a row of inverted semi-cylindrical ones over the joint to keep out the wet. In the Middle Ages tiles were

TIE-BEAM. In a roof-truss, a beam which rests on the walls and extends completely across. It was anciently termed *roof-*beam, *chamber-beam, binding-beam, footing-beam,* and *footing-dormant.*

extensively employed in this country for covering buildings, though they seem always to have been considered

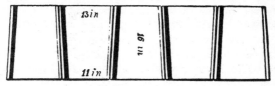

Roman Tiles, Wheatley.

an inferior material to lead.   It does not appear that any
but flat plain tiles, with such
others as were requisite for
the ridges, hips, and valleys,
were used; the ridge-tiles,
or crest, formerly also called
roof-tiles, were sometimes
made ornamental. [See

A. Roof-tiles.   B. Crest-tiles.   C. Pan-tiles.

Crest.] It is not unusual to find the backs of fireplaces
formed of tiles, and in such situations they are sometimes
laid in herring-bone courses, as in the great hall, Kenilworth: most of the fireplaces in Bodiam Castle, Sussex,
are constructed in this manner, and the oven by the side
of the larger fireplace in the hall is also built of tiles.

(2.) Glazed decorative tiles were anciently much used
for paving sacred edifices; they are sometimes called Norman tiles, possibly from the supposition that they were
originally made in Normandy; and, considering the age
and variety of specimens that exist in northern France,
this idea may not be wholly erroneous. It is doubtful,
however, whether any tiles have been discovered in England that present the features of the Norman style of
architectural decoration, the most ancient being apparently
of the thirteenth century. The name of encaustic has
also been given to these tiles, and it would not be inappropriate, were it not applied already to denote an antique
process of art, of a perfectly different nature; whereas
a method wholly distinct, and peculiar to the glazed tiles
of the Middle Ages, was commonly adopted in northern
Europe. The process of manufacture which, as it is supposed, was most commonly employed, may be thus de-

scribed. The thin squares of well-compacted clay having been fashioned, and probably dried in the sun to the requisite degree, their ordinary dimension being from four to six inches, with a thickness of one inch, a stamp which bore a design in relief was impressed upon them, so as to leave the ornamental pattern in *cavetto;* into the hollows thus left on the face of the tile, clay of another colour, most commonly white, or pipe-clay, was then inlaid or impressed; nothing remained except to give a richer effect, and, at the same time, ensure the permanence of the work by covering the whole in the furnace with a thin surface of metallic glaze, which, being of a slightly yellow colour, tinged the white clay beneath it, and imparted to the red a more full and rich tone of colour. In the success of this simple operation, much depended upon this, that the quality of the two kinds of clay that were used should be as nearly similar as possible, or else, if the white was liable to shrink in the furnace more than the red, the whole work would be full of cracks; in the other case, the design would bulge and be thrown upwards; imperfections, of which examples are not wanting. To facilitate the equal drying of the tile, deep scorings or hollows were sometimes made on the reverse, and by this means, when laid in cement, the pavement was more firmly held together. Occasionally, either from the deficiency of white clay of good quality, or perhaps for the sake of variety, glazed tiles occur which have the design left hollow, and not filled in, according to the usual process, with clay of a different colour; a careful examination however of the disposition of the ornament will frequently shew that the original intention was to fill these cavities, as in other specimens, but instances also present themselves where

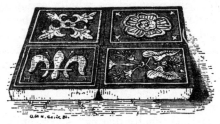

Westleigh, Devon.

the ornamental design evidently was intended to remain in relief, the field, and not the pattern, being found in *cavetto.* It must be observed, that instances are very frequent. where the protecting glaze having been worn away, the white clay, which is of a less compact quality than the red, has fallen out, and left the design hollow, so that an impression or rubbing may readily be taken. It appears probable that the origin of the fabrication of decorative pavements, by the process which has been described, is to be sought in the mediæval imitations of the Roman mosaic-work, by means of coloured substances inlaid upon stone or marble. Of this kind of *marqueterie* in stone, few examples have escaped the injuries of time; specimens may be seen on the eastern side of the

Canterbury Cathedral.

altar-screen in Canterbury Cathedral, and at the abbey church of St. Denis, and the cathedral of St. Omer.

Amongst the earliest specimens of glazed tiles may be mentioned the pavement discovered in the ruined priory church at Castle Acre, Norfolk, a portion of which is in the Britism Museum. These tiles are ornamented with scutcheons of arms, and on some appears the name THOMAS; they are coarsely executed, the cavities are left, and not filled-in with any clay of different colour.

A profusion of good examples still exists of single tiles, and sets of four, nine, sixteen, or a greater number of tiles, forming by their combination a complete design, and presenting, for the most part, the characteristic style of ornament which was in vogue at each successive period; but examples of general arrangement are very rare and imperfect. To this deficiency of authorities it seems to be due, that modern imitations of these ancient pavements have generally proved unsatisfactory, in the resemblance which they present to oil-cloth, or carpeting; and the intention of producing richness of effect by carrying the ornamental design throughout the pavement, without any intervening spaces, has been wholly frustrated. Sufficient care has not been given to ascertain the ancient system of arrangement: it is, however, certain that a large proportion of plain tiles, black, white, or red, were introduced, and served to divide the various portions which composed the general design. Plain diagonal bands, for instance, arranged fretwise, intervened between the compartments, or panels, of tiles ornamented with designs; the plain and the decorated quarries were laid alternately, or in some instances

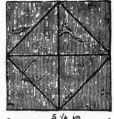

Woodperry, Oxon.

longitudinal bands were introduced in order to break that continuity of ornament which being uniformly spread over a large surface, as in some modern pavements, produces a confused rather than a rich effect. It has been supposed, with much probability, that the more elaborate pavements were reserved for the decoration of the choir, the chancel, or immediate vicinity of an altar, whilst in the aisles, or other parts of the church, more simple pavements of plain tiles, black, white, or red, were usually employed. It may also deserve notice, that in almost every instance when the ornamented tiles have been accidentally discovered, or dug up on the site of a castle or mansion, there has been reason to suppose a consecrated fabric had there existed, or that the tiles had belonged to that portion of the structure which had been devoted to religious services. We meet often with the item "Flanders tiles" in building accounts of castles, but these were for the fireplace only. The lower rooms were usually "earthed," the upper rooms boarded.

TINNING of ironwork was practised in the Middle Ages to preserve it from rust, and perhaps for ornament sake. Thus the iron gate which enclosed the shrine of St. Erkenvald was tinned over.

Timber-built House, or Half-timber House. Timber-houses were in use at all periods, from the earliest known records to the present time, though stone and brick houses have gradually become more common. From the perishable nature of the material we have probably no timber-work remaining earlier than the thirteenth century, and of that period it is rare; although several roofs and beams

Newgate, York, c. 1380.

with the mouldings and ornaments of that style are judged to be of that time, no perfect timber-house is known either of the thirteenth or fourteenth century. A house in the Newgate at York, of this description, is believed to be of the fourteenth century in its main construction, as the details of the stone-work are of that period, and the timber-work appears to belong to the same construction.   The upper part of this house is carried on a massive *breast-summer*, with upright posts from it to the *tie-beam* of the roof, from which there is a king-post to the *wind-beam*, and *braces* to the *principal timber*. Other timber-houses are called *sile-built*, when the lower beam is close to the ground, forming a *sile* or *cill*, instead of being raised as a *breast-summer* over the ground-floor.

King Richard's House, Leicester, c. 1450.

Those of the fifteenth and sixteenth centuries are very numerous, and belong generally to the class called *Half-timber* houses, in which the ground-floor is of stone or brick and the upper part only of wood, which usually over-hangs, or is corbelled out very boldly, sometimes on stone corbels, but more often on wood only.

A very common practice was to build, so to speak, the skeleton of the house with timber, and fill up the interstices with brick, many examples of which are very picturesque, particularly in midland towns, such as Shrewsbury, Coventry, &c.   The space between the timbers in other examples was filled with plaster-work, but in them the woodwork was always left prominent.   The *Barge-board* also was a striking feature in timber-built houses, and frequently very richly carved.

Tomb and **Tombstone** (Gr. *Tumbos*). In its first sig-nification a grave of any kind, but in the second a mark of a grave, or a *monument*, to remind the passer-by that a person is buried beneath. In the earliest ages a heap of stones, or a single upright stone, such as the *Menhir*, seems to have marked the resting-place of the dead. Amongst the early Britons the *cromlech*—that is, two or three stones standing upright, with one or more across them on the top—was a common form of tomb. But contemporary with them was the simplest of all struc-tures, the mound of earth.

When the Romans came, they brought over with them, amongst other customs, their modes of burial. Consider-ing the time of their occupation, the remains of their tombs belonging to this period are not so numerous as might be expected; but still there are several, and in most cases they consisted of a single stone, with an inscription commonly ad-dressed to one or more of the heathen gods. A few instan-ces of stone cof-fins of this pe-riod have been found, as at York. To this kind of tomb, or rather stone

Roman Coffin, York.

coffin, the name of *Sarcophagus* is usually applied; and we find that in some cases, e.g., at Westminster, the tomb has been used over again in some later times.

The marks of interment adopted by the heathen in-vaders of this country, in the fifth century, were probably mounds of earth only; and it is only by the nature of the pottery or other implements and articles of dress found in the graves that these burial-places can be dis-tinguished from those of the Britons. Of course amongst

To-FALL, Too-FALL : a shed or building annexed to the wall of a larger one, the roof of which is formed in a single slope with the top resting against the wall of the principal building. A term retained in use in the north. Sometimes called a *Lean-to*.

the later Saxons, when Christianity prevailed, and they were buried in the churchyard, more lasting memorials were erected.

The sepulchral monuments throughout the Middle Ages were of great importance from an architectural point of view; and while we find them following the prevailing style, we frequently find also that on them was lavished the most elaborate work possible. The examples which remain to us are those which were placed within the church. No doubt there were many tombs of no mean design or work placed in the churchyard, but they have, for the most part, perished.

Of the former we have many of the twelfth century (some perhaps of the eleventh). The covers of these were at first simply coped, afterwards frequently ornamented

Flat Gravestone, Great Milton, Oxon.

with crosses of various kinds, and other devices, and some-times had inscriptions on them: subsequently they were sculptured with recumbent figures in high relief; but still generally diminishing in width from the head to the feet, to fit the coffins of which they formed the lids. Many of the figures of this period represent knights in armour with their legs crossed; these are supposed to have been either Templars, or such as had joined, or vowed to join, in a crusade to the Holy Land. The figures usually had canopies, which were often richly carved over the heads, supported on small shafts, which ran along each side of the effigy, the whole worked in the same block of stone. This kind of tomb was sometimes placed beneath a low arch or recess formed within the substance of the church wall, usually about seven feet in length, and not more than three feet above the coffin, even in the centre: these arches were at first semicircular or segmental at the top, afterwards obtusely pointed, they often remain when the figure or brass, and perhaps the coffin itself, has long disappeared and been forgotten. On many tombs of the thirteenth century there are plain pediment-shaped canopies over the heads of the recumbent effigies, the earliest of which contain a pointed trefoil-arched recess : towards the end of the century, these canopies became gradually enriched with crockets, finials, and other architectural details.

In the reign of Edward I. the tombs of persons of rank began to be ornamented on the sides with armorial bearings and small sculptured statues, within pedimental canopied recesses; and from these we may progressively trace the peculiar *minutiæ* and enrichments of every style of Gothic architecture up to the Reformation.

Altar, or table-tombs, called by Leland "high tombs," with recumbent effigies, are common during the whole of the fourteenth century; these sometimes appear beneath splendid pyramidical canopies, as the tomb of Edward II. in Gloucester Cathedral, Hugh le Despenser and Sir Guy de Brian, at Tewkesbury; or flat testoons, as the tombs of Edward III. and Richard II. at Westminster, and Edward the Black Prince at Canterbury. Towards the middle of the thirteenth century the custom commenced, and in the earlier part of the fourteenth prevailed, of inlaying flat stone with brasses; and sepulchral inscriptions, though they had not yet become general, are more frequently to be met with. The sides of these tombs are sometimes relieved with niches, surmounted by decorated pediments, each containing a small sculptured figure, sometimes with arched panels filled with tracery. Other tombs about the same period, but more frequently in the fifteenth century, were decorated along the sides with large square panelled compartments, richly foliated or quatrefoiled, and containing shields.

Many of the tombs of the fifteenth and sixteenth centuries appear beneath arched recesses, fixed in or projecting from the wall, and inclosing the tomb on three sides; these were constructed so as to form canopies, which are often of the most elaborate and costly workmanship; they

are frequently flat at the top, particularly in the later
period. These cano-
pies were sometimes
of carved wood, of
very elaborate work-
manship; and some-
times the altar-
tomb of an earlier
date was at a later
period enclosed
within a screen of
open-work, with a
groined stone cano-
py, and in a few
instances an upper
storey of wood, form-
ing a mortuary
chapel or chantry.

Tomb, Waterperry, Oxon., c. 1400.

In the early part
of the sixteenth cen-
tury the monuments
were generally of
a similar character
to those of the pre-
ceding age; but
alabaster slabs with
figures on them, cut
in outline, were fre-
quently used. The
altar - tombs with
figures in niches, carved in bold relief, were also frequently of alabaster, which was extensively quarried in
Derbyshire. Towards the middle of this century the
Italian style of architecture had come into general use;
Wade's monument, in St. Michael's Church, Coventry,
1556, is a good example of the mixture of the two styles
which then prevailed.

In the two following centuries every sort of barbarism
was introduced on funeral monuments; but the ancient
style lingered longer in some places than in others. The
tomb of Sir Thomas Pope, founder of Trinity College,

Oxford, who died in 1558, in the chapel of that society, shews the altar-tomb in its debased form, after the true era of Gothic architecture had passed away.

Of remains of square tombs in our churchyards, but few are found, and in all cases are decayed by the weather. There is a kind of stone known as a Head-stone,

Bredon, Worcestershire.

which is chiefly used in modern times, but while there are few mediæval examples remaining, there is no reason to suppose but that they were very numerous. One at Temple Bruer is probably of the twelfth century; another at Lincoln is probably of the thirteenth. A very simple example from Handborough churchyard is possibly of the fifteenth century.

Handborough, Oxon.

Tooth Ornament (called also *Dog-tooth* ornament). This name is given to an ornament very extensively used in the Early English style of architecture, consisting of a square four-leaved flower, the centre of which projects in a point. This form is called by the French *violette*, and often bears a very close resemblance to that flower. There are minute differences in the manner of cutting it, and sometimes the sides are so perfectly flat, and it is formed with so much stiffness, as to resemble a pierced pyramid rather than a flower. It is characteristic of the Early English style, in which it is often used in great profusion, though occasionally met with in late Norman work, as at the west window of the south aisle of the nave of Rochester Cathedral; it is generally placed in a deep hollow moulding, with the flowers in close contact with each other, though they are not unfrequently placed a short distance apart, and in rich suites of mouldings are often repeated several times. In some parts of France it is commonly used in work of the twelfth century.

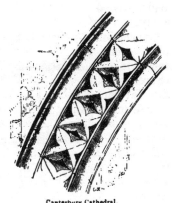

Canterbury Cathedral.

West Door, St. Cross, Hants.

Torus (Lat.), a large round moulding commonly used in the bases of columns, &c.: called also a *Round*. It occurs by itself chiefly in the Classical style, but it is not uncommon in the Norman, and is used thus sometimes in the Gothic styles.

TONGUE, the name given to the ornament in the *Echinus* moulding which alternates with the egg-shaped figure; hence the name *Egg-and-Tongue moulding*.

Touch-stone, a name sometimes applied to compact dark-coloured stones, such as Purbeck and Petworth marble, and others of similar kind, which are frequently used for fine work in Gothic architecture; some of these are capable of receiving a high polish: the term does not appear to have been in common use for any very long period. It is believed to have been so called from its supposed identity with, or resemblance to, the *lapis Lydius*, or Touch-stone, used by goldsmiths in assaying the quality of gold by the test of aquafortis. There is a fine effigy in the church at St. Denis, near Paris, of Catherine de Courtenai, who died in 1307, sculptured in limestone, nearly as black as the real touch-stone, and erroneously supposed to be of that material.

Tower. Any attempt to particularize the various kinds of towers which have been adopted by different nations in former ages, would far exceed the scope of this work: the following observations, therefore, are chiefly confined to those which were in use in the Middle Ages in England and the adjacent parts of Europe, and more especially to the towers of churches. Among the Greeks and Romans, towers were employed of various forms and for different purposes, but by no means so abundantly as in after ages, and in general they appear not to have been so lofty as those of mediæval date; the tower of Andronicus Cyrrhestes, called also the Temple of the Winds, at Athens, is octagonal; at Autun, in France, a considerable part of a large and lofty square tower of late Roman work exists. The tower for the use of bells is supposed not to have been introduced till the fifth century, and hence the term *Campanile*, applied to the Italian towers.

In the Middle Ages the towers of castles were numerous and of striking character. During the prevalence of the Norman style the *Keep* often consisted of a large rectangular tower, with others of smaller size, or turrets, attached to the angles, and these last-mentioned generally rose higher than the main building, as at the White Tower of London, and the castles of Rochester and Guildford; the keep tower of Conisburgh Castle in Yorkshire, which is of the latest Norman work, is circular, with large buttresses on the outside; in other examples, especially in those of *later* date, the keep towers are of various forms, often irregular, apparently so constructed as being considered best adapted to the peculiarities of the sites, and the systems of defence in use at the periods of their erection. Besides these main towers, many others, which, though of less magnitude than the keep, were often of very considerable size, were employed in different parts of fortifications, especially at the entrances, where the gateways were generally flanked by towers projecting considerably before the main walls; these were pierced with loop-holes and oillets, and were commonly surmounted with machicolations. The round towers of Ireland have been the subject of so much controversy that it is impossible to notice the different theories respecting them in a work like the present.

Church towers of all dates are greatly diversified, not only in their details but also in general proportions and form; they are occasionally detached from the building to which they belong, but are usually annexed to it, and are to be found placed in almost every possible situation except about the east end of the chancel; the most frequent position is at the west end. In all later cases their use was for hanging the bells, and hence the name *Belfry*; though at first it is not impossible that they served for defensive purposes also, especially when near the walls of towns, e.g. St. Michael's, Oxford. Large churches have often several towers, especially when the plan is cruciform, and in this case there are generally two at the west end, and one, of larger dimensions, at the intersection of the transepts, as at the cathedrals of Canterbury, York, and Lincoln. Ordinary parish churches have usually but one tower. In some examples, where there is an entrance to the church through the lower storey of a tower, it is made to form a porch with an open archway on one side, as at Cranbrook, and many other churches in Kent; or on three sides, as at Newnham, Northamptonshire: in towns, towers are sometimes placed over public thoroughfares, and in such situations are built on open archways. It is not unusual to find church towers which batter, or diminish upwards; these are generally of Norman or Early English date, but in some districts, as in

Northamptonshire, this mode of construction was continued to a later period.

The towers belonging to the style described in the article on *Saxon* architecture are square and massive, not of lofty proportions, and apparently never were provided with stone staircases; some of them are considerably ornamented, while others are very plain: the tower of the church of Sompting, Sussex, which belongs to this style, terminates with a gable on each of the four sides, and is surmounted by a wooden spire, but whether or not this was the original form may be doubted.

In some parts of the kingdom circular church-towers are to be found; these have been sometimes assumed to be of very high antiquity, but the character of their architecture shews that they commonly belong to the Norman and Early English styles; they are built of rough flints, generally of coarse workmanship, with very little ornament of any kind, and that little, for the most part, about the upper storey; one of the best examples is that of Little Saxham

Little Saxham Church, Suffolk.

Church, Suffolk. Plain round towers in the counties of Norfolk and Suffolk are of all periods: the only materials readily accessible being flints, and these not admitting of square corners, the towers were built round, and this practice is continued even to the present day.

Norman towers are generally square, and of rather low proportions, seldom rising much more than their own breadth above the roof of the church, and sometimes not so much; they generally have broad flat buttresses at the angles, and are usually provided with a stone staircuse carried up in a projecting turret attached to one of the angles; this is very commonly rectangular externally, but the form is not unfrequently changed towards the top, especially if the turret is carried up the whole height of the tower; occasionally polygonal Norman towers are to be met with, as at Ely Cathedral. In Normandy a few examples of village church towers of this style exist, which are capped with pyramidal stone roofs, like low square spires, but in general the roofs and parapets are additions of later date. Many Norman towers are very considerably ornamented, the upper storeys being usually the richest, while others are very plain: good specimens remain at St. Alban's Abbey, the cathedrals of Norwich, Exeter, and Winchester; Tewkesbury Abbey; Southwell Minster; the churches of Castor, Northamptonshire; St. Clement, Sandwich; Iffley, Oxfordshire; Stewkley, Buckinghamshire, &c.

In *Early English* towers much greater variety of design and proportion is found than in those of prior date. The prevailing plan is square, but some examples are octagonal, and occasionally the upper part of a square tower is changed to an octagon. Projecting stair-turrets are almost universal, though

Middleton Stoney, Oxon., c. 1220.

they are frequently so much masked by buttresses as to be in great measure concealed. Many towers in this

style are of lofty proportions, while others are low and
massive. The best examples are generally more or less
ornamented, and some are very highly enriched. The
belfry windows are often large, and deeply recessed,
with numerous bold mouldings in the jambs, and appear
sometimes to have been
originally left quite open.
Considerable variety of
outline is produced by
the different arrange-
ment, sizes, and forms
of the buttresses at the
angles of towers in this,
as well as in the later
styles of Gothic archi-
tecture, and sometimes,
instead of buttresses,
small turrets are used,
which rise from the
ground and generally
terminate in pinnacles.
Many towers of this date
are finished at the top
with parapets, some of
them with pinnacles at
the angles, a few with
two gables, called pack-
saddle roofs, as Brook-
thorpe, Northampton-
shire, and many are
surmounted with spires,
which, although perhaps
in the majority of cases
they are of later date

Brookthorpe, Northamptonshire, c. 1260.

than the towers, appear to have been originally contemplated. Examples remain at the cathedrals of Oxford
and Peterborough, the churches of St. Mary, Stamford;
Ketton and Ryhall, Rutland; Loddington and Raunds,
Northamptonshire; Middleton Stoney, Oxfordshire, &c.

In the *Decorated* and *Perpendicular* styles towers differ
very considerably, both in proportions and amount of enrichment, and considerable diversity of outline and effect

is produced by varying the arrangement and form of the subordinate parts, such as windows, buttresses, pinnacles, &c., but in general composition they do not differ very materially from Early English towers. Many are very lofty, and others of low proportions, some highly enriched, and some perfectly plain; a large, and probably the greater number, are crowned with parapets, usually with a pinnacle at each corner, and sometimes with one or two others, commonly of rather smaller size, on each of the sides; many also terminate with spires, or, especially in the Perpendicular style, with lanterns. Decorated towers remain at Lincoln Cathedral, the churches of Heckington and Caythorpe, Lincolnshire; Newark, Nottinghamshire; Finedon, Northamptonshire; St. Mary's, Oxford, &c. Perpendicular towers are very numerous in all parts of the kingdom, especially in Somersetshire; among

Brislington, Somersetshire.

such as are best deserving of attention may be mentioned those at Canterbury, York, and Gloucester Cathedrals, and the churches at Boston and Louth, Lincolnshire; Kettering, Northamptonshire; Taunton, Somersetshire; Cirencester, Gloucestershire; Great Malvern Worcestershire; and those of St. Mary Magdalen College, and Merton College, Oxford.

TRABS (Lat. *Trabes*), a beam, but especially applied to the *Wall-plate*.

TRACHELIUM (Gr.), the neck; applied to part of the space beneath the more solid portion of the capital in an Ionic or Doric column.

Tracery (? Old Fr. *Tracer*), the ornamental stonework in the upper part of Gothic windows, formed by the ramifications of the mullions; also the decorations of corresponding character which are abundantly used in Gothic architecture on panellings, ceilings, &c. The term is not ancient. Tracery has been very satisfactorily divided by Professor Willis into two classes, the early kind, called *Plate-tracery*, consisting merely of openings cut through a flat plate of stone, and the later kind resembling bars of iron twisted into the forms required. Plate tracery begins in the late Norman period, when small circular openings are pierced through the spandrel between two round-headed arches under one circum-

scribing arch. The earliest example that has been noticed is in the triforium of the choir of Peterborough Cathedral, A.D. 1145. Several windows of the same figure occur in the later Norman buildings and in the period of transition, and plate-tracery continues in use in the earlier part of the Early English style, by piercing the spaces between or above the heads of the windows when two or more were grouped together under one arch. These piercings seldom followed the figure of the space pierced, and very often, if not generally, had different mouldings from them; but the system of making the mul-

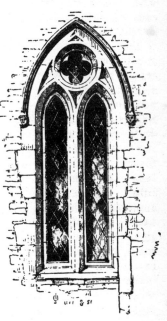

Charlton-on-Otmoor, Oxon.

lions branch off into circles, quatrefoils, and other geometrical figures above the springing of the arches, speedily superseded this expedient, and established the use of tracery: its character, at first, was often rather heavy, and the larger openings only were feathered, but this defect was rapidly corrected, and it became one of the most marked and beautiful characteristics of the Decorated style.

Bar-tracery begins in the later part of that style, and at first consists of foliated circles only, as in the cloisters and other parts of Salisbury Cathedral. Soon afterwards trefoils and quatrefoils, not enclosed in circles, and their other forms, came in.

The heads of the windows were at first trefoiled only, and cut out of the solid, but afterwards were pierced, and became part of the tracery.

The early Decorated tracery is arranged principally in circles, quatrefoils, and other regular figures, with the featherings for the most part confined to the larger piercings; this is usually called *geometrical* tracery: in the matured examples of the style it is generally more complicated, and the patterns are designed

Meopham, Kent, c. 1260.

with greater freedom and elegance. Many windows of this date have the heads filled with most elaborate tracery, branching off into a variety of graceful curves, without any admixture of geometrical forms, though very commonly portions of flowing and geometrical tracery are combined in the same window. Two of the Decorated windows most celebrated for their tracery are the west window of York Minster, and the east window of Carlisle Cathedral. Some idea of the great variety of design in the tracery of English windows may be found in the work on the subject by Mr. E. A. Freeman.

One of the earliest indications of the approach of the Perpendicular style is perceived in the introduction of straight lines in the tracery, sometimes horizontal, but more frequently vertical; these, on their first appearance, are not numerous, and in general not very striking, but they are found rapidly to increase as the style becomes developed, until the flowing lines of the Decorated tracery are exploded. There are very great varieties in the window-tracery of the Perpendicular style; occasionally transoms are introduced in it, particularly in some districts, and an effect very

King's Sutton, Northants.

similar to that of a transom produced by arching the small lights at a uniform level across a considerable part, or the whole breadth of the window, is common. Although the leading lines are vertical, it is very usual to find some of the piercings formed of curved patterns, and the principal mullions are frequently arched and carried through the window-head, so as to divide the tracery into several distinct portions.

In addition to its use in

windows, tracery is also extensively employed as a decoration in Gothic architecture in various other ways. In general character it always more or less resembles that of the windows, though the patterns are often necessarily modified to suit the spaces to which it is applied. Panels are sometimes entirely covered with it, and present, in fact, epitomes of blank windows; parapets often, especially on the Continent, consist of a range of tracery; ceilings, both vaulted and flat, are very commonly ornamented with it; in screens it is almost invariably introduced; it is also made to decorate a variety of small objects, such as locks, door-handles, &c. The use of the word *tracery* (as well as *mullion*) by modern writers is derived from Sir Christopher Wren, who employs them habitually in his reports, and it may be supposed therefore that the word was used by the workmen of that day. His cotemporaries, Dr. Plot and Randle Holmes, both use it, and from these authorities it derives its present universal employment. "*Tracery* is the working of the top part of a window into several forms and fashions," says Holmes (Acad. of Armory, p. 112, pt. iii.); and Wren, describing Salisbury Cathedral windows, admires them because the light is not obstructed "with many mullions and transoms of *tracery-work.*" (Parentalia, 302, 304, 307.) But in mediæval contracts the term does not appear, and instead of it we find *form-pieces* and *forms.*

There were different kinds of pierced work in metal plate largely introduced into the goldsmith's work, and into other brass and ironwork; as, for example, the lock-plates which are often seen upon doors, which are formed of thin iron plate, upon which ornamental patterns are traced, and the ground pierced through and coloured cloth placed behind it. It is in them that it is thought we may look for the origin of the name, if not of the design. Often the patterns are the same as those of the stone tracery, and the subordination of the mouldings is produced by placing two or more plates upon each other.

TRAIL, a running enrichment of leaves, flowers, tendrils, &c. [See *Vignette.*]

Transept: any part of a church that projects at right angles from the body (that is, the high central portion either of nave or choir), and is of equal or nearly equal height to it, is termed the transept. The transept gives to the church its cruciform arrangement, but its position varies in different ages and styles. Large churches also have several transepts. The transept is always so arranged that the projection southward is accompanied by a corresponding projection northward, and although from delays in building and alterations the two are frequently dissimilar in style and plan, as at Chester, it must always be supposed that the two are contemplated. Hence, while the word transept includes both the north and the south branches, it is frequently used to designate one only, and when both are meant, it is used in the plural number. In the basilican churches of Rome, and others of that class but not so early, the transept is at the altar extremity of the building, and the head of the cross is only marked by an apse. Gradually, however, the eastern limb of the cross became elongated in successive structures, until, as at York, it is made equal to the western limb. This western limb, in describing the building, is usually termed the nave, and the eastern the choir, without reference to the actual position or extent of the real choir considered with respect to its liturgical meaning, for the latter is often placed west of the Transept, as at Norwich and Westminster. Often a small secondary transept is placed east of the principal transept, as at Cluny, Canterbury, Salisbury, Lincoln, and several other examples. Occasionally the western front is developed into a transept, as at Ely, or a transept is placed at the extreme east end, as at Durham, Fountains, and Peterborough. The transepts were sometimes called "cross isles," (transversæ insulæ.) [See *Aisle.*] In Latin more usually the *Cross* (Crux.) [See *Cathedral.*]

Transition: this term is employed in reference to mediæval architecture, while it is in progress of changing from one style to another. There are three periods of transition, viz. from the Romanesque or Norman style to the Early English; from the Early English to the Decorated; and from the Decorated to the Perpendicular: buildings erected at these particular times frequently have the features of two styles so blended together that they cannot be properly considered to belong to either; sometimes the details of the later style are associated with the general forms and arrangements of the earlier, and *vice versa.*

Mediæval architecture was at all times undergoing a gradual progressive change, as is evident from the difference between early and late work in each of the styles, but these alterations are, for the most part, only modifications of the distinguishing characteristics, though many of them indicate the more important changes to which they eventually led. This term is more usually applied to the first great period of transition, from the Romanesque to the Gothic.

Transom (Transommer, or cross-beam), a horizontal mullion or cross-bar in a window, &c. The most ancient examples of transoms are found in the Early English style: of this date they are extremely rare, and appear only to have been used occasionally in glazed windows which were provided with casements, and in the unglazed openings of belfries, turrets, &c., for the sake of strength. At this period they were mere straight bars of stone, and except in unglazed windows of very great length, were introduced but once in the height of the opening: as church windows were seldom made to open, specimens of the first-mentioned kind are to be sought for in domestic buildings; they exist at Battle Abbey, Sussex, and at Woodcroft and Longthorpe, Northamptonshire. In the Decorated style the use of transoms increased, and examples of them in the unglazed openings of towers and spires are by no means uncommon, as in the churches of Exton, Rutland; St. Mary, Stamford; King's Sutton, Northamptonshire, and St. Mary, Oxford. In glazed church windows they were still very rarely employed, though they may be seen in the cathedral at Bristol, and in the churches of Albrighton, Shropshire, and Dodford, Northamptonshire; but in

Bampton, Oxon.

domestic buildings they were very generally adopted, doubtless from the convenience which they afforded for the application of casements. At this period they were introduced only once in the height of the window, and the lights were usually arched and feathered beneath them. In the Perpendicular style the use of transoms was very general in windows of all kinds, and they were often repeated several times in the height; they were also sometimes introduced in the tracery: the lights were almost always arched and feathered under them. They also occur in *Lowside* windows, in which probably the lower division of the window was provided with a shutter. During the reigns of Elizabeth and James I., and even later, transoms continued to be frequently used, but they were seldom more than plain bars, like horizontal mullions. In continental Gothic transoms were much less employed than in this country.

Headcorn, Kent.

TRAVERSE, a kind of screen with curtains used in halls, chapels, and other large rooms to give privacy to dignified persons.

TRELLIS, Trellice, an open grating or lattice-work, either of metal or wood; the name is usually confined to such as are formed of straight bars crossing each other.

TRESAUNTE, a passage in a house, &c. (? that between the screen at the lower end of the hall and the offices), or a narrow passage in a wall. In monastic rules the *trisantia* is often mentioned, and appears to have been near the chapter-house and a part of the cloister. In large monasteries there were several *trisantiæ*, as there were several *cloisters*. Amongst others it is probable that the covered passage which so usually lies between the transept gable and the chapter-house, usually called *the Slype*, was a *trisantia*.

Trefoil (Lat. *Tres* = three, *folium* = a leaf), ornamental feathering or foliation used in Gothic architecture in the heads of window-lights, tracery, panellings, &c., in which the spaces between the cusps represent the form of a three-lobed leaf. [See *Foil*.]

Tribune, or Tribunal. A word in its first signification used to denote the seat of the Ruler or Judge (*tribunus*) in the Apse of a Basilica, where justice was administered. Afterwards, when the basilican arrangement was applied to churches (see *Basilica*), it signified the seat of the bishop, or that of the bishop and clergy, which was usually round the apse. That at Torcello is perhaps as good an example as can be given. The word at a later date came to signify any elevated part of a church or public building; hence the French use it to this day for any gallery; or for the triforium in a church. It is also used for the Pulpit, although in

Tribune, Torcello.

this sense it retains more of the primary idea as the place of authority; also for the President's seat in French Assemblies. In Norwich Cathedral the bishop's throne still exists, on the east end of the choir wall; though built round and hidden, it shews that before the twelfth century the basilican arrangement was adopted in this country.

Triforium. The Triforium, whether it be a corrupt reading of the last word (*Tribunum*) or not, means very much the same thing, namely, a gallery in a church. We are indebted for the word to Gervase, a writer of the twelfth century, and in describing the rebuilding of Canterbury Cathedral he applies the word to the space formed between the sloping roof of the aisle and the vaulting beneath it, which then being open, formed a sort of gallery or tribune to the church. To this space, which is often very capacious, and occurs in most of the cathedrals both in England and on the Continent, the name is now usually applied. But Gervase says, in distinguishing between the old work and the new, that in the latter the architect made "another triforium" above the lower one, and this now exists at Canterbury also, but would in an ordinary way be called the clerestory passage; the word may, therefore, be legitimately applied to both.

Triforium, Winchester.
C. Clere-story.
T. Triforium.
P. Pillars.

The lower, or chief triforium (or blindstory, as it is sometimes called), although in the first instance merely an architectural necessity arising from the construction of the aisle-roof, came to be used for various purposes. The blank wall above the nave-arches was, as we gather from Gervase, in Anselm's church, covered with arcading, and pierced with only small openings. In the new work we find the elegant series of arches, amounting practically to arcading, occupying and adorning the whole of the wall-space. In several cases we find the spaces, or long galleries, to be used for purposes of worship, as altars exist in them; and we know from documentary evidence it was used as such, as in the history of Charles the Good, where it is called the solarium, or upper chamber of the church. We also know that it was sometimes used as a gallery for women, answering to the actual galleries in the Roman basilicas. At times it is now used in some cathedrals abroad by the congregation when any great function is going on, and seats are placed there. Besides this, it always afforded easy means of reaching the upper part of the wall, for placing or removing hangings and such like.

The ornamental arrangement of the lower triforium differs considerably. In the *Norman* style it is often formed of one arch occupying an entire bay of the building, or of one arch subdivided into smaller ones supported on small shafts, as at Malmesbury Abbey. In the *Early English* style a range of small arches is not uncommon, and sometimes two or more larger arches subdivided are used. In the *Decorated* and *Perpendicular* styles, in which the aisle-roofs are frequently flatter than is usual at earlier periods, the space occupied by the triforium is often much reduced, and in some

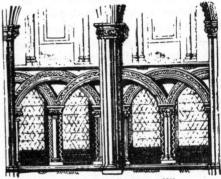

Triforium, St. Cross, Hampshire, c. 1200.

buildings, especially in the latter style, it is altogether abolished.

In some instances, even in parish churches, a passage or gallery is carried round the nave or chancel in the thickness of the walls, where there are no aisles, as e.g. Nun Monkton, Yorkshire, and in the church of St. Peter-in-the East in Oxford. In large churches, too, and in cathedrals, passages in the thickness of the wall, more or less open to the church, occur. To all these the name triforium may properly be applied. When, however, the back of the passage is open, so to speak, to the sky, by means of the windows behind, the name clearstory or clearstory-passage, is perhaps more appropriate.

The theory deriving the word triforium from *tres-fores*, or three openings or doors, is not probable, as the general rule was for a Norman triforium arcade to have two or four openings, as was the case where the name is first applied. Nor is the Latinization of *thoroughfare* a more probable derivation; nor yet that of *turri-forium*, or tower-passage, though nearly all the upper passages lead to and from the towers.

Trigylph: an ornament used in the Doric frieze, consisting of three vertical angular channels, or flutes, separated by narrow flat spaces. They are not worked exactly in the same manner in the Grecian and Roman examples; and in the latter, when placed over columns, are invariably over the centre of them, but in the former, at the angle of an entablature, are placed close up to the angle, and not over the centre of the column.

Truss: (1.) The collection of timbers forming one of the principal supports in a roof, framed together so as to give mutual support to each other, and to prevent any straining or distortion from the superincumbent weight; they are usually placed at regular intervals, and are formed in various ways, according to the size and nature of the roof with which they are connected; diagrams of two, of the simplest kind, are given in the article on *Roof*. (2.) Wooden partitions and other works in carpentry are sometimes strengthened with framed trusses of similar kinds. (3.) *Ancones, brackets,* and *consoles* are sometimes called trusses.

Tudor Style: this name is used by some writers on Gothic architecture, but they do not agree in the application of it. It is variously employed to designate the Perpendicular style throughout its continuance—the latter period of this style—and the mixed style which sprang

TRICLINIUM, the room in which the Romans ate their principal meals; also the couch on which they reclined at their meals.

TRIMMER: this is an ancient term in carpentry, but it is doubtful whether it was formerly used in precisely the same sense as at present; it now signifies a piece of timber inserted in a roof, floor, wooden partition, &c., to support the ends of any of the joists, rafters, &c., which cannot, from particular circumstances, be made to bear upon the walls or upon any of the main timbers: thus floors are trimmed at the fire-places and for the passage of stairs. The joists, rafters, &c., into which the ends of the trimmers are framed, are called trimming-joists, and trimming-rafters.

TRIPTIC, a sort of tablet, in three divisions, to open and shut, the two outer folding over the centre when closed, as contrasted with Diptych. See *Leaves*.

TROCHYLUS, a hollow moulding frequent in the bases of Classical orders. Same as *Scotia*.

up on the decline of Gothic architecture usually called Elizabethan. The term is not very extensively used, and is most commonly understood to mean late Perpendicular work, and Henry VII.'s Chapel at Westminster is looked upon as the most perfect specimen in this style. The *Tudor Flower* is a flat flower, or leaf, placed upright on its stalk, much used in Perpendicular work, espe-

cially late in the style, in long suites as a crest, or ornamental finishing, on cornices, &c.; the examples differ considerably in detail, but the general effect does not vary much.

Turret, Touret, Turette, a small tower: the name is also sometimes given to a large pinnacle. Turrets are employed in Gothic architecture for various purposes, and are applied in various ways: they also differ very greatly in their forms, proportions, and decorations. In many cases they are used solely for ornament; they are also often placed at the angles of buildings, especially castles, to increase their strength, serving practically as corner buttresses. Occasionally they carry bells, or a clock, but one of the most common uses to which they are applied is to contain a *newel*, or spiral staircase; for this purpose they are usually found attached to church towers, forming an external projection,

Beckley, Oxon.

which very frequently terminates considerably below the top of the tower, but in some districts turrets of this kind generally rise above the tower, and are finished with a parapet or small spire. Turrets of all dates are sometimes perfectly plain, and others variously ornamented, according to the character of the prevailing style of architecture, the upper part being the most enriched, and not unfrequently formed of open-work. In the *Norman* style, the lower part is usually square, and this form is continued to the top, but the upper part is sometimes changed to a polygon or circle; few turrets of this date retain their original terminations, but they appear to have been often finished with low spires, either square, polygonal, or circular, according to the shape of the turret. In the *Early English* and later styles they are most usually polygonal, but are sometimes square,

St. Mary's, Beverley.

and occasionally circular. The upper terminations are very various; in the Early English style spires prevail, but in the *Decorated* and *Perpendicular* not only spires but parapets, either plain, battlemented, panelled, or pierced, and pinnacles are used. The peculiar kind of turrets often found attached to small churches and chapels, which have no tower to receive the bells, are described under the term *Bell-gable*.

TUN, a term used in some parts of the west of England for the shaft of a chimney.

TURNPIKE-STAIR, a name sometimes applied to a spiral staircase or *Vise*. See also *Newel*.

TURNGRECE, also a winding stair. See *Step*.

Tufa, Tufo, Tuff, a porous stone either deposited by calcareous waters, or formed by successive layers of volcanic dust, as in Rome and the Campagna around it. Much of it is exceedingly light, and resembles petrified sponge; it is extremely durable, and was extensively used by the Romans for the external facing of buildings, as at the theatre at Lillebone, in Normandy, and the Pharos in Dover Castle. In the Middle Ages it was sometimes used in walls in localities where it could be easily procured, but it was principally employed in vaulting, for which, from its lightness, it was peculiarly suited. Gervase, in his account of the rebuilding of the choir of Canterbury Cathedral, after the fire in 1174, describes the vault to be "ex lapide et *tofo levi*." It is used in the vaulting of the late Norman porch on the north side of the nave of Bredon Church, Worcestershire, and in many other buildings.

Tympanum (Lat.), the triangular space between the horizontal and sloping cornices on the front of a pediment in Classical architecture; it is often left plain, but is sometimes covered with sculpture. This name is also given to

Tympanum of Doorway, Essendine, c. 1130.

the space immediately above the opening of a doorway, &c., in mediæval architecture, when the top of the opening is square and has an arch over it; this arrangement is not uncommon in this country in Norman work, and on the

Continent is to be found in each of the styles; tympanums of this kind are occasionally perfectly plain, but are generally ornamented with carving or sculpture; in continental work the subjects are usually arranged in tiers one above another, and often embrace a great number of figures. Also when an arch is surmounted by a gable-moulding or triangular hoodmould, the space included between the arch and the triangular hoodmould is termed the tympanum of the gable.

Type, or Tippe: the canopy over a pulpit, according to Nicholson's Dictionary. It seems to have been also employed for the capping or cupola roof of a turret, which resembles the usual form of the pulpit canopy, although this term is seldom used. A very beautiful example is given under the article *Tabernacle*. The term seems to be applied also to other structures of the same form. In the account, for instance, of the repairs of the White Tower, 23 Hen. VIII., there are particulars of the repair and construction of "four types on the top of the White Tower with their ordenances about them," which are manifestly the roofs of the four corner turrets, which upon this occasion were "hythened with brycke work every type a yarde hye," plastered, roughcast, the woodwork re-constructed, and the lead re-cast.

Valley. In a roof where there is more than one ridge, the internal angles formed by the meeting of the sides are termed *Valleys*, and the timbers supporting these sides are termed *Valley Rafters*. Also the intervals in a vault, the space between the ridges of the vault as seen from above.

TUSSES, projecting stones left in a wall to which another building is intended to be added, in order to connect them securely together. The term is not in general use at the present day. They are sometimes called *Toothing-stones*.

TYLLE-THAKKERS, tile-thatchers or tilers.

TYMBRE, a herald's term for the crest, which in an achievement stands on the top of the helmet, or on the top of a fumerell or lantern, on the roof of a hall, &c., or on the finial of a turret. The *Vane* from Stanton Harcourt, on the next page, affords an illustration.

UNDERCROFT, a subterranean chapel or apartment. At Hereford, in the cloisters, there is a place called the Mary-croft.

Vane (written also Fane, Lat. *Vannus*), a plate of metal turning on a vertical spindle so as to shew the direction of the wind, frequently fixed on the tops of spires and pinnacles, and other elevated situations; it is often in the form of a cock, and from this circumstance is very commonly called a weather-cock. Vanes were in use in the times of the Saxons, and in after ages were very extensively employed. They were sometimes perfectly plain, and sometimes cut into ornamental forms, which were not unfrequently heraldic devices. During the prevalence of the Perpendicular and Elizabethan styles, figures supporting vanes were often placed on the tops of pinnacles, and in other elevated situations; these were usually in the form of small flags, and were sometimes pierced with

Stanton Harcourt, Oxon.

a representation of some armorial bearing. Occasionally the vane was shaped like an heraldic device.

Vault (Fr. *Voûte*, and Lat. *Volutus*). The simplest and most ancient kind used over a rectangular area is the *Cylindrical*, called also a *barrel*, and sometimes *wagon - vault;* this springs from the two opposite walls, and presents a uniform concave surface throughout its whole length. The term 'cylindrical' properly implies the form of a segment of a cylinder, but it is applied to pointed vaults of the same description.

Cylindrical Vault.

Vaults of this description were used by the Romans, and also by the builders in this country, to the end of the Norman style. The Romans also first introduced groining, formed by the intersection of vaults crossing each other at right angles, and some of their constructions of

this kind were of very large size. In groined vaults the
arches which cross each
other do not always cor-
respond in width; in
such cases they some-
times spring from the
same level, and conse-
quently are of unequal
heights; and sometimes
the springing of the nar-
rower vault is raised so
that the tops are on the
same level.

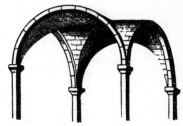

Groined Vault.

Domical, or hemispherical vaulting over a
circular area was likewise practised by the Romans, of
which the Pantheon at Rome exhibits a magnificent example of 142 ft. in diameter. The decorations employed
on Roman vaulting consist chiefly of panels, and flat bands
of ornament following the curve of the arch : the application of ribs at that period was unknown.

In the *Norman* style cylindrical or barrel vaulting, as
well as groined vaulting, is used; the former of these is
either perfectly devoid of ornament, as in the chapel in
the White Tower of London, or has plain and massive ribs
at intervals, following the direction of the curve of the
arch. In groined vaulting the cross-vaults are not unfrequently surmounted, or stilted, when they are of narrower span than the main vault, though sometimes, in such
cases, they are both made to spring from the same level;
but in general the parts of the building are so arranged
that both vaults are of nearly or quite the same breadth.

In the *Early English* style, when the use of the pointed
arch was permanently established, the same form was also
given to the vaulting; and groined vaults at this period
were universally adopted. In buildings of this date ribs
are invariably employed, especially on the groins : the
simplest arrangement of them consists of the diagonal or
groin ribs, cross-springers, and the longitudinal and trans-
verse ribs at the apex of the main and cross-vaults; but
these two last, in some examples, are omitted. Additional
ribs are sometimes introduced between the diagonals and
cross-springers. In some buildings in this country, and

in many on the Continent, the vaulting is constructed with
the main vault double the width of the cross-vaults, with

Westminster Abbey, c. 1260.

the diagonal ribs embracing two bays or compartments of
the cross-vaults, as in the choir of Canterbury Cathedral.

Decorated vaults for the most part differ but little from
those of the preceding style: the longitudinal and trans-
verse ribs are occasionally, but not often, omitted, and the
number of those on the surface of the vaulting is sometimes
increased; and in some examples ribs are introduced crossing the vaults in directions opposite to their curves, so as
to form in some degree an appearance of net-work upon
them. The short ribs which connect the bosses and intersections of the principal rib and ridge-ribs, but which do
not themselves either spring from an impost or occupy the
ridge, are termed *liernes,* and the vaults in which they
occur, *lierne vaults.*

In the *Perpendicular* style the general construction is much the same as in the Decorated, but the ribs are often more numerous, and pendants are not uncommon. Towards the latter part of this style *fan-tracery* vaulting was commonly introduced: this has no groins, but the pendentives are circular on the plan, and have the same curve in every direction, resembling inverted curvilinear conoids, and are generally covered with ribs and tracery branching out equally all round them. The middle of the upper part of the vault, between the pendentives, is usually domical in construction, and frequently has a pendant in the centre of each compartment. A fine example of this is found in Henry the Seventh's Chapel, Westminster.

Vaulting-shaft: a term proposed by Professor Willis for a shaft, small column, or pillar, which supports the ribs of a vault. Shafts of this kind sometimes rise from the floor, and this is specially the case in most Norman, and some Early English work; at other times from the capital of a larger pillar, or from a corbel or other projection, and this is become more common in the fourteenth century. The most usual arrangement is that shewn in the example here given, where the shaft rises between the springings of the arches of the nave.

Vaulting-shaft, Netley Abbey, c. 1300.

Vesica Piscis (Lat.): a name applied to a pointed oval figure, formed by two equal circles, cutting each other in their centres, which is a very common form given to the *aureole*,

VENT in an embattled wall is either the *Crenel* or the *Loophole*, for its exact meaning is somewhat ambiguous.

VERGE, a mediæval term sometimes applied to the shaft of a column, or to a small ornamental shaft in Gothic architecture.

VERGE-board = Barge-board.

or *glory*, by which the representations of each of the three Persons of the Holy Trinity and the Blessed Virgin are surrounded in the paintings or sculptures of the Middle Ages. It has been conjectured (though without much probability) that it was adopted from the idea that this figure is symbolical, and significant of the Greek word ἴχθυς (a *fish*), which contains the initial letters of the name and titles of the Saviour. This form is sometimes found in panels and other architectural features, and is extremely common in mediæval seals, especially those of bishops and monastic establishments.

Vesica Piscis, Ely Cathedral.

Vestibule, a hall or ante-chamber next to the entrance, from which doors open to the various rooms or passages of a house. This is the Vitruvian and the modern sense, but the latter includes any lobby, porch, or ante-room, through which a larger apartment or a house, &c. is entered. *Vestibulum* in mediæval Latin is also used for the *vestiarium* or *vestry*, and sometimes for the nave, the *ecclesia* being strictly the choir only. The origin of the word is disputed, but it is probable that it first signified the entrance-chamber to the baths, where the clothes of the bather were laid aside; and hence the entrance to a house or any public edifice.

Vignette (Fr.), a running ornament consisting of leaves and tendrils, such as is frequently carved in the hollow mouldings in Gothic architecture, especially in the Decorated and Perpendicular styles; called also *Trail.*

Vignette.

Vethym, or Fethym, a fathom; a measure of six feet.

Vomitoria (Lat.), the principal exits of an amphitheatre.

Voussure (Fr.), a vault.

Vyse. See *Vise* and *Step.*

Vestry, or **Revestry:** a room attached to the choir of a church, sometimes called the *sacristy*, in which the sacred vessels and vestments were kept, and where the priest put on his robes. In ordinary parish churches it was usually an adjunct on one side of the choir, but was sometimes at the east end, behind the altar, either within the main walls of the building, as at Crewkerne, Somersetshire, and Arundel, Sussex, or forming a projection beyond them, as at Hawkhurst, Kent, and in several churches in the city of York.

Vise (old form *Vys* = a screw), a spiral staircase, the steps of which wind round a perpendicular shaft or pillar called the newel. The majority of ancient church towers are provided with staircases of this kind, and they are to be found in various situations in most middle-age buildings. During the prevalence of the Norman style, the steps were formed of small stones supported on a continuous spiral vault, reaching the whole height of the stairs, one side of which rested on the newel, and the other on the main wall; subsequently to this period the steps were each made of a single stone, one end of which was inserted into the main wall, and the other rested upon and formed part of the newel. See also *Newel*.

Vitruvian Scroll, a peculiar pattern of scroll-work, consisting of convolved undulations, used in Classical architecture. The name given after the great architectural writer Vitruvius.

Vitruvian Scroll.

Volute (Lat. *Volutus* = turned), a spiral scroll forming the principal characteristic of the Ionic capital. Volutes are also used on the capitals of the Corinthian and Composite orders. Examples will be found in the illustrations accompanying the article *Order*. At the same time, in the pattern of

Volute.

the Norman capitals, the volute seems to be frequently retained; in the thirteenth century it takes the form of foliage, and is practically lost.

Voussoir, a name adopted from the French for the wedge-shaped stones (or other material) with which an arch is constructed, as marked in the engraving, *a, a, a;* the upper one, namely *b*, at the crown of the arch, is termed the *Key-stone.* The lowest voussoir, or that which is placed immediately above the impost, is termed the springing-stone, or *springer.*

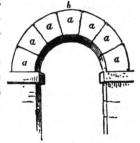

Voussoirs.

Wainscot, this term originally seems to have implied rough planks of oak timber, and subsequently to have been given to wooden panelling, to which they were converted, for lining the inner walls of houses and churches. It was very extensively employed during the reigns of Queen Elizabeth and James I., and for a long period afterwards. The name has long ceased to be confined to *oak* panelling. It is also called *Seeling-work.*

Wall-painting, the large spaces which are sometimes left without any ornamentation in our churches, and which,

Wall-painting, Ringstead, Northants.

when whitewashed, appear so cold and unsightly, were originally covered with colour, either in the shape of floral or geometrical patterns, or of figures and emblems. The painted glass when treated in conjunction with the wall, as may be seen at the Sainte Chapelle, has a beautiful effect. The bands of colour on the wall were no doubt in continuation of the transoms, or the sill, or a continuation of a band carried round the arches, and taking the place of a dripstone and string. Examples are frequently discovered on removal of whitewash from our old churches, but they are seldom in such a state as to admit of preservation. [See *Polychrome.*]

Window: the windows employed in Classical architecture are usually rectangular openings without any internal splay, with architraves and other ornaments on the exterior, very similar to those of the doorways, but sometimes they have arched heads; and occasionally small circular and semicircular windows are used. In modern buildings, windows called Venetian windows are sometimes introduced; they are of large size, divided by columns, or piers resembling pilasters, into three lights, the middle one of which is usually wider than the others, and is sometimes arched; in the arrangement and character of their ornaments they resemble the windows used in Classical architecture.

In mediæval architecture the windows vary most materially in the several styles. In the class of buildings spoken of in the article on *Saxon* architecture they are generally small, and when in situations to require glazing have often a large splay both externally and internally; but sometimes the inside only is splayed, and the external angle of the jamb merely chamfered. In church towers, and situations where *glazing* is not necessary, they are frequently of two or more lights, divided by small pillars, or piers, usually resembling balusters, with the jambs constructed without any splay either internally or externally. The heads of the windows in this style are formed of semicircular arches, or of long stones placed on end upon the imposts, and leaning against each other at the top, so as to form a triangle.

WAGON-VAULT. See *Vault.*
WALL-PLATE. See *Plate* and *Roof.*
WELL-HOLE of a staircase.

See *Step.*
WINDERS in winding stairs. See *Newel* and *Step.*

In buildings of the early *Norman* style the windows are generally of rather small proportions, but in those of later date they are often of considerable size; the most ancient examples are usually very little ornamented, having only a small chamfer or a plain shallow recess round them externally, and a large splay within, but sometimes there is a small shaft on each side in the external recess, and a label-moulding over the arch; this mode of decoration prevails throughout the style, and is made to produce a bold and rich effect by the introduction of mouldings and other ornaments in the arch, and

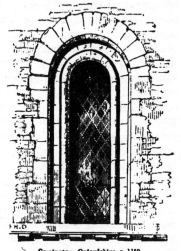

Cassington, Oxfordshire, c. 1150.

sometimes in the jambs; the number of shafts also is sometimes increased. The richest examples are met with in buildings of late date, although numerous specimens remain of all periods, up to the very end of the style, which are perfectly plain, or have only a few simple mouldings on the outside. There are some Norman windows divided by shafts, or small piers, into two or more lights; these are often placed in shallow recesses with arched heads, embracing the whole breadth of the window; they are found principally

Bucknell, Oxon., c. 1160.

in towers, and in situations where glazing is not required.

A few examples of circular windows of this style remain; some are without mullions or tracery of any kind, but other specimens are divided by small shafts, or mullions, arranged like the spokes of a wheel. The insides of the windows of this period, except those in belfries and in other situations where they are not intended to be glazed, are almost invariably splayed, and are frequently without any kind of ornament; when decorations are used, they

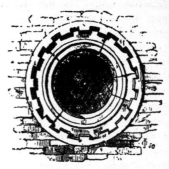

Lambourne, Berks., c. 1160.

are similar both in character and mode of application to those of the exterior, though generally inferior to them in richness and amount. The proportions of the openings are very various throughout the existence of the Norman style, but the most elongated specimens are usually late. They are sometimes placed in pairs, and occasionally in triplets, towards the end of the style, so close to each other that the space between the internal splays is not more than sufficient to receive the decorations with which the windows are surrounded.

In the *Early English* style the proportions of windows vary very greatly, but the majority of them are long and narrow; they are used singly, or combined in groups of two, three, five, and seven. When grouped in this manner, they are not unfrequently placed so near to each other that the stonework between them is reduced to a real mullion, and in such cases they are generally surmounted by a large arch embracing the whole number of lights; but in the majority of examples the spaces between the windows are more considerable, except in those of late date, many of which are separated by mullions, and have the space between the

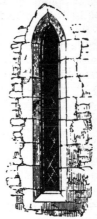

Burwash, Sussex.

heads of the lights and the arch over them pierced with circles, quatrefoils, or other openings, producing very much the effect of the windows of the succeeding style. In belfries, spires, &c., where glazing is unnecessary, two or more openings, separated by small shafts, placed under one arch, are not uncommon. A very prevalent mode of ornamenting the windows of this style, especially on the insides, is with small shafts, which are usually detached from the other stonework, and stand quite free; they are often made of a finer material than the rest of the window, and polished. The amount of decoration employed is very various: many examples are perfectly plain within, and have only a single or double chamfer, or small splay, externally; others, when equally plain on the exterior, have shafts and mouldings within; some again have the interior and exterior equally enriched, and some have the greatest amount of decoration externally, but

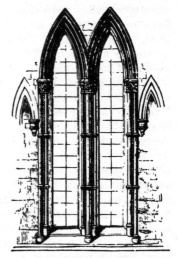

Lincoln Cathedral, c. 1220.

Shipton Olliffe, Gloucestershire, c. 1220.

in general, when there is any difference, the inside is the most highly ornamented. The jambs are always splayed on the inside, and the inner arch is most commonly unconformable to that over the actual opening of the window, springing usually from a lower level; this arch, even when the jambs are perfectly plain, has a chamfer on the inner edge, or a small suite of mouldings, which generally project below the soffit, and either die into the jambs, or rest upon a corbel on each side. A few examples have the heads of the open-

Luddenham, Kent.

ings formed of trefoil or cinquefoil arches; and occasionally, in those of late date, they are feathered. There are various beautiful specimens remaining of circular windows of this style. Triangular windows are also occasionally to be met with, but they are usually small, and in the subordinate parts of buildings.

In the *Decorated* style the windows are enlarged, and divided by mullions into separate lights, and have the heads filled with tracery. [See *Tracery*.] Occasionally windows are met with of this date with transoms, but they are very rare

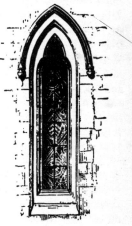

Stanton St. John's, Oxon.

except in domestic work, and in spires and towers where not intended to be glazed. The heads of the windows in this style are of various forms; the most prevalent are two-centred pointed arches of different proportions, but besides these, segmental arches, both plain and pointed, are used, and ogees; square heads are also common. The inner arches are very frequently of different shapes and proportions from those over the tracery, and, even when the inner jambs are perfectly plain, are generally chamfered or moulded in the same manner as the corresponding ing arches in the Early English style. Many Decorated windows which have elaborate tracery are almost destitute of mouldings: the mullions are often only splayed, and the jambs provided with one or two additional mouldings of the simplest character: but in enriched buildings there are generally several subordinations of mullions, and the jambs are filled with a variety of mouldings; in common with those of the preceding and following styles, they are always splayed in the inside. The rich ballflower moulding of the period is very commonly used, and in some cases the ornament is carried along the mullions and the tracery, as at Leominster and Gloucester, though generally only along the outside. There are some circular windows of this date, of which a magnificent example remains at Lincoln Cathedral; squares, triangles, and other unusual forms, are also

Great Haseley, Oxfordshire, c. 1300.

Ashby-Folville, Leicestershire, c. 1340.

occasionally to be met with, but they are generally small.

The principal differences between the windows of the *Perpendicular* and the preceding style consist in the altered arrangement of the tracery, the frequent introduction of transoms, and the shapes of the heads, which are very often formed of four-centred arches, and ogees are nearly or quite disused; in other respects they do not differ materially, although the character of the mouldings becomes changed, and some of the subordinate parts are modified, as the style gradually emerges from the Decorated. Small circles, quatrefoils, and squares, are not very unusual. Sometimes the transoms and sills of the windows are ornamented with small battlements, a feature peculiar to England. As the Perpendicular style

St. Mary's, Devizes, Wilts., c. 1450.

becomes debased, the heads of the windows grow gradually flatter, until they cease to be arched, and the opening is divided by the mullions into plain rectangular lights; this kind of window prevails in buildings of the time of Queen Elizabeth and King James I., and is found in work of the time of James II. and even later, until superseded by the modern sash-window.

There is a very remarkable window found in a great number of churches: it is of small size, below the level of the other windows, and at a convenient height from the floor for a person to look out through it; the usual situation is at the western end of the south side of the chancel, but it is sometimes on the north, and is occasionally found on both sides. It is called a *low side window.* The purpose of it has been much disputed, but it is now generally considered to have been for the administration of the Sacrament to lepers, or to sick persons during time of plague: they are sometimes called lepers' windows. In many cases, instead of a small window of this description, the large window over the place which it would occupy is elongated, and the additional portion at the bottom is parted off by a transom. No example of these windows has been noticed of a date prior to the Early English style, and the majority are

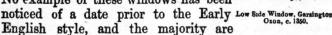

Low Side Window, Garsington, Oxon, c. 1350.

later, though they are found inserted in Norman churches. The theory adopted by some Ecclesiologists was that a light was burnt on the altar which might be seen from

WICKET, a small door formed in a larger one, to admit of ingress and egress, without opening the whole.

WIND-BEAM, a cross-beam used in the principals of many ancient roofs, occupying the situation of the *collar* in modern king-post roofs. See *Roof.*

WINGS of a moulding. See *Fillet.*

WITHDRAWING - ROOM. See *Chamber*

the outside through these windows, whence they gave to them the name of *Lychnoscope.*

A very elegant form of window, not uncommon in cathedrals and large churches in the Middle Ages, is called by the name of a *Rose Window.* It is a circular window, and the mullions converge towards the centre something like the spokes of a wheel; hence the name Catherine windows, or Wheel windows, is sometimes given to them.

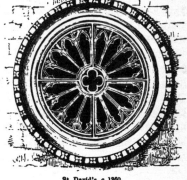

St. David's, c. 1360.

Zig-zag, a decoration peculiar to the Norman style of architecture, consisting of mouldings running in zig-zag lines: very considerable variety is given to this class of ornaments

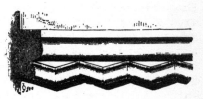

Peterborough Cathedral, c. 1175.

by changing the arrangement of the different suites of mouldings, and by turning the points of the zig-zags in different directions; in some examples the prominent parts stand out quite free,

Iffley, Oxon, c. 1160.

and are entirely detached from the wall, as at Cuddesdon

XENODOCHIUM (Gr.), a room in a monastery for strangers. The house of the abbot near the entrance seems to have been frequently used for this purpose, as at Fountains Abbey, Yorkshire.

XYSTUS = Ambulatory.

YARD, Yerde: this name was sometimes given formerly to long pieces of timber, such as rafters, &c.

YLE = aisle.

YMAGE = Image.

ZOCLE = Socle.

ZOPHORUS, the Vitruvian name for the frieze in Classical architecture.

Church, Oxfordshire, and St. Joseph's Chapel, Glastonbury Abbey. This kind of decoration is not found in
buildings of the earliest Norman work, but in the more
advanced specimens; it is most abundantly employed about
the doorways, windows, arches, &c. Examples are to be
found in most churches of the Norman style. It is more
commonly used in the arch-mouldings of doorways than
in any other part of the building, and in rich examples
there are sometimes three courses of zig-zag mouldings,
as in the Norman doorway at Middleton Stoney, p. 173.
In that instance they are continued down the sides of
the doorway also, but that is not equally common. The
arch of a Norman window is also sometimes enriched in
the same manner, as at St. John's, Devizes, p. 174.

TOPOGRAPHICAL INDEX TO ILLUSTRATIONS.